'To maintain international peace and security'

(Article 1.1)

'To achieve international co-operation in solving international problems of an economic, social, cultural, or humanitarian character' (Article 1.3)

'The Trusteeship Council, operating under the authority of the General Assembly, shall assist the General Assembly in carrying out these functions.' (Article 85)

'In discharging these duties the Security Council shall act in accordance with the Purposes and Principles of the United Nations' (Article 24)

NIJHOFF LAW SPECIALS

VOLUME 43

The titles published in this series are listed at the end of this volume.

A Better United Nations for the New Millennium

The United Nations System –
How it is now and how it should be in the future

by

Kamil Idris

and

Michael Bartolo

KLUWER LAW INTERNATIONAL
THE HAGUE / LONDON / BOSTON

A C.I.P. Catalogue record for this book is available from the Library of Congress.

ISBN 90-411-1344-4

Published by Kluwer Law International,
P.O. Box 85889, 2508 CN The Hague, The Netherlands.

Sold and distributed in North, Central and South America
by Kluwer Law International,
675 Massachusetts Avenue, Cambridge, MA 02139, U.S.A.

In all other countries, sold and distributed
by Kluwer Law International,
P.O. Box 85889, 2508 CN The Hague, The Netherlands.

Cover photo: CORBIS/Kit Kettle.

Printed on acid-free paper

DEDICATION

To Our Children
Michael and Daniela Bartolo,
Mohamed, Dinas, Dalia, and Dahd Idris,
who, at the dawn of the new millennium,
deserve a *Better United Nations*,
for themselves and their children, and
who, we are certain, would also make better use of it.

FOREWORD

GLOBALIZATION WITHOUT MARGINALIZATION

In spite of the phenomenal technological advances of this century, one out of every six human beings continues to live in abysmal poverty. Even their basic needs of food, shelter and clothing are not adequately met. Nearly a billion of them suffer from chronic malnutrition. In the absence of disposable income, which is a basic requirement for participation in the increasingly market-oriented economies of today, a large number of our fellow human beings are unable to lead a dignified life. Insecurity and deprivation pervade all facets of their daily lives. To make matters worse, during the last part of this century the income inequalities have increased. According to one estimate, over the past three decades, the share of global income of the world's richest 20 per cent rose from 70 percent to 85 percent, while the share of the poorest 20 percent fell from 2.3 percent to 1.4 percent.

Against this background, it is hardly surprising that the unfolding global information and communication revolution has unleashed social, political and economic forces which are strengthening the resolve and the desire of the disadvantaged and deprived sections of our global society to share in the fruits of technological, social, political and economic progress that only a small percentage of the world's population has enjoyed so far. Often such aspirations, when not fulfilled, have manifested in disruptive and violent ways. Even in democratic societies the social strife, the political upheavals, the violent outbursts, the injustices, the brutalities and the wars in different parts of the world seem to be consuming more and more time, energy and resources, and this with such alarming regularity as to require intervention by the international community, and especially by the United Nations, through its peacekeeping and peacemaking activities; Kosovo and East Timor are two recent examples.

A Better United Nations for the New Millennium

No doubt, the whole United Nations System represents an institutionalized political enterprise of mankind, after two wars on a *quasi*-global scale, to eliminate such conflicts and to bring economic and social progress to all. Over the last five decades, it has continued to engage the attention of its Member States, to prevent war and other conflicts or, in the event of failure, to contain and resolve them through diplomatic and other means. At the same time, a tremendous amount of work has been done within and by the United Nations System in the social and economic spheres, and much has been achieved. Even so, we do not seem to be moving significantly, if at all, towards economic justice and social equity at the world level. The persistent and widespread poverty and increasing inequalities around the globe, require reconsideration of strategies and policies on many fronts, since the process of global economic integration continues to intensify the marginality of many individuals, groups and even nations.

For example, the number of Least Developed Countries has gone up to 48, at present. On the one hand, the rate of growth of the world economy has been slowing down. On the other hand, the speed of communication and the flow of information have been increasing, along with the widening gap between the rich and the poor. The world economy grew at a rate of 5 percent during the 1960s, 3.6 percent during the 1970s, 2.8 percent during the 1980s, and 2 percent during the 1990s. There are many signs that only a small number of countries are involved in the globalization process in terms of their effective participation in the so-called global market. Apart from the OECD countries, less than a dozen developing countries are active partners in this process of globalization.

At the same time, income inequalities between countries are increasing. The gap in *per capita* incomes between the developed countries and developing countries has tripled from USD5 700 in 1960 to USD15 400 in 1993. By 1994-1995, the Gross National Product (GNP) *per capita* in the world was USD4 600. However, this resulted from a GNP *per capita* of USD24 000 in the richest countries, with a total population of some 850 million, and a GNP *per capita* of less than USD400 in the poorest economies, where more than 3 billion people live.

The increasing information flows and interdependence of the peoples have put very complex challenges before the leadership at the national and international levels. At no time in human history has the need for international cooperation and coordination been greater than it is today. The greatest challenge before the world is to create conditions and systems, which allow such cooperation and coordination in an effective and efficient manner, to help build and sustain a more egalitarian and equitable world order.

The international institutions and structures created in the aftermath of the Second World War have served us rather well. To meet the challenges of the new millennium, however, these institutions and structures will have to evolve and adapt to the emerging situations, so that they become more relevant and, at the same time, provide effective and efficient tools for achieving the desired results.

To improve substantially the quality of life of all humanity, a conducive, enabling environment is a prerequisite. In creating and maintaining such an environment the international institutional framework will, in my view, play a much larger role than it has played so far. At the same time, the voice of the private sector as well as of the civil society organizations will become very forceful and, if ignored, strident and ominous. I say so because the present international institutional framework is limited to dialogue, discussion and debate amongst the politicians, bureaucrats and technocrats, with a marginal role for the businessmen, farmers, workers, and other economic, social and political actors. To find satisfactory solutions to the myriad and complex problems of the present-day, highly interdependent and rapidly evolving reality, we require the cooperation and coordination of all types of interests in society, in the framework of flexible, adaptable and evolving institutional mechanisms which are able to respond in a timely and holistic manner.

I am deeply touched by the sincerity and commitment of the authors of this book to deal with the challenge of reforming the United Nations so that it becomes an effective instrument in reaping the benefits of globalization for all mankind. I share many of their underlying concerns and assumptions and, therefore, am able to empathetically relate to their cause of a better United Nations for the new millennium.

The United Nations System succeeded in realizing its goals in the political, social, economic, cultural and legal arenas on the world stage whenever its actions were based on a consensus. In other words, whenever it was backed by the political will and the resources required for accomplishing the task at hand. However, its failures have been as spectacular as its successes and that is part of the reason why the need for reforming it has been felt, practically throughout its history.

We do not have to wait for a major conflict or catastrophe to wake up to the miserable existence of a vast proportion of mankind. Our empty rhetoric and platitudes provide them no solace or satisfaction. Therefore, the debate on reform of the United Nations System must move beyond the cost-effectiveness and efficiency issues, to that of relevance. If the United Nations System has to become more relevant, then its purpose, actions, and achievements must be judged by their success in improving the conditions of all mankind. The social, political, legal and economic environment must be conducive to bringing forth the best in every human being, in a cooperative, collaborative and synergistic ambience. The political will and commitment must be matched by appropriate resources for the United Nations System of organizations to rise to this challenge. If the system continues to be hamstrung by the non-payment of dues by certain Member States, then the best possible ideas for reform cannot materialize.

The issue of reform has been addressed over the years, both within and outside the United Nations from a plethora of perspectives. The authors of this book, by testing every proposal on the yardstick of relevance, have provided a clarity and direction which is remarkably noteworthy. The spirit of democratic principles underpins many of the reforms suggested by the authors. The proposed reforms for redefining the relationship between the United Nations, the Specialized Agencies, and especially the Bretton Woods Institutions and the WTO, should be seen in this light. The new role for the Trusteeship Council, suggested by Malta and included in the Secretary-General's comprehensive reform proposals referred to in this book, is a very novel and creative suggestion and, therefore merits very serious consideration.

The suggestions concerning the realignment and reorganization of certain Organs, Programs and of some of the Specialized Agencies have been mooted on the basis of great clarity and practical insight, and appear to be both rational and practicable. But in my view, this book, which follows a considerable amount of work from all quarters on the reforms required in the United Nations System, is a unique contribution to the debate on the United Nations reform for the following four reasons.

First and foremost, it has a very pragmatic and realistic agenda. For example, by devoting a substantial amount of effort to reforms of the Administrative Committee on Coordination (ACC), the authors have shown a practical way to make headway in implementing the reform process in the United Nations System, which is capable of paying handsome dividends with minimal costs. By focusing on the ACC, the authors have touched upon a hitherto low priority aspect of United Nations reform. There has been constant criticism of the inability of the United Nations and the Specialized Agencies to function effectively as a system, and yet very little attention has been devoted to making the system work.

Second, the conflict of national versus global priorities and the gap between what we world leaders say and do are, in my view significant and need to be highlighted in any serious effort at reform of the United Nations.

Third, the authors have been and are a part of the system, and, therefore, have an insight into its actual operation, its coordinating mechanisms, its political dynamics, and, above all, a sense of what is realistically achievable in the next ten years or so. Many of the ideas on the ACC expressed in the book have been tested on the anvil of the ACC itself, and have also benefited from comments and feedback from interested circles within the United Nations System.

Fourth, the authors link their analysis and proposals closely to the original dreams and hopes as enshrined in the Charter of the United Nations, and more importantly, they do this without changing a word of the Charter itself.

The decentralized system of the United Nations and the Specialized Agencies has its coordinating link in the ACC. Strengthening the ACC would in no way detract from the decentralized nature of the system. However, in the evolving information society towards which mankind is rapidly moving, a strengthened ACC can play the role of an efficient and effective conductor of an orchestra, so that the United Nations System, with its various Organs, Programs, Funds, Specialized Agencies and the Bretton Woods Institutions, sings a harmonious tune which our future generations can enjoy. This is my aspiration and hope in the sunset years of my life.

The book provides a blueprint for a more democratic United Nations System which would reduce the odds against the developing countries in their access to resources, ideas, information and practical knowledge for their 'catch up' efforts on many basic developmental fronts. If the international system of institutions and relations continues to strengthen, or even merely perpetuate, the *status quo*, then the continuation of current patterns of production, consumption and wealth distribution will result in even greater turmoil and disruption in the world, to the detriment of all. It is, therefore, in the larger interests of humanity as a whole that I support efforts at reform at all levels of political organization, from the local to the global, for globalization to proceed with a human face which is compassionate and caring, especially for those downtrodden, weak and destitute brothers and sisters of ours in all parts of the world.

For making a unique contribution to this noble endeavor through this book, I wish to thank the authors for their penetrating foresight and deep concern for the underprivileged sections of our society. May God bless them in all their future efforts in this direction.

Mandela

Nelson Mandela,
Johannesburg, South Africa
Former President of South Africa

PREFACE

BEYOND THE SECOND GENERATION UNITED NATIONS

The reform of the United Nations has been the subject of debate and discussion for some time. Apart from deliberations, which have been underway within the intergovernmental machinery itself, important contributions have been made and continue to be made by those who work both outside and within the United Nations System.

The fact that so many scholars, academics and politicians have dedicated themselves to studying and scrutinizing the system is symbolic of the hope that '*we the peoples*' still have a place in this Organization. This hope has been the inspiration of millions, spurring many to contribute to the wealth of ideas and proposals to better the system. For never has public opinion called for the abolishment of the United Nations. But public opinion has repeatedly cried out for its reform.

Like any other international institution, and indeed any national government, the United Nations System could not escape the winds of change that have swept the world in recent years. The United Nations was tested and tried throughout the Cold War and yet it survived. New opportunities in international cooperation have buttressed the determination to make it more effective; a determination driven not only by the will of those who may wish to see more done with less, but also by the conviction that much more can be done.

We look to the United Nations as the body best able to address the threats to international peace and security that our planet now faces. Over the past several years, the nature and extent of these threats have changed dramatically. With the end of bipolar world politics, great hope was ignited that the United Nations – freed from the shackles of power diplomacy – would grasp the opportunity to rejuvenate itself to meet the plethora of challenges facing mankind, be they social ills, widespread poverty, bitter internecine civil wars, AIDS epidemics, and the like.

It was during this unprecedented time of change that I was honored to serve as President of the General Assembly of the United Nations. It was a time when the promise of a new international order was shattered by the stark reality of conflict and territorial invasion. The Gulf War lurked in the shadows and later took center stage on our agenda. Rather than providing us with a taste of frustration at our inability to forestall such conflict through preventive diplomacy, it provided us with the assurance that the international community could indeed act in concert when the political will to do so was present.

Yet, visions of misery and internal strife continued to heighten our concerns. The ills confronting the dignity of millions came to the fore as the Organization sought to reorient itself at a time of rapid change.

It was at this time that the development agenda came to the fore. How best could this Organization instill a sense of dignity and well-being in those peoples still suffering from starvation and misery? It was at this time when we demonstrated the determination to start looking with conviction and commitment at the root causes of conflict and tension, in the hope of building a better world, not only for the present but also for future generations.

Within this context, I pursued the idea of purposeful reform. A reform that required not merely tinkering with the institutional set-up of the Organization but rather a reorientation of the principles projected in the Charter so as to enable them to be applied to current realities.

The transformation of the role of the Trusteeship Council was one such proposal. After having completed its mandate in terms of the territories entrusted to it, this principal organ could take into its fold that principle of trust as a notion which reflects a grounding in the past and a link to the future.

The concept of the common heritage of mankind, first codified in the Law of the Sea Convention, has since been incorporated into a number of conventions and international legal instruments. It demonstrated the awareness of the international community, that each generation could not act in isolation but had to rethink its notions of a static world view. It was the ultimate recognition that humankind was not dependent on actions of a particular generation at any given time; rather it was the guardian of the heritage that was handed down from the past and which it held in trust for the future generation.

Thus, the Trusteeship Council, which already incorporated this notion of trust and tutelage, could be the organ to be entrusted with the 'common heritage'. At a time when institutional reform was widely recognized as a must, the incorporation of this notion in its various institutional arms, was an obvious progression. Since then the idea has been pursued within the Organization and has begun to gain ground.

Most recently, the Secretary-General included it in his comprehensive report on reform, as one of the longer-term and possibly high impact proposals. It is my conviction that such a proposal could be at the root of a reformed United Nations. Rather than skirting around the institutional rim, it goes to the core of reform where the concept of trusteeship is applied to peoples rather than to territories.

The Secretary-General's reform program, launched only last year, has started to bear fruit. This is unprecedented, in the sense that for the first time a personality at the head of the system, has taken a proactive and comprehensive view of reform. His program is built on a number of previous proposals made within the international system. It is my sincere hope that the intergovernmental process will bring such proposals to fruition in the interests of a stronger and more relevant United Nations – *A Second Generation United Nations*. For it is with this sense of regeneration that we must continue to look to the future if we are to fulfil that sense of promise with which the fathers of the Charter endowed the United Nations.

This study, produced by authors who are both, in their own right, familiar with the United Nations System, will certainly contribute to the discussions now underway regarding United Nations reform. They seek to build relevance into an Organization often accused of inertia and ineffectiveness. They seek to identify those problems that stem from a lack of coordination and breathe a new political impetus into the system to help it to fulfill its role.

Centered on a blueprint of reform, such a study will undoubtedly provoke much discussion and deliberation. The proposal for the eventual restructuring of committees into commissions seeks to establish an issue-based approach as the basis of an organizational structure rather than have the organizational structure impose itself on the issues dealt with.

The proposed tripartite structure of the General Assembly is an ambitious one, which requires analysis and deliberation in the context of a forum for civil society. Involvement of civil society in the work of the United Nations has become a priority, in the knowledge that as we move into a world based on subsidiarity, involvement of grass-root decision-making becomes paramount. Taking such a structure from the International Labour Organization system and adapting it to that of the General Assembly is challenging, bearing in mind the diversity of issues which the latter discusses.

What remains of paramount value to governments will be the universality of the General Assembly and its working committees. The General Assembly is the only principal organ within the United Nations in which all members are permanent members. It is this feature of permanence and continuity, which must be emphasized – for it is in this manner that we can truly trace the patterns of consensus-building for the benefit of the present and future.

The emphasis put by this study on the need for better coordination within the United Nations System is timely. Innovative tools are at our disposal, such as cheaper and faster means of communication, which have enabled cost-cutting and enhanced effectiveness. It is up to the United Nations to make the best use of such means and set an example for other organizations and governments to follow.

A Second Generation United Nations is a goal, which cannot be denied to the Organization as it enters the new millennium – beset with problems, yet full of promise, and still relevant in today's world. This is what the authors tried to highlight in the publication 'A Second Generation United Nations'; in the conviction of the paramount relevance of this Organization, we tried to develop further ideas on how the United Nations could truly reflect the aspirations of the people it represents.

A Better United Nations for the New Millennium

The road to success is long. The commitment is unwavering. Problems continue to emerge. We must continue our efforts to confront those challenges that the present and the future will bring.

The terrible human tragedy of 'hunger refugees' is one such challenge. How long are we to face the picture of people in flight – homeless, penniless and desperate? Images of the exhaustion and fatigue of those undertaking journeys into an unknown future, as they embark upon our shores, are profoundly shocking. Can we afford to look the other way when so many of us are affected? Such scenes of misery are not an isolated incident on some distant shore, but affect each and every one of us. Can we afford to bequeath to our children a future characterized by populations in flight, where stability and economic well-being are perpetually threatened? Can we really take comfort from our successes while being aware that millions continue to suffer from deprivation, persecution and want?

There is no longer a single government or people which can combat this phenomenon alone. Ultimately, it is the long-term development strategies of countries and peoples that will provide an answer. However, in the knowledge that our world is far from perfect, we must combine our efforts in our search for solidarity. For solidarity alone will provide the base for fulfilling our obligation to ensure human dignity. Millions of humans cannot be allowed to wander the planet in search of a better future, at the risk of life itself.

These millions, like us, look to the United Nations for an answer – an answer we must provide. International cooperation is key to fostering the kind of environment in which human rights and dignity are ensured, not on paper but in practice. We have hailed and demanded respect for human rights – progress has been made but more needs to be done. Let us look together at that aspect of the human person that requires protection – from want, poverty and illness. Let us seek to develop strategies that will truly address these threats – address them not purely on security considerations but based on the sense of dignity that we all aspire to for ourselves, our children and our neighbors around the globe.

As we embark on such efforts, we must also confront the concerns and challenges that are currently before the Organization. Recent events in Europe point to the major challenges that the United Nations is still unable to cope with. Of concern is the seeming lack of direction and orientation in the face of challenges which threaten to make this Organization an instrument of afterthought – whose services are sought only after political processes outside its control have decided the nature and fate of events that will influence international peace and security.

Rather than see such unfolding events reinforce the will to ensure that this universal Organization play its rightful role in such international matters, we have witnessed that an issue clearly within the mandate of the United Nations, by design or default, has been completely excluded from its ambit. This raises serious concern for the future as such recent events could set in motion dangerous trends that might jeopardize the very future of the United Nations as an organization.

Clearly, equally challenging to our future is the question of the balance of approaches by the United Nations. To what extent do grave violations of human rights justify the use of force? Traditional concepts of human rights, national sovereignty and justification for the use of force have become intertwined in a tangled web, and the means to unravel this is not yet clearly perceived.

The extent to which the United Nations and its Member States choose to confront these issues, is key to the future of the Organization. Simply treating events as the act of turning yet another page of history will not provide the sense of direction that is needed in this period of transition. Individually and collectively, we must guard against complacency and irrelevance, so that the United Nations may continue to provide us with the international security system that guarantees global stability.

The regeneration of a determination for engagement, solidarity and cooperation regarding our common goal, may provide us with the political will which is indispensable for making future changes in a developing world context.

I wish to thank the authors of this book for reiterating some of the views and recommendations of *A Second Generation United Nations* and applaud their timely contribution to the debate on the reform of the United Nations at the dawn of a new millennium.

Guido de Marco
The Palace, Valletta, Malta
President of Malta

TABLE OF CONTENTS

ACKNOWLEDGMENTS

The authors wish to show their appreciation to all those who had encouraging words and particularly those who, beyond their call of duty, assisted in one way or another in the preparatory work of this book.

Particular mention has to be made of Dr. Guriqbal Singh Jaiya, Ms. Tamara Nanayakkara, and Ms. Anuradha Madhavan, for their dedicated assistance in all aspects of this project. Dr. Jaiya coordinated the research, and took it upon himself to put right anything that in a project of this magnitude is bound to go wrong. Our appreciation also goes to Ms. Lesley Sherwood, and Ms. Odile Conti, who helped with the diagrams, cover design and the layout, and to Mr. Emmanuel Spiry, Ms. Preeta K. Muthalali, Mr. Pablo Espiniella, and Mr. Jose Blanch who assisted in the research. Our thanks also goes to Mr. Khamis Suedi.

We take full responsibility for any errors and mistakes that inadvertently remain in the book.

Finally, the views and positions in the book are ours and do not necessarily represent the views and positions of the Government of Malta or the World Intellectual Property Organization (WIPO).

INTRODUCTION

TAKING THE SECOND GENERATION UNITED NATIONS INTO THE NEW MILLENNIUM

SUMMARY

Reform of the United Nations has hardly ever been put in a theoretical framework. Some say that the reason for this has been the lack of theories for reforming the Organization.[1] In the area of peacekeeping and security, the United Nations Charter has proved to be less than a democratic constitution, giving the edge to a few countries at the expense of the majority of the Member States. The democratization of the United Nations Charter can be a framework for significant reform.

In the economic and social fields, an appropriate framework follows in the tracks of earlier research[2] which shows the lack of technology transfer as the real cause of underdevelopment, and shows how the United Nations, through its technical assistance programs, seems to have perpetuated the *status quo* rather than helping the poorer countries to break the vicious circle of underdevelopment. Therefore, some of the same tenets and arguments are revisited, particularly the question of the relevance of the United Nations which is the underlying theme of this work.

---

[1] Petersmann E.U., How to Constitutionalize the United Nations? Lessons from the 'International Economic Law Revolution', in *Liber Americorum Günther Jaenicke-Zum*, Springer, 1998, p. 321.
[2] See particularly two Ph D dissertations at the New School for Social Research in New York, one by Merhav in 1966, and the other by Bartolo in 1976.

Two important disparities are discussed, namely the disparity of national versus global priorities,[3] and the disparity of what countries state, at the highest levels, and what they are actually ready to do.[4]

To date, no reform proposals have addressed the question of the whole United Nations System. Some studies and reports on United Nations reform, including the proposals of the Secretary-General, make passing references to the system at large but stop short of making specific proposals on how the system of United Nations, including its Specialized Agencies, can function as a whole rather than in an *ad hoc* way as it does now.

The name 'Specialized Agency' is today a misnomer, since there is hardly any agency which truly specializes in a subject without some other entity duplicating some of the work. In some instances, one may find areas where the work of not only one or two agencies overlaps, but of a number of agencies – for example, in the development field and in the area of humanitarian affairs. The term 'United Nations System' is itself a misnomer, since it certainly does not work as a system.

Another problem in this respect is the problem of definition. One cannot answer with any certainty what is really meant by the term 'United Nations System'. Some include the Bretton Woods Institutions, like the World Bank and the International Monetary Fund (IMF); others, more familiar with their work, do not. The World Trade Organization (WTO) is not part of the United Nations System, although there were efforts by the United Nations to bring it into its fold.

In Chapter 1, the reform of the United Nations is put into the correct perspective. This chapter also includes a summary of the proposals of the Secretary-General and comparisons with other proposals for reform that have been made in other quarters.

Chapter 2 analyzes how the system works now and particularly focuses on the legal agreements that bind, or should bind, the United Nations System together. The recent reforms in the various institutions also give an insight into the original objectives of the organizations and how these have changed, if, in fact, they have.

In this book, relevance takes precedence over efficiency. No irrelevant organization should be allowed to exist, irrespective of how efficient it is. Once the relevance of the organization is beyond doubt, then the quest for efficiency should be pursued without hesitation. Chapter 3 is devoted to the challenges and various levels of relevance; it develops a yardstick of relevance against which all organizations and their activities need to be measured.

Even though, since the publication of '*A Second Generation United Nations*', the question of relevance has become very topical, there is hardly any work that deals with this matter comprehensively. The earlier statements and the preliminary reports, which preceded the comprehensive proposals of the Secretary-General (Renewing the United Nations: A Program of Reform) looked very promising in this regard, but did not live up to expectations, since the proposals never explained the meaning of relevance in the

---

[3] de Marco, Guido and M. Bartolo, *A Second Generation United Nations*, London and New York, Kegan Paul International, 1997, Chapter 9.
[4] For example, see speeches by President B. Clinton, Prime Minister Tony Blair and others, made at the Summit commemorating the 50th Anniversary of The Multilateral Trading System. WTO Publication, p. 16 and p. 76.

context of the United Nations. The question seems to have been completely overlooked in the details of the proposals and the final recommendations. This work explains the various levels of relevance that would be essential for *A Better United Nations for the New Millennium*. Without relevance, the United Nations cannot expect to live up to the noble aspirations of its Charter. The aspirations of 'we the peoples' must mean all the peoples and not just some of the peoples.

The Charter is analyzed and discussed as it relates to matters of coordination and reform in Chapter 4, to set the stage for the chapters on the ACC, as well as later chapters. The book also deals at length with the present machinery for coordination, in Chapters 5 to 8. The ACC is evaluated and put through rigorous analysis to bring out the results of the frequent meetings of the ACC and its subsidiary machinery. What is the cost, in terms of human and financial resources, of such coordination? What does the ACC administer? What does it coordinate? An attempt is made to answer these and other questions to see the relevance of such a committee, and even if this is the right title.

Alternative ways of coordination are investigated. However, if the United Nations System could be sufficiently focused to enable anyone to see the mission or *raison d'être* of every agency, then there may be very little need for coordination. The wonders of the latest developments in information technology would make the necessary coordination possible at the least possible cost.

Coordination should not be the monopoly of the United Nations, or of any other agency for that matter. Coordination should be a transparent affair, with the agency most concerned with the subject playing a lead role.

A Better United Nations for the New Millennium would have to be different from the United Nations of the twentieth century. The current political will to reform the United Nations should not be lost by making merely cosmetic changes, or changes which may affect its efficiency rather than its relevance or direction. This may be the only chance we have to give the United Nations the needed responsibility and authority to achieve the noble ideals of the Charter and to safeguard such ideals for the future. This chance must not be lost, because it may not come again soon.

This new millennium United Nations must be equipped to be the centerpiece of a United Nations System, including all Specialized Agencies and entities working for peace and development, both governmental and nongovernmental. Such a United Nations would give no excuse to anyone to withhold funding because its motto would be that, if an activity could be undertaken more economically and more efficiently anywhere else, it would not be a job for the *better* United Nations.

The blueprint for *A Better United Nations for the New Millennium* is proposed in Chapter 9. This 'better' United Nations would be a more realistic alternative to the fully transformed United Nations referred to in Annex III, which would require drastic changes in the Charter, if not a completely new Constitution.

Chapter 10 puts to the test the new role of the proposed *Better United Nations for the New Millennium* by relating it to the other institutions and making the best use of existing institutions to prevent duplication and waste.

The concluding chapter presents the blueprint with diagrams and the vision of a truly relevant United Nations System.

DEVELOPMENT OR UNDERDEVELOPMENT

The Age of International Institutions

The headlines at the end of the second millennium continue to announce the ever-increasing gap between the rich and the poor. These headlines usually quote figures from the annual reports of the various institutions that were established, primarily after the Second World War, to assist in the reconstruction of those countries that had been ravaged by the war. This reconstruction was primarily expected to rehabilitate the countries of Europe, to ensure and guarantee the continuing expansion and development of the world economy, driven by the expansion of the economies of the developed countries.

The last century of the second millennium could easily be referred to as the Age of International Institutions. The International Labour Organization (ILO), the League of Nations and later the United Nations and its family of Specialized Agencies, the Bretton Woods Institutions and the WTO may be considered the most significant. However, a number of other institutions, regional in nature, also contributed to this age of supra-national institutions.

These institutions and others may have prevented a third world war, but they have certainly not prevented the many regional conflicts that still plague the people directly involved. These institutions have also failed to raise the living standards of the great majority of peoples, and have also failed to ameliorate the life of the poorest of the poor or the destitute of this world. In fact, the promise and hope of self-reliance has only faded with time, as the poor continue to struggle to have access to the most basic necessities. Particularly in developing countries, a very sizeable percentage of the population still does not have access to means of wealth creation or to opportunities for acquiring the knowledge and skills that could enable the poor to graduate, as it were, to a level where they have a decent livelihood and live a life of dignity and self-respect.

The objective of this book is to analyze why the United Nations and the related Specialized Agencies could not assist more effectively the countries in need, particularly in the area of economic and social development. This is particularly important now, when everyone seems to be concerned with the future of the United Nations. In fact, the First General Assembly of the United Nations of the next millennium, starting in September 2000, is expected to look into this matter with the objective of launching a more effective United Nations for the future.

This book is primarily concerned with the relevance of the United Nations and the Specialized Agencies, as reiterated during the 45th Session the General Assembly of the United Nations, and further develops some of the ideas of '*A Second Generation United Nations*' [5] in this regard.

---

[5] As pointed out in Chapter 1, some of the proposals of '*A Second Generation United Nations*' have already been implemented, and others earmarked for implementation.

Increasing Gap Between the Rich and the Poor

The United Nations, and the Specialized Agencies for that matter, cannot solve all the problems of the world. In over fifty years of work in the area of technical cooperation, the United Nations does not have much to show by way of results. Its own figures continue to show, year after year, a picture of severe poverty and the increasing gap between the rich and the poor.

According to the Human Development Report of 1997,[6] although poverty has been dramatically reduced in some parts of the world, a quarter of the world's people remains in abject poverty. About 1.3 billion people live on incomes of less than USD1 a day. The global expansion of trade and investment is proceeding speedily, but largely for the benefit of the more dynamic and powerful countries. It is pointed out that, unless globalization is carefully managed, poor countries and poor people will become increasingly marginalized.[7] Already, annual losses to developing countries from unequal access to trade, labor and finance have been estimated at USD500 billion, or ten times what they receive in foreign aid.[8]

The 1998 edition of the same report[9] points out that globalization is hurting poor people, not just poor countries. While globalization has helped reduce poverty in some of the largest and strongest economies, the developing world has seen the gap between 'winners' and 'losers' widening. The share of the poorest 20 percent of the world's population has shrunk from 2.3 percent of world income in 1960 to 1.1 percent today, and it is still falling. The 1999 version of the report continues with the stark statistics, pointing out that the assets of the world's top three billionaires are more than the combined GNP of all the Least Developed Countries and their 600 million people.[10]

The United Nations is marginalized by the Bretton Woods Institutions and the WTO in international economic and trade matters. In the area of political affairs and security, the recent events in Kosovo[11] underline the inability of the United Nations to influence developments of importance to its Member States, in their region and beyond.

A relevant United Nations would know its limitations, and, therefore, its Member States would only expect realistic results, and it would not be blamed for everything that is bad in the world. More importantly, a United Nations that is relevant to the concerns of its Member States would deal with such concerns more easily, and probably with better results.

This book endeavors to propose ways to make the United Nations at large more relevant. It is not too concerned with efficiency as an end in itself, because an efficient organization that is not relevant would do worse and not better.

One should resist the temptation to blame all the ills of the world on the United Nations. There should be no hesitation in stating that the primary responsibility for

---

[6] *Human Development Report, 1997*, published by UNDP, Oxford University Press, 1997, p. 23.
[7] *Ibid.*, p. 87.
[8] *Ibid.*, p. 87.
[9] *Human Development Report, 1998*, published by UNDP, Oxford University Press, 1998, pp. 33-37.
[10] *Human Development Report 1999*, published by UNDP, Oxford University Press, 1999, p. 3.
[11] See particularly Security Council resolutions S/1999/517 of 14 May 1999 and S/RES/1239 of 14 May 1999.

national economic development rests with the respective countries themselves. The United Nations and the Specialized Agencies may, and should, assist countries in their development efforts whenever possible. This is particularly important in the light of the framework referred to above, and the conventional wisdom that the introduction of technology in the developing countries is the *primum mobile* of economic development.

The Technical Cooperation Programs of the United Nations

The technical cooperation programs of the United Nations and the Specialized Agencies were the ideal channel to transfer some of the necessary technology to assist the poor countries in breaking the vicious cycle of underdevelopment. Put in a different way, the poor countries needed their *comparative advantage* shifted to products which would have given them a competitive edge in international markets, rather than maintaining their existing specialized areas, usually primary products. This left them victim to the phenomenon of 'adverse terms of trade', and limited their role in international trade and the gains from it.

The increase in the number of 'Least Developed Countries' is in itself a strong indication of the failure of the technical cooperation programs of the United Nations.[12] This failure, among other reasons, led to the decline of resources for United Nations technical cooperation and for Overseas Development Assistance (ODA) in general, in the last decade. The numerous evaluations of the technical cooperation programs of the United Nations during the last fifty years failed to identify the problems, because these evaluations were always formulated in terms of the efficiency of the programs themselves, rather than the impact they had on the countries involved. Some of the reasons for this are referred to briefly, to put the present debate on United Nations reform in the right perspective.

The United Nations' programs of technical cooperation failed not because they were not efficient but because they were not relevant.[13] The lack of a meaningful definition of development prevented the formulation of useful criteria for impact evaluation of United Nations programs and projects of technical cooperation, or technical assistance, as they were called earlier.

It is felt that the same mistake should not be made in the present debate on the reform of the United Nations. The United Nations needs to be made relevant before it is made efficient. In the case of United Nations reform there is no excuse, since it is clear what the Member States expect of it. In this respect, the Charter of the United Nations is unambiguous and speaks for all the peoples of the Member States.

---

[12] Of the 48 Least Developed Countries, 33 are in Africa; 9 in Asia; 5 in the Pacific; and 1 in the Caribbean. UNCTAD has the responsibility of keeping track of the number of Least Developed Countries.
[13] See Bartolo, op. cit.

The Neoclassical View

The early years of the formative stage of the international institutions, particularly the United Nations and the Bretton Woods Institutions, coincided with a very intense and productive period in the evolution of economic thought on development. Although this evolution saw its most compelling scholarship as a result of the research of Raoul Prebisch[14] and of the research and discussions of the Economic Commission for Latin America (now ECLAC) on the terms of trade of developing countries in that region, it had a much wider significance beyond Latin America. The relationship between the developing and the developed countries, thanks to Prebisch and his followers, could be seen in the context of neoclassical economic thought which predominated at that time, and which produced a prolific amount of literature on the relations between the *center* and the *periphery*.[15]

As mentioned in Annex 1, Adam Smith's classical view of trade was followed by the more comprehensive neoclassical interpretation based on the David Ricardo's theory of *comparative advantage*. It was in this framework that Prebisch, and others that followed, tried to show the adverse effect on developing countries of the terms of trade. This led to the belief that trade between unequal partners tended to be more to the benefit of the stronger partner. Prebisch showed that this was mainly due to the income inelasticities of demand for raw materials and the basic asymmetries in the way labor markets functioned.[16]

Some, particularly those who were defending the concerns of the developing countries, felt that the United Nations, and more importantly the Bretton Woods Institutions, ignored the important intellectual developments in the area of economic thought referred to above. More importantly, they felt that they ignored the empirical evidence that showed that the terms of trade moved against the weaker partner, namely, the developing countries. The United Nations and the other institutions did not adjust their technical cooperation programs to assist the developing countries out of the neoclassical trap referred to above.

It is exactly in this context that the question of the relevance of the United Nations needs to be seen. No one denies that this is only one aspect of the work of the United Nations. The other important work in the political and security area should not be ignored, but there is now unanimous understanding and agreement that the economic and social well-being of the people of this planet is essential for universal peace and security. For this reason it was considered essential to develop the intellectual framework against which real United Nations reform, in this important area, may be seen.

Relevance of the United Nations cannot be seen in the abstract, and if there is an area that is as far from the abstract as one can go it is the area of economic and social development. Extreme poverty and destitution are very real and too common in this

---

[14] Refer to the bibliography for some of the work of Prebisch, particularly his seminal article of 1951.

[15] For additional information, see also works by Singer and Sunkel in the bibliography.

[16] For an excellent summary of the historical background on the economic thinking on development, the predominant theories of underdevelopment (pp. 24-33) and the Prebisch hypothesis (pp. 333-357) one may want to refer to Sunkel, Osvaldo, *Development from Within*, Boulder & London, Lynne Reinner Publishers, 1993.

world. The eradication of poverty should certainly be a major yardstick for the relevance of the United Nations.

It is believed that, in the last fifty years, the United Nations has not adequately addressed the issue of the poverty that predominates in our world. It has not adequately addressed the elements of the neoclassical paradigm of development while formulating technical cooperation programs to assist developing countries. This is so in spite of the fact that the foremost proponents of the effects of such a paradigm on the developing countries came primarily from one of its regional arms, namely, the ECLAC, and later the United Nations Conference on Trade and Development (UNCTAD).

It is true that the power and significance of the terms of trade debate seemed to have dissipated by mid 1970s. The valiant attempts by the followers of Prebisch to continue in his tradition became less frequent as time passed, and apart from the efforts of Sunkel[17] and his collaborators and a few others, very little else was done. This does not mean, however, that the underlying premises of the era are no longer valid.

Terms of Trade of Manufactures

In fact, recent work by the UNCTAD[18] and others,[19] shows the same phenomenon of adverse terms of trade for the developing countries, this time for manufactures rather than for primary products. This would probably rekindle some interest in the earlier debate, since it would appear that the UNCTAD figures could prove to be more significant, if further empirical work continued to show such a trend.

The UNCTAD Report quoted emphasized that the indications of deterioration in the terms of trade 'do not provide an adequate test of the Prebisch-Singer thesis as it applies to manufactures, because they are based on aggregate data for manufactured exports from all developing countries, including both labor- and technology-intensive products, which according to this thesis should be subject to different price dynamics'.[20] But it appears that there is enough evidence to show that the relative price of manufactured exports for developing countries has fallen during the past two decades, alongside the rapid expansion of their volume.[21]

Moreover, calculations by the UNCTAD Secretariat seem to conclude that 'Export volumes from the South increase by more than 80 percent , but the terms of trade for their manufactures drop to less than one half of their previous level. Thus, real export earnings of the South (i.e., in terms of the imports they can procure from the North) fall considerably'.[22]

Although UNCTAD warned that the results obtained are highly sensitive to the assumptions made with respect to consumption substitution elasticities, it was concluded

---

[17] Sunkel, *op. cit.*
[18] *Trade and Development Report, 1996*, UNCTAD, pp. 146-152.
[19] Minford, P., J. Riley and E. Nowell, 'The Elixir of Growth: Trade, Non-traded Goods and Development', *CEPR Discussion Paper* No.1165, London, May 1995.
[20] UNCTAD, *op. cit.*, p. 147.
[21] UNCTAD, *op. cit.*, p. 149.
[22] UNCTAD, *op. cit.*, p. 152.

that 'the degree of immiserization is widely recognized in the case of primary products, but it is no less for labor-intensive manufactures'. [23]

This development of the adverse terms of trade of manufactures, if it can be sustained, would also be very significant in the context of the present debate at the WTO on globalization and the marginalization of developing countries. The discussions on the follow-up to the Uruguay Round and the possible next round of trade negotiations would be a good reason for the UNCTAD, on behalf of the United Nations, to develop a new paradigm of economic development. This paradigm would go beyond and yet not ignore the neoclassical concerns so ably advanced by Prebisch and the Latin American School.

Relevance in the economic and social sectors of the United Nations and the Specialized Agencies has to be seen in the context of whether the United Nations may play a role in changing the international economic and financial architecture to level the playing field. It has also to be seen in the context of whether the United Nations can assist the developing countries in participating in the new world order, without the constraints imposed upon them by the neoclassical paradigm of trade and development.

WAR OR PEACE

A Theory for United Nations Reform ?

The United Nations is primarily a political organization, irrespective of the areas of work it is involved in. Everything at the United Nations depends on the political will of Member States. To be more accurate, it is the political will of some of the Member States, namely, those that have the most influence, due to their advanced stage of economic development and the high level of their assessed contribution to the budget of the United Nations.

The successes of the United Nations, which should not be downplayed, have occurred when the national priorities of the most influential Member States coincided with international priorities. We saw this happening, for example, in the drive towards decolonization, the fight against apartheid, and the emergence of Namibia into Statehood. In a great many other instances of United Nations work, the words and statements at the highest level were not matched with deeds or any concrete follow-up action. In such cases, the United Nations remains at a stalemate.

We think that, in spite of the criticisms of the United Nations and its Charter, we are not ready yet to support a call for a completely new organization or a new Charter. Even the complete transformation of the United Nations proposed in Annex III, although probably requiring major changes in the Charter, would still safeguard the dreams and hopes of its drafters, by maintaining those elements which eloquently reflect universal participation and global governance responsibility.

As far as *A Better United Nations for the New Millennium* is concerned, we do not foresee any major changes in the Charter, if any changes at all. But we do call for a

---

[23] *Ibid.*

democratization of the Charter, by emphasizing the parts that call for wider participation in the work and decisions of the United Nations, for example, it is possible to do so in the Security Council, and, by reinterpreting its global governance responsibility, in the case of the Economic and Social Council (ECOSOC).

We think that it is only fair to give the Charter of the United Nations a chance, by exploiting its potential before it is declared a failure and replaced. This could be done by interpreting relevant parts, like the Preamble[24] and Chapter III, Article 8,[25] to introduce tripartite representation in the General Assembly and at all levels of the United Nations. This tripartite system would include the *civil society* and parliaments, in addition to the Governments. Universal participation in the work and decisions of the United Nations is in both the spirit and the letter of the Charter. In addition, it should not be too difficult to reinterpret the spirit and letter of the Charter to give the General Assembly a legitimate function to govern the whole United Nations System, including the Bretton Woods Institutions and the WTO.

Political Developments due to the Cold War

A theoretical framework certainly gives the discipline and the advantage of scholarship to facilitate clear and lucid analysis. However, any analysis that involves the United Nations must also be put in the correct historical context. The 'Age of International Institutions' also coincided with political developments dominated by the Cold War. This gave rise to other institutions, like the North Atlantic Treaty Organization (NATO), the Warsaw Pact and the Organization for Security and Cooperation in Europe (OSCE), previously known as the Conference on Security and Cooperation in Europe (CSCE).

More importantly, these developments had an impact on the work and effectiveness of the United Nations, dominated by a Security Council that was rendered ineffective, especially when the two superpowers took different positions on major conflicts.

The disintegration of the USSR and the transition to the post-cold war era did not make the United Nations more effective. If anything, it made it less so, primarily because of the influence of the only superpower left, namely the United States. This made the other Member States suspicious of the role of the United States in the United Nations, even when there was no clear or valid reason for it.

Kissinger's statement[26] that 'In the twentieth century, no country has influenced international relations as decisively and at the same time as ambivalently as the United States' could as well have been said about the influence of the United States on the United Nations. This should not come as a surprise to anyone, considering the role of the United States as the only remaining superpower and the fact that it pays one fourth of the United Nations regular budget.

---

[24] As everyone should know, the preamble of the Charter of the United Nations starts with the words, 'We the Peoples of the United Nations Determined'.
[25] Chapter III, Article 8, states, 'The United Nations shall place no restrictions on the eligibility of men and women to participate in any capacity and under conditions of equality in its principal and subsidiary organs'.
[26] Kissinger, Henry, *Diplomacy*, Simon and Schuster, 1994, p. 17.

The relevance of the United Nations in the political and security areas has to be seen in the context of national versus global priorities. This means that some countries would support the United Nations as long as the objectives and priorities of the Organization coincided with their national ones. This was difficult to achieve. In this context, we feel that the relevance of the United Nations has to be seen as representing the objectives and priorities of the majority of the Member States rather than only of a few, even if these few finance the bulk of the budget. In other words, countries should accept the fact that the United Nations becomes more relevant only if the gap between national and global priorities and targets is bridged.[27]

There could not be a more striking example of such a test of relevance for the United Nations as the recent conflict in Kosovo. It may be hasty to conclude that the credibility of the United Nations has received a fatal blow by being completely left out of the decision to take military action. In fact, this could serve as a 'wake-up' call for the United Nations and might result in its resurgence, to launch its role in the spirit of its Charter. We hope that it is the latter and that it is realized that conflict resolution by peaceful means is the ultimate objective of the United Nations, if it is to be relevant.

THE UNITED NATIONS AND DEVELOPMENT

The International Development Strategy and the United Nations Development Decades

The developments in both the economic and political areas referred to above served as the backdrop for the so-called North-South debate and the East-West conflict at the United Nations. The political debates and ensuing actions at the United Nations were the things that made the headlines, and as such were the things that people heard about. On the other hand, the discussions and decisions that resulted from the North-South debates on economic and social matters hardly ever made the headlines and, therefore, were scarcely known to the outside world.

Few people have heard about the International Development Strategies or the United Nations Development Decades,[28] launched in the 1960s and continuing until the end of this millennium. These decades came about as a result of an international consensus that a new approach and impetus were needed to deal with the urgent development problems. The International Development Strategy that was eventually formulated as a result of intensive debate at the United Nations between the countries of the North and the South never really had a chance of success. The major shortcoming was the failure to agree on realistic targets for the strategy, both as concerns growth targets and an increase in

---

[27] de Marco and Bartolo, *op. cit.*, p. 119.
[28] For a summary of what the strategies and the decades were supposed to accomplish, and the various dates and deadlines, see *Basic Facts About the United Nations*, United Nations Publication, 1998, p. 127.

Overseas Development Assistance (ODA). Moreover, not even the most modest targets agreed upon were met.

It was believed that a major shortcoming of the International Development Strategy, apart from the lack of financial resources, was the lack of a meaningful definition of development. This made it difficult to set realistic targets and to develop useful development indicators. As a result, it was difficult to develop useful evaluation criteria to identify the shortcomings of both the Strategy and the technical cooperation programs of the United Nations.

This concern, that the measure of development in terms of GNP and other national accounting techniques did not provide a meaningful measure of development, divided the so-called United Nations System into two camps. The United Nations, with some of its Funds and Programs that dealt with operational activities for development and humanitarian purposes, emphasized this concern and did something about it. On the other hand, the Bretton Woods Institutions seemed to accept these measures, in spite of wide criticism that they were ignoring for a long time the social consequences of their Structural Adjustment Programs (SAPs).

Development with a Human Face

The United Nations, led primarily by the United Nations Children's Fund (UNICEF) called for 'development with a human face', which meant that any adverse social consequences of the development programs should be simultaneously addressed. This campaign was conducted in the context of the SAPs of the Bretton Woods Institutions. UNICEF and some other parts of the United Nations kept pointing out the social inequities and hardships that the SAPs caused in the relevant countries. They showed how the poorest segments of the population of these countries were bearing the brunt of the economic sacrifices which were produced by the implementation of programs to restructure their economies.

As a result of this determination of the United Nations, the enlightened leadership of some of the Bretton Woods Institutions, yielding to the pressure, started taking these social realities into consideration while formulating their SAPs, even if the net result was that the SAPs took a little longer to meet their objectives. Thus, *development with a human face* became more than a slogan.

The firm belief of a number of senior officials of the United Nations, that economic and social consequences of development cannot be considered separately, also led to a breakthrough with the formulation of a more meaningful definition of development. This, in turn, facilitated the production of a set of useful and significant development indicators.

The Human Development Index (HDI)

This breakthrough came with the publication of the Human Development Report[29] in 1990, which defined human development as the process of enlarging people's choices. The now generally recognized Human Development Index or HDI takes into consideration a number of development indicators, both economic and social.

Before the HDI there was always a recognition of the deficiencies in the prevailing measurement of development. In fact, there were various efforts and recommendations in this regard, which emphasized a type of 'quality of life' index[30] and a 'degree of transfer of technology'[31] index. But it was only in 1990, with the publication of the Human Development Report, that the HDI was recognized as the most comprehensive and equitable measure of development. It seems now, about ten years later, that the HDI continues to be the generally recognized and acceptable yardstick for measuring development.

The understanding and definition of development, as it has evolved, augers well for a more effective role of the United Nations and the United Nations System in facilitating a more equitable participation in international relations for the majority of its Member States. It is in this context that the United Nations can become relevant to the needs and concerns of all of its Member States, rather than to those of only a few of them.

This would require, of course, a strong political will. While it would require some basic rethinking of the present framework for development and some basic changes in the United Nations and the System at large, it is realistic to expect that it can be accomplished, to everyone's satisfaction, in both developed and developing countries.

The development debate of the next millennium must be conducted in a more candid and less antagonistic manner than has been the case in the last fifty years. No one should expect or call for an overnight revolution in this regard.

The development debate must be conducted at the United Nations. That is where all Member States have an equal status.

The debate at the United Nations has to be more candid, at two levels. At the first level, the United Nations has to recognize that it is not helping developing countries in their efforts to participate equitably in international economic, financial, and trade relations. So far, the United Nations has not been able to do so and should not pretend otherwise, as it is clear that the Bretton Woods Institutions and the WTO have the primary influence in international economic, financial and trade issues.

At the second level, it must also be recognized that, in the past, gains from trade and other international activities, such as finance, went only marginally to the majority of developing countries. This matter should be discussed without recrimination. Only cool heads may come out with a formula that takes into consideration the past inequities and provides for more equitable participation in the future.

---

[29] *Human Development Report, 1990*, UNDP, Oxford University Press, 1990.
[30] Liu, B., 'Quality of Life: Concept, Measure and Results', in the *American Journal of Economics and Sociology*, January 1975, vol. 34, No. 1.
[31] Bartolo, *op. cit.*

What is certain is that such a debate has to take place within a *Better United Nations System* that is relevant to the concerns and requirements of the majority of Member States. This book is a modest contribution to this end.

UNITED NATIONS REFORM AND ITS ROLE IN FACILITATING A GLOBAL ENVIRONMENT FOR EQUITABLE DEVELOPMENT IN PEACE AND FREEDOM

The framework and rationale developed above should facilitate the discussion on United Nations reform, as it puts the subject in the context of economic and political thinking prevalent during the formative years of the international institutions. The first few chapters put reform in the correct historical context, both in the United Nations proper and in the so-called United Nations System. The question of relevance is then dealt with at length, before analyzing what the Charter of the United Nations says about reform and coordination.

This is followed by a series of chapters dealing with a new and relevant ACC, to be called the Policy and Coordination Board (PCB), which is considered pivotal in keeping the United Nations System together and functioning as a whole.

A blueprint for the *Better United Nations* is followed by a discussion and a set of recommendations on how this *Better United Nations* may bring out the best in the rest of the United Nations System and other institutions. The conclusion presents the blueprint with diagrams and the vision of a United Nations oriented in the right direction and having a clearer focus.

CHAPTER 1

THE REFORM
OF THE UNITED NATIONS

SUMMARY

After a brief description of the organigram of the current United Nations System, United Nations reform is put in the correct perspective. What has been reformed so far is analyzed to identify what the status of United Nations reform really is. Considering the present plans for the changes anticipated, what are the United Nations and the United Nations System going to look like at the beginning of the new millennium? This chapter also includes a comparison between the proposals of the Secretary-General and the *Second Generation United Nations*, and particularly on how much the former drew upon the latter for ideas.

The proposals in *A Second Generation United Nations* formed part of a rich harvest of reform proposals. The Secretary-General, in preparation for his Comprehensive Report, had at his disposal a wealth of analyses and recommendations. The most important recommendations came as a result of a number of *ad hoc* working groups which were established soon after the 45th Session of the General Assembly and dealt with a number of important sectors and subjects.

The Secretary-General of the United Nations issued his comprehensive report entitled *Renewing the United Nations: A Program of Reform* in July 1997. The recommendations in this report and recommendations from other sources are analyzed.

The highlights of the Secretary-General's proposals are also compared with some of the proposals in *A Second Generation United Nations.*

There is certainly a gap between the number of recommendations and proposals available and what has actually been implemented so far. This phenomenon is discussed with the objective of trying to find the main reasons behind this. Most of the reform developments have occurred at the level of the Secretariat, and very little else has been reformed.

Proposals to reform the main organs of the United Nations, namely, the Security Council, the ECOSOC, and the Trusteeship Council, are also reviewed to determine the stage of progress, if any.

The Present United Nations

Since this is a book about the United Nations, it is important for us to understand what is the United Nations. In this book, when we refer to the United Nations, we mean the General Assembly and the major organs represented in Diagram 1 entitled the 'Current United Nations System'. In addition to the General Assembly, the major organs consist of the Security Council, ECOSOC, the Trusteeship Council, the Secretariat, and the International Court of Justice (ICJ). The major organs normally have a number of committees, *ad hoc* bodies and subsidiary organs. The United Nations also has a number of Funds and Programs, which (although headed by a senior person, who reports to an executive board) are under the responsibility of the Secretary-General, who heads the Secretariat. Diagram 2 gives the details of how the Secretariat is organized. Although some would understand the Secretariat to be the major departments and the various offices in New York, Diagram 2 includes also some entities situated outside of New York, but which still are considered part of the Secretariat. Sometimes we refer to the United Nations proper, to distinguish it from the United Nations System as a whole.

The United Nation System includes the Specialized Agencies like the International Labour Organization (ILO), the International Monetary Fund (IMF), and the International Bank for Reconstruction and Development (World Bank). The degree of closeness between the United Nations proper and the Specialized Agencies is determined by the agreements signed by the individual Specialized Agencies with the United Nations. The IMF and the World Bank have agreements, which differ from most of the other Specialized Agencies' agreements. The World Trade Organization has no agreement at all. In Chapter 2, the agency agreements are analyzed. Ideally, it is desirable to have a United Nations that would require no agreements to hold it together; in other words, a holistic United Nations.

UNITED NATIONS REFORM SINCE THE 45TH SESSION OF THE UNITED NATIONS (1990-1991) TO THE PRESENT TIME

The debate on the reform of the United Nations picked up momentum during the 45th Session of the General Assembly (1990-1991) and this momentum has not let up since. It reached a peak during the 50th Anniversary of the United Nations in 1995. The lack of any concrete changes to the United Nations as a result of this debate left some

Diagram 1. Current United Nations System

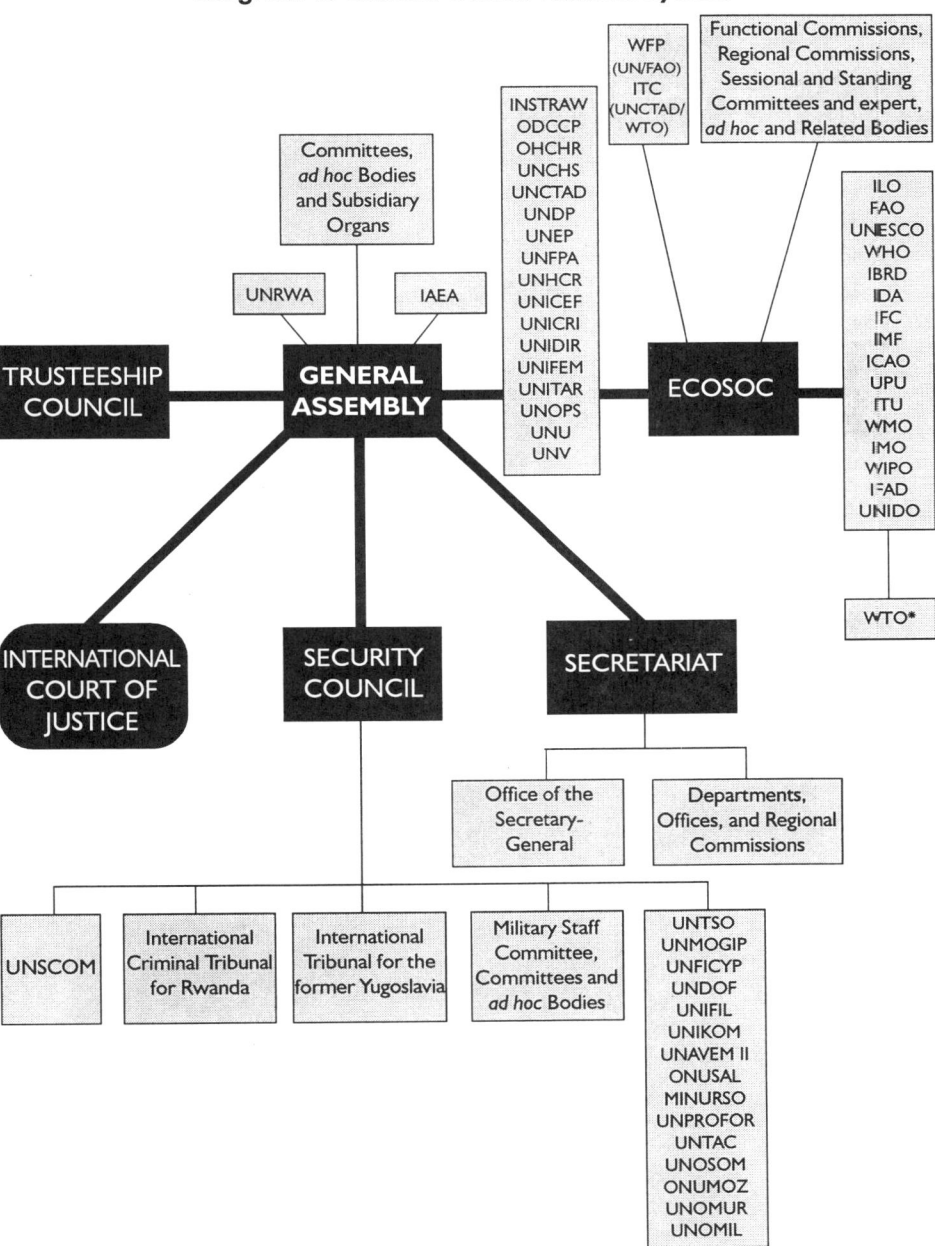

* Not part of the United Nations System although has cooperating arrangements and practices with the Organization.

Diagram 2. United Nations Secretariat

Secretary-General

Executive Office
of the Secretary-General

Office of Legal Affairs

Department for Disarmament Affairs

Office for the Coordination
of Humanitarian Affairs

Department of General Assembly Affairs
and Conference Services

Department of Management
Office of Programme Planning,
Budget and Accounts
Office of the Human Resources Management
Office of Central Support Services

Office of the Iraq Programme

United Nations Fund for International Partnership (UNFIP)

Office of the United Nations
Security Coordinator

Office of Internal Oversight Services

Department of Political Affairs

Department of Peacekeeping Operations

Department of Economic and Social Affairs

Department of Public Information

Office of the Special Representative
of the Secretary-General for Children
and Armed Conflict

United Nations Joint Staff Pension Fund

Secretariat of the United Nations Conference
on Trade and Development

Secretariat of the United Nations
Environment Programme

United Nations Centre for Human Settlements

Office for Drug Control and Crime Prevention

Secretariat of the Economic Commission
for Africa

Secretariat of the Economic and Social
Commission for Asia and the Pacific

Secretariat of the Economic Commission
for Europe

Secretariat of the Economic Commission
for Latin America and the Caribbean

Secretariat of the Economic and
Social Commission for Western Asia

Office of the United Nations High
Commissioner for Human Rights

Office of the United Nations High
Commissioner for Refugees

United Nations Relief and Works Agency
for Palestine Refugees in the Near East

UN Office at Geneva

UN Office at Vienna

UN Office at Nairobi

disenchantment, and created the environment for the change of leadership, which took place in January 1997. The new Secretary-General came to his task with a commitment to make an impact in the area of United Nations reform, and shortly thereafter presented his comprehensive proposals that are analyzed later on in this chapter.

Despite various setbacks in the attempts to reform the United Nations, we agree with the view of the Secretary-General that this matter is of the utmost importance. We think that there should be no letting up in our bold efforts to make the United Nations work for all the peoples of the world rather than for a few, as at present.

We know that it is not easy for the countries that have influenced the United Nations since its inception to give up some of this influence. We know of the gap between rhetoric and action in this regard. We have referred already to the conflict between national and global priorities. We have emphasized the importance of relevance over efficiency. We think that eventually we will succeed in having a *Better United Nations* for the future, because there is no other alternative.

THE SECOND GENERATION UNITED NATIONS

The Book, entitled '*A Second Generation United Nations*' was published in 1997 when the debate on the United Nations reforms was at its peak. In January 1997, when a new Secretary-General of the United Nations was appointed, he had a rich harvest of reform proposals before him, including those of the *Second Generation United Nations.* The proposals of *A Second Generation United Nations* are summarized in Diagram 3, entitled Second Generation United Nations, and Diagram 4, entitled Second Generation Economic and Social Institutions of the United Nations. The book gives predominance to the General Assembly and proposes the streamlining of its structures as well as those of the Secretariat, as indicated in Diagram 3. This predominance of the General Assembly, reinvigorated by the decennial summits, is extended to the economic and social areas, as seen from Diagram 4. This is elaborated later in the book.

The Secretary-General presented his comprehensive proposals on reform in his report entitled, *Renewing the United Nations: A Program of Reform,* which was issued on 14 July 1997.[1] The Secretary-General had at his disposal a wealth of analysis and recommendations, the most important of which came as a result of a number of *ad hoc* committees which were established soon after the 45th Session of the General Assembly and which dealt with a number of important sectors and subjects of the United Nations. Work is still continuing in some form or another on some of these sectors and subjects, for example, on the Security Council.

Other contributions came from individuals, Governments, groups (like the European Union) and other organizations (like the South Centre). Some of the ideas of *A Second Generation United Nations* were reflected in the report of the Secretary-General referred to above.

---

[1] A/51/950, 14 July 1997.

Diagram 3. Second Generation United Nations*

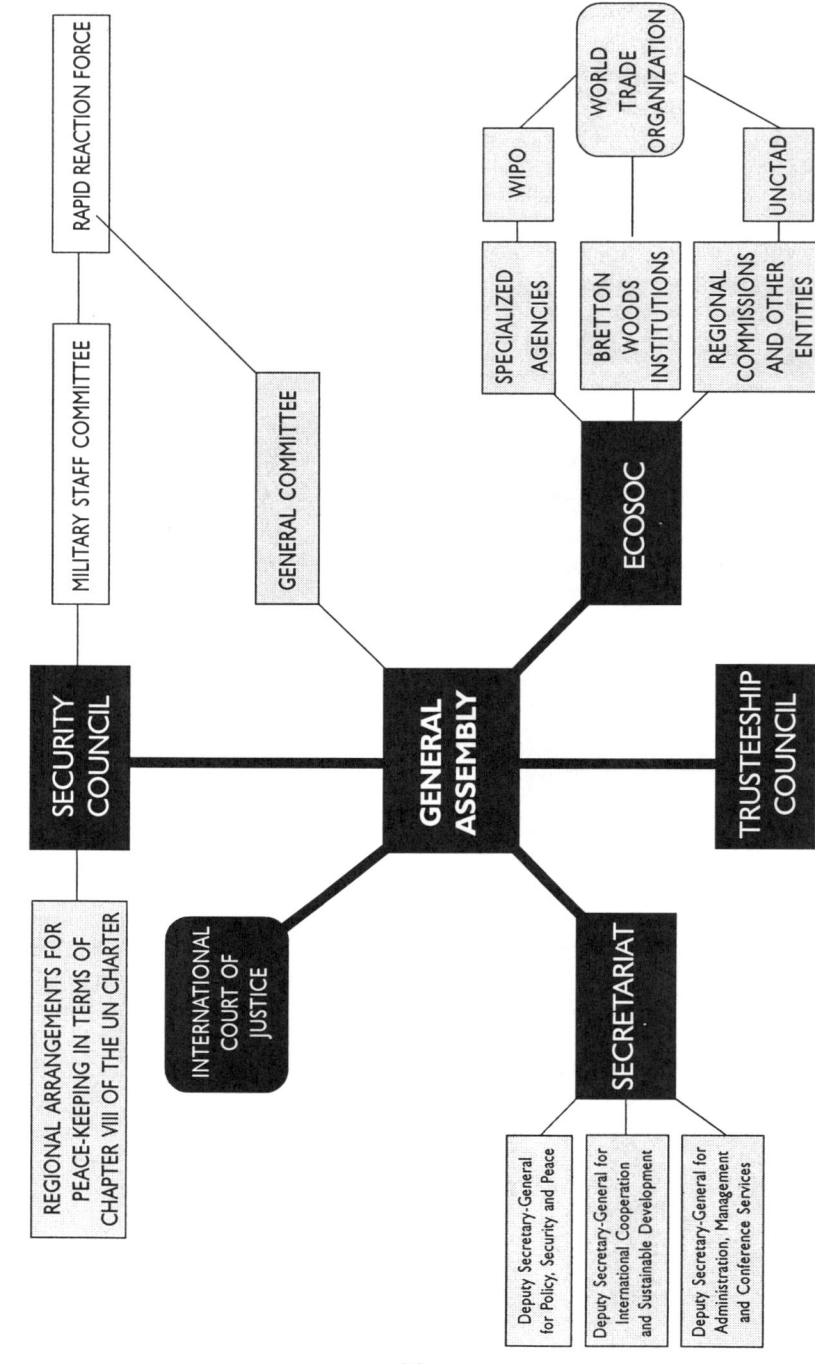

* See de Marco, Guido and M. Bartolo, *A Second Generation United Nations*, London and New York, Kegan Paul International, 1997, p. 125.

Diagram 4. *Second Generation Economic and Social Institutions of the United Nations**

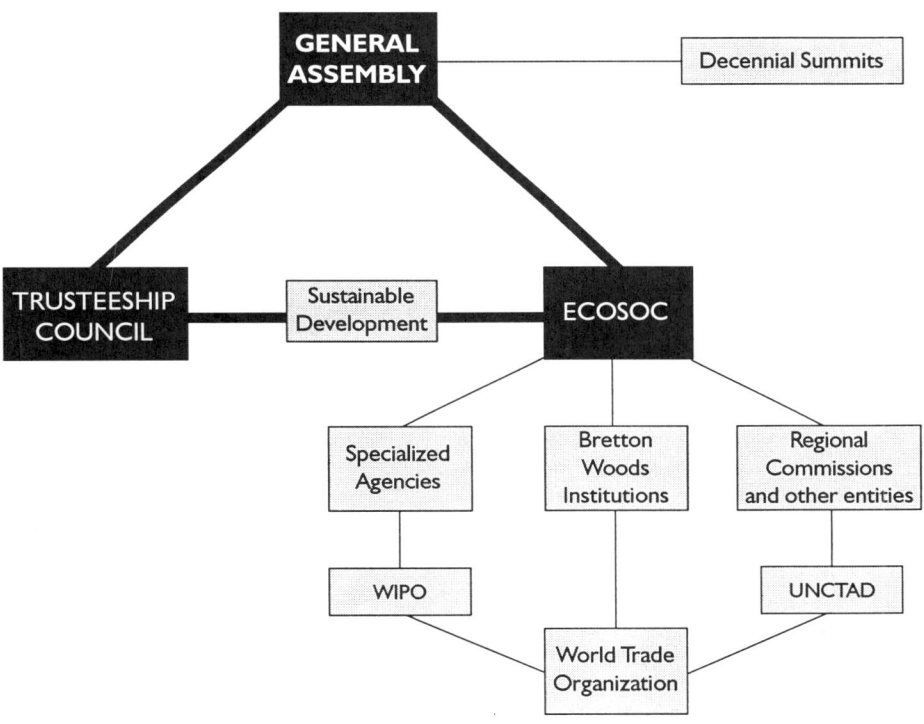

* See de Marco, Guido and M. Bartolo, *A Second Generation United Nations*, London and New York, Kegan Paul International, 1997, p. 99.

AN IMPRESSIVE NUMBER OF PROPOSALS FROM WITHIN THE UNITED NATIONS

The Presidential *ad hoc* Committees

Some of the *ad hoc* committees on United Nations reform under the President of the General Assembly continued their work and some submitted their conclusions to the General Assembly. Other developments in the area of United Nations reform, like the comprehensive report of the Secretary-General mentioned above, may be considered as landmarks, although the implementation of the recommendations leaves a lot to be desired.

The open-ended 'High-Level Working Group on the Strengthening of the United Nations System', was the last of the five closed-door groups created to address different aspects of United Nations reform. This Group, created in September 1995, dealt with the General Assembly and the Secretariat. It presented its comprehensive recommendations to the General Assembly on 1 May 1997. Other Groups dealt with the Agenda for Peace, the Agenda for Development, the Financial Situation of the United Nations, and, of course, the Security Council. The Group on the Security Council submitted its recommendations[2] before the end of the 52nd General Assembly in September 1998. The salient points of all these groups are worth keeping in mind although, without exception, very little of a concrete nature has been put forward.

Some of the Groups were split further into sub-groups. The 'Working Group on the Agenda for Peace', for example, had four sub-groups, with only two ending up making some sort of recommendations. The sub-group on coordination made recommendations on troop-contributing States, regional arrangements, NGOs and coordination within the United Nations System itself. The only other sub-group with any significant results was the sub-group on the question of United Nations Imposed Sanctions. In response to the Secretary-General's report entitled *Supplement to an Agenda for Peace* (3 January 1995), the sub-group made some recommendations[3] on the subject of sanctions, emphasizing the conditions that ought to be respected and the humanitarian aspects of the sanctions.

The 'Working Group on the Financial Situation of the United Nations' discussed three inter-related issues,[4] without being able to propose concrete recommendations to the General Assembly. These issues were the cash-flow situation, the payment of contributions in full and on time, and the scale of assessment.

The 'Working Group on an Agenda for Development' did substantial work in the form of an *Agenda for Development* that was adopted by the General Assembly.[5] This interesting document dwells heavily on the coordination within the United Nations System and gives a role to the *civil society*. This document, however, typical of United

---

[2] A/AC.247/1998/WP.1/Rev. 2, 11 August 1998.
[3] WGAP/96/2, 6 September 1996.
[4] WGFS/28, 15 December 1995 and WGFS/30, 26 January 1996.
[5] A/AC.250/1, 16 June 1997.

Nations consensus documents of this kind, skirts the issue of changes in the relationship between the United Nations and the Bretton Woods Institutions.

Another group which produced substantial material in areas where there seemed to be consensus was the 'Working Group on the Strengthening of the United Nations System'.[6] Some of the recommendations of this Group deal with ways of 'Improving the capacity of the General Assembly to discharge effectively its functions, role and powers and of the Secretariat to carry out effectively and efficiently the mandates of intergovernmental processes with the necessary transparency and accountability'.

These recommendations, if implemented, would certainly help towards a better and more efficient functioning of the United Nations, but they fail, in our opinion, to address the question of relevance. Admittedly, this is not an easy issue, especially when one needs the cooperation of all the Member States to adopt recommendations by consensus.

The Presidents of the 52nd and 53rd General Assemblies

The President of the 53rd General Assembly, Didier Operetti Badan, Foreign Minister of Uruguay, stated after his election that the 'winds of reform' were blowing at the United Nations. He said that no one could say that the United Nations did not want reform. According to him, the central question was as to how Member States could help move the reform process along. He added that he imagined that that was a difficult task, noting that when there was a problem, the first step was to identify it. Urging a sense of optimism, he said that fresh impetus for reform should be fostered through new approaches.

The President had just listened to a disappointed Hennadiy Udovenko, the outgoing President. After stating that if there was one single topic that distinguished the 52nd General Assembly from others, it was the issue of revitalizing the United Nations. He said that the hope inspired by the comprehensive report of the Secretary-General and the ensuing two encouraging resolutions had not led to any substantive progress. After nine months of intensive consultations, he said that all that could be offered was a resolution sending the bulk of reform proposals to the next General Assembly for additional consideration.

What was particularly regrettable, the outgoing President said, was that the delays do not concern only the long-term proposals (like the Trusteeship Council) but also the Secretary-General's recommendations on vital and urgent measures on the administration and the budget. He did not accept the excuses for these delays. He regretted the inability to move beyond the narrow positions of individual delegations and groups.

He noted the failure to make progress in the area of Security Council reform, in spite of 'all the eloquent appeals'. There was no political will and courage in this area, he said. He also pointed out that no conclusive results had been reached on 'The Agenda for Peace'. He said that considerable differences remained on the issue of reconciling the principle of national sovereignty with the possibility of launching timely preventive

---

[6] WGUNS/CRP.16, 2 June 1997.

action without obtaining the consent of the government concerned. Further, he said that post-conflict peace-building also remained controversial. There was no agreement to assign the key role in this area to the General Assembly.

This stalemate came as no surprise since, as early as 6 May 1998, the General Assembly had already deferred action on most of the reform proposals of the Secretary-General, and there was never any expectation that the *ad hoc* Working Groups would come up with proposals of any significance that the Assembly could act upon.

Only one proposal of the Secretary-General, to designate the 55th General Assembly in the year 2000 as the Millennium General Assembly, was accepted in principle. In this context, it may be recalled that it was recommended in *A Second Generation United Nations* that a future General Assembly should be designated as the 'enabling or implementing' Assembly and that the year of that Assembly should also be designated the year of the *Second Generation United Nations.*

All that the Assembly did in May 1998 was to defer several proposals (mainly of an administrative and financial nature) to its Fifth Committee. These included proposals on the Revolving Credit Fund, the Core Resources for Development, the Development Account, Sunset Provisions and Pilot Projects. Some of these proposals, like the streamlining of the agenda of the General Assembly, were also dealt with in *A Second Generation United Nations.* Among these was also the proposal on the need to make better use of the Trusteeship Council, on the lines of the Malta recommendations on this body, which are also reflected in *A Second Generation United Nations.*

The Secretary-General himself was much quicker than the General Assembly. By May 1998 he had already made substantial changes in the Secretariat, albeit mainly of an administrative and efficiency nature, as detailed below.

The 52nd General Assembly could only decide on a few matters of reform, which were not considered controversial and were certainly not major developments. These included a new Code of Conduct for the Staff, some changes in the timing and the agenda of the Disarmament Commission and some changes in the Subsidiary Bodies and Functional Commissions of the ECOSOC. The Assembly also approved an agreement on cooperation between the United Nations and the International Tribunal for the Law of the Sea, which has its headquarters in Bonn and was established under the 1982 United Nations Convention on the Law of the Sea.

THE HIGHLIGHTS OF THE SECRETARY-GENERAL'S PROPOSALS

A Comprehensive Program of Reform with Promise

The Secretary-General's report, *Renewing the United Nations: A Program for Reform,* made three kinds of recommendations. The first set dealt with the administrative and financial management of the Secretariat, Programs and Funds. These he started to implement immediately. The second set dealt with recommendations which needed the agreement of the governments, and the third set contained longer-term proposals like the one on the Trusteeship Council, which very closely resembles Malta's blueprint for that Council.

The highlights of the Secretary-General's proposals include:

(a) Creation of a Development Fund, to be made up of savings expected as a result of the reforms.
(b) Creation of a new post of Deputy Secretary-General (for a woman).
(c) Cabinet-style administration under four managers – for peace and security, humanitarian affairs, development, and economic and social issues.
(d) Consolidation of the work of six aid agencies into two groups – one for development and the other for humanitarian affairs.
(e) Consolidation of programs to combat drugs, money laundering and terrorism in one department.
(f) Amalgamation of human rights activities, under a High Commissioner for Human Rights.
(g) A new department for disarmament.
(h) Zero-growth, result-based budgeting.
(i) New priorities and rationalization of the agenda for the General Assembly.
(j) No activity of the United Nations to go beyond its useful purpose.
(k) United Nations System to be reviewed.
(l) The establishment of a Revolving Credit Fund to prevent insolvency of the United Nations.

The Secretary-General's report was received with much enthusiasm but, as indicated earlier, so far the results have not been encouraging. His original plea for relevancy fell well short of expectations and the results, as in other past efforts for reform, have been in the area of efficiency only. This, as in the past, raises the concern that the United Nations needs to be relevant before being efficient. Or, as indicated on various occasions in the past by the President of the 45th Session of the General Assembly, 'efficiency without relevance is a step backwards'.

A COMPARISON WITH THE PROPOSALS IN THE SECOND GENERATION UNITED NATIONS

A Number of Similarities

The Secretary-General seems to have followed some of the ideas of *A Second Generation United Nations.* His proposals on the new Trusteeship Council reflect very closely those in the book on the same subject. Other ideas, like the 'Summit General Assembly', the question of 'relevance', and the changes in the humanitarian area and the technical cooperation area are also similar.

A Second Generation United Nations has as its centerpiece a more relevant and efficient General Assembly. The Secretary-General has also recognized the importance of this, but has not gone as far as *A Second Generation United Nations* General Assembly. He did not consider making better use of the General Committee and the Office of the President. Nor did he deal with the issue of streamlining the various committees as proposed in *A Second Generation United Nations*. He did, however, propose the streamlining of the agenda. He also recognized the importance of the summit potential of the General Assembly and of involving ministers in decision-making on topics of great importance, like the review of the Charter.

In the area of peacekeeping, he gave importance to building a rapid reaction capacity but did not go as far as *A Second Generation United Nations*, which related this force to the General Committee as well as to the Security Council. As in *A Second Generation United Nations*, the Secretary-General made some proposals for better coordination between the General Assembly, the Security Council and the Secretary-General.

Similar proposals to those in *A Second Generation United Nations* were made by the Secretary-General in the areas of humanitarian affairs, technical cooperation and disarmament. *A Second Generation United Nations* did not include the post of Deputy Secretary-General since it was believed that such a post would neither increase the United Nations relevance nor its efficiency. *A Second Generation United Nations* included a more rational reorganization of the most senior staff.

A Second Generation United Nations did not foresee that development activities could be separated from economic and social affairs. The Secretary-General's proposals do not go far enough in the area of the ECOSOC.

The Secretary-General's proposals on the Trusteeship Council seem to rely heavily on those of *A Second Generation United Nations*. While *A Second Generation United Nations* Trusteeship Council could be launched without any necessary changes in the Charter, the Secretary-General's proposals foresee changes in the Charter, making it very difficult, if not impossible, to reach a consensus on the matter.

As in *A Second Generation United Nations*, the Secretary-General's proposals give importance to decentralizing operational activities, in the areas of peacekeeping, and economic and social affairs, from the Secretariat in New York to the already established regional institutions.

A Second Generation United Nations gives the utmost importance to relevance and warns that efficiency without relevance is a step backward. The Secretary-General's proposals take a similar stance and emphasize relevance. The Secretary-General went out of his way to make this point both in his report and in the preparatory period prior to the report. Some find that the Secretary-General's proposals are long on efficiency and short on relevance. This is not intended to be a criticism of the Secretary-General. He certainly needs the support of the Member States to tackle the question of relevance.

As the history of United Nations reform shows, it is much easier to deal with efficiency than with relevance when it comes to changing the United Nations. Most of the developed countries want the *status quo* for the United Nations and relevance means changing the United Nations to respond to the needs and priorities of the majority rather than responding, as it is now, to the needs and priorities of only a powerful minority. It is, therefore, not surprising that the Secretary-General probably realized that any chance of progress in United Nations reform is only possible in the area of administrative and financial restructuring. So far this is the only area where some progress has been achieved.

SOME OTHER REFORM PROPOSALS

One should not give the impression that no reform proposals were made and discussed before the 1990s. One needs only to refer to the bibliography for a selection of texts that deal with reform since the creation of the United Nations in 1946. The texts by Joachim Müller[7] are a good example, and describe ten reform efforts launched in the 1980s. At the beginning of the decade, the North-South confrontation had become a central theme in the United Nations. Disappointed third-world countries deplored the 'ignorance of the minority', while the industrialized countries rejected the 'tyranny of the majority'.[8] Joachim Müller refers to the Palme Commission, and Bruntland Commission, and pays special attention to the Group of 18 and the process of reform initiated after the 40th General Assembly in 1985.

The Group of 18

The last major effort to reform the United Nations before Kofi Annan's comprehensive proposals, referred to earlier, was launched in December 1985 by a decision of the General Assembly to establish the Group of 18, to review the efficiency of the administrative and financial functioning of the United Nations.

The 40th Session of the General Assembly is remembered for bringing together about 100 Heads of States and Governments to commemorate the 40th Anniversary of the United Nations, and for resolution 40/237, whereby a group of high-level experts, known as the Group of 18, was established. This Group was mandated to conduct a review of the administrative and financial matters of the United Nations, with a view to identifying measures for further improving the efficiency of its functioning. It was to submit its findings within a year.

Almost simultaneously, in late 1985, the then Secretary-General, Javier Perez de Cuellar, recommended a set of economy measures, which he considered to be under his authority. The economy measures were approved by the General Assembly (resolution 40/472). They were perceived to be of a temporary nature, with the expectation that they would provide short-term cash flow relief and help in regaining the confidence of the Member States.

The final report of the Group of 18, entitled the *'Report of the Group of High-Level Intergovernmental Experts to Review the Efficiency of the Administrative and Financial*

---

[7] Müller, Joachim, *Reforming the United Nations; New Initiatives and Past Efforts;* Kluwer Law International, The Hague, 1997.
[8] *Ibid.,* Preface.

Functioning of the United Nations',[9] was issued in August 1986. It was submitted for consideration to the 41st Session of the General Assembly.

The Group of 18 made 71 recommendations for improving the efficiency of the United Nations. Some believed that the Group had been particularly influenced by pressure from the United States, whose criticism of the Organization had reached a high point.[10] The report noted parallel growth in the intergovernmental machinery and that the multiplication of committees, commissions and expert groups resulted in 'overlapping of agenda', duplication of work, and an overly complex structure that suffered from lack of cohesion which made coordination difficult.[11]

Further, it noted that the frequency and duration of conferences and meetings had reached a point where it presented many difficulties to all Member States, and that the considerable resources allocated for conferences and meetings were not put to maximum use, which amounted to wastage. The Group recommended substantial reductions in the number of conferences and meetings, and in their duration, without affecting the substantive work of the Organization.[12] It also pointed out that the Secretariat's structure had become too complex, fragmented, and top-heavy, while the qualifications of its staff, particularly in the higher categories, were inadequate and the working methods were not efficient.[13]

After consideration of the report of the Group of 18, and a lengthy discussion on the recommendations by the General Assembly, the ECOSOC and a Special Commission, some of the recommendations were eventually implemented. The Group of 18 was also significant in that it ushered in a number of other reform initiatives by national institutions like the United States Association of the United Nations, and by individuals like Mikhail Gorbachev, Brian Urquhart, Erskine Childers, and others. Initiatives on reform also came from other institutions, like the South Commission (1990), the Nordic United Nations Project (1991), and the Commission on Global Security and Governance (1991).[14]

Boutros Boutros-Ghali and Reform

Earlier, in 1992, Boutros Boutros-Ghali was presented with a multitude of reform proposals generated from within the United Nations and from outside, on his appointment as Secretary-General of the United Nations. He immediately launched a major restructuring of the Secretariat of the United Nations, which was subsequently endorsed by the General Assembly.[15]

---

[9] A/41/49, 8 August 1986.
[10] Saksena, K. P., *Reforming the United Nations: The Challenge of Relevance*, New Delhi, Newbury Park, Sage, 1993, p. 110.
[11] Report of the Group of 18, *op. cit.*, Supplement No. 49, Introduction.
[12] *Ibid.*, para. 3.
[13] Saksena, *op. cit.*, p. 111.
[14] For more information on the Group of 18 and other reform initiatives, refer to Müller, *op. cit.*
[15] General Assembly Res. 46/232, 2 March 1992.

This restructuring was also aimed at efficiency rather than at relevance. The objective was to reduce bureaucratic layers, eliminate duplication, abolish a number of high-level posts and reinforce offices by giving them greater and clearer responsibilities. In the political sector, emphasis was given to strengthening the support provided to the Secretary-General in matters related to peace and security, and to enabling the Secretariat to respond efficiently to the mandates of the Security Council and the General Assembly. In the economic and social fields, the aim was to achieve integration and enhance the capacity for coordinated responses to complex emergencies and the delivery of humanitarian assistance.

One of the highlights of this reform was the abolishment of the post of the Director General of International Economic Cooperation and his department. This is significant for two reasons. First, because the General Assembly had, a decade or so earlier, established this post to coordinate the largely dispersed economic and social activities within the Secretariat and beyond, as a result of the landmark recommendations of an earlier celebrated group of eminent persons.[16] Second, because the present Secretary-General has again consolidated these same activities of the Secretariat; only this time it is headed by an Under Secretary-General instead of a Director General. To add a bizarre twist to all this, some time earlier, his predecessor did the same thing, to break the activities down again within months.

Reform efforts continued in the early 1990s, and the General Assembly undertook action to enhance its own capacity and merged the Special Political Committee and the Fourth Committee to form a new Special Political and Decolonization Committee.

THE GAP BETWEEN THE NUMBER OF PROPOSALS AND IDEAS AND THE CONCRETE ACTION TAKEN TO IMPLEMENT SOME OF THEM

Change Never Comes Easy

Why is it so difficult to make progress in the implementation of some of the ideas, even though there is a near unanimity on their merit? No doubt there is no lack of excellent ideas and proposals for reform. There also seems to be nearly unanimous agreement that the United Nations System has to be made more effective, whether it is in the area of economic and social development or in the political and security area. The gap between the rhetoric of reform and the extent to which this reform is allowed to proceed, referred to earlier, is sometimes confusing and discouraging. This phenomenon can only lead one to the conclusion that proposals dealing with an increase in the relevancy of the Organization touch upon the shifting of the *status quo,* which the more powerful countries are not inclined to alter in spite of their speaking out in favor of it.

---

[16] The Group of 25. See the *Gardner Report*, United Nations, New York, 20 May 1975, para. 71 and GA Res. 32 / 197 of 20 December 1977.

Faced with this dilemma, the only proposals that have a chance of implementation are those dealing with administrative and financial matters. Since such proposals may not make the United Nations more relevant, therefore, they may not be in the interest of the majority of the Member States. Good examples are the changes undertaken in the United Nations Secretariat as a result of the proposals of the Secretary-General, referred to above. Such proposals do not seem to improve the relevance of the Organization, even though they may sound and appear to be impressive; however, they may improve somewhat the efficiency of the United Nations.

No one should underestimate the difficulty of making changes, including those changes that may appear straightforward, such as those concerning the Secretariat that are under the authority of the Secretary-General. In this respect, no other Secretary-General of the United Nations has done so much as the present one, and that too in such a short period of time.

The Senior Management Group

The Senior Management Group, made up of the senior officials of the Secretariat and the Funds and Programs and its sectoral executive committees, have brought a degree of consolidation in the day-to-day work of the United Nations. This could also have implications for the ACC, since it would no longer be necessary for the United Nations to be represented by all the senior officials, who usually outnumber the heads of the Specialized Agencies, a fact that made the agencies unhappy in the past. It did not take too much time for the Secretary-General to appoint a woman Deputy Secretary-General to assist him in the running of the Secretariat and the new groups referred to above. This machinery for better coordination in the United Nations proper should facilitate better coordination system-wide, and make the task of the ACC in this regard much easier. This should be a yardstick by which the effectiveness of the new machinery in the Secretariat of the United Nations should be measured.

Steps have been initiated to reform the United Nations human resources management and the budgetary procedures. These will take a number of years to complete. The reduction of resources is in itself an incentive to become more efficient, although efforts towards efficiency will always be necessary. The 'Development Account' proposed by the Secretary-General will probably continue to be discussed for some time by the General Assembly, although some recommendations have already been made in this regard. The creation of the Office of the Inspector-General, before the present Secretary-General took office, may be considered as a step in the right direction, although no efforts have been made to reduce duplication in this area, for example, with the work of the Joint Inspection Unit (JIU).

Consolidation in Economic and Social Areas

Soon after he took office, the Secretary-General did some consolidation in the area of economic and social affairs. This area is so dispersed and disintegrated that it offers scope for immediate progress. At least this was recognized and a start has been made.

Reform in some programs and departments augured well at first, especially in the Regional Commissions, but seems now to be slowing down.

The reform proposals regarding the ECOSOC do not tackle the basic problems. The reform efforts and results, as these concern the ECOSOC, will be referred to again later in this chapter. At the risk of using a cliché, it is believed that reinventing the wheel in the area of economic and social affairs will not work. This is an area that offers the Secretary-General the most scope in making proposals that would have a major impact on the work and relevance of the United Nations. It is unfortunate that reform in this area is seen as separate from that in the area of operational activities.

Operational activities at the United Nations are divided into those for development and those for humanitarian and emergency purposes. In the area of development, not too many things have changed. Various coordinating efforts have now been centralized in the context of the executive committees referred to earlier. The change from the old Department of Humanitarian Affairs to the new Office for the Coordination of Humanitarian Affairs, was a first step to rationalize United Nations activities in this important area that directly affects the most needy of the world's peoples.

The two areas of economic and social affairs and operational activities should be considered as one, to facilitate future reform and to make further economies in staff costs. The consolidation of these two areas would certainly facilitate post-conflict consensus-building. It is also in these two areas that the Secretariat would find the most scope to divest itself of some of the activities that are becoming more difficult to undertake, due to the continuous reduction of resources.

A most welcome sign of the latest wave of reform, resulting from the Secretary-General's comprehensive proposals, is the increasing openness to the *civil society* (including the business community) to participate in the work of the United Nations at some levels. This must continue and the level of debate must be intensified so that decisions are taken and translated into concrete action.

Two Perspectives on Resources

In the context of reform, the question of resources can be seen from two perspectives. Some believe that unless resources are cut, no reform will ever take place at the United Nations. On the other hand, some think that orderly reform can only take place if the necessary funds are available for the reformed machinery and activities. We believe that resources will always be found for worthwhile activities.

As mentioned earlier, no one would disagree that the reform exercise of the United Nations was given a fresh impetus by the comprehensive proposals of the Secretary-General. No one would blame or criticize the Secretary-General for implementing only the first category of reform proposals, namely those dealing with administrative and financial management, for those are the easiest to implement. This is because such reform depends only on the Secretary-General, and the Member States need only to be kept informed. Moreover, no one would deny that the changes just discussed might improve the efficiency of the United Nations, but that they may not affect its relevance at all.

Member States have a major say in other changes and reforms that could make the United Nations more relevant. These include those of the second and third categories of the Secretary-General's proposals. However, as the officials representing the Member States at the United Nations do so for only brief periods, therefore, it is still the responsibility of the staff in the Secretariat of the United Nations to come up with imaginative ideas. The continuity has to come from within the United Nations, whose staff is usually appointed for longer periods, if not on a permanent basis.

While the type of reforms just referred to seem to be proceeding on, or nearly on, schedule, one has still to see any tangible results. Results cannot be judged on the basis of statements made by senior officials. It is also not in any one's interest to reject criticism on the slowness of the reform process. In fact, such a practice is in itself proof that little progress has been made in making the United Nations more effective.

The Proof is in the Results

No one needs to be told how much has been accomplished and how many things have changed for the better at the United Nations. The only proof is in the end results, and not in the improvements made in the means to arrive at such results. The end results should be obvious, and no one needs to be told about them.

One must not forget that United Nations reform started before the present Secretary-General presented his welcome comprehensive report.[17] Some of these efforts on the reform of major organs of the United Nations are indicative of the various reform initiatives that started in earnest during the 45th Session of the General Assembly (1990-1991).

As seen earlier, in spite of a number of concrete proposals from various quarters for reforming the General Assembly, very little progress was made beyond some improvements in its agenda. The same may be said of the other major organs; although an enormous amount of discussion has taken place, for example, on the proposals to reform the Security Council, but nothing concrete was achieved.

REFORM OF THE MAJOR ORGANS

COMMENTS ON THE DEVELOPMENTS ON THE SECURITY COUNCIL

No Progress in the Reform of the Security Council

It is for the reasons referred to earlier that we believe that the discussions on the Security Council are at a stalemate. It was not surprising that the last group to present its report to the General Assembly was the Group on the Security Council. It was also not

---

[17] See fn. 1.

surprising that no progress has been made on the reform of the Security Council. This was one definite area that touched upon the relevance of the United Nations rather than on administrative restructuring of the Organization. Looking back at the lack of significant progress in United Nations reform during the last 50 years or so, one finds that, in the end, lack of political will has always resulted in governments rejecting significant proposals that would have made the United Nations more relevant. In the past, the governments, in general, have accepted only those proposals that, at best, would make the United Nations more efficient. This seems to give the excuse to governments to avoid the crux of the matter while, at the same time, giving the impression that something worthwhile is still being done.

The present exercise does not appear to be different. On 24 August 1998, the General Assembly received a rather lengthy report from the 'Working Group on the Security Council' on the basis of which it decided to extend the work of the Group for another year, without taking any substantive decisions on the matter.[18]

The Group considered its work under the following five headings:

(a) Working methods of the Security Council and transparency of its work.
(b) Decision-making in the Security Council, including the veto.
(c) Expansion of the Security Council.
(d) Periodic Review of the enlarged Security Council
(e) Majority required for taking decisions on Security Council reform.

The Group could only summarize to the General Assembly the positions of the different delegations, under the above five headings, and proposed postponing further consideration of the matter to the 53rd Session of the General Assembly. The General Assembly, however, managed to pass a resolution[19] on item (e) above, stating that any decisions on the reform of the Security Council would require at least a two-thirds majority.

The frustrations of having yet another inconclusive General Assembly on such an important matter is reflected in the following summary of President Udovenko's statement at the end of the 52nd General Assembly. He stated that while progress has been made in some areas, there was no compelling evidence to believe that there had been any breakthrough in the reform exercise. In fact, he was not even encouraged to hope that there would be any results before the end of the millennium.

He said that some of the stumbling blocks include opposition to the creation of new permanent seats, disagreement over the issue of the total size of the enlarged Council, different approaches to the issue of rotational arrangements for new permanent seats, and finally, considerable differences on the problem of veto rights with respect to both current and prospective permanent members.

He added that what was, indeed, unfortunate on the subject of Security Council reform was the fact that the intensive discussions, which have not led to any practical

---

[18] A/AC.247/1998/WP.1 REV.2, 11 August 1998.
[19] A/53/L.46, 20 November 1998.

results, give the impression to the outside world that the reform exercise merely reflects conflicting interests between different groups in pursuit of their respective goals. The final outcome of this exercise, he continued, could perhaps inflict even damaging consequences on the Organization. He made the plea that, in the reform of the Security Council, there should be one predominant interest – to enhance the relevance of the United Nations to the requirements of a changing world.

The outgoing President reminded everyone of the declaration on the occasion of the 50th anniversary of the United Nations, in which it was clearly stated that the Security Council should change to respond to the needs of a changing world. He concluded by saying that it was likely that the next session of the General Assembly might pose some difficult questions for delegations. It was quite possible, he said, that they might be challenged with the need to give an answer to whether the exploration of different aspects of the reform of the Security Council should not be brought to an end, in one form or another. If there was still a need, he added, for something to be explored after five years of extensive discussions, perhaps it was the ability to see beyond national interests, and the ability to measure this reform against the historical imperatives of today's world. That, he said, could well be another important question.

Strong words indeed, from a frustrated, outgoing President of the 52nd Session of the General Assembly.

We think that, in spite of all the efforts that went into the work on the reform of the Security Council, the entrenched position of the major players on such an important and crucial subject for the future of the United Nations has been too quickly accepted. No one disagrees that it is only fair for Member States to expect a Security Council that is more representative of the present world.

SOME IMPROVEMENTS IN THE FUNCTIONING OF THE ECOSOC

Revitalization is Still Proving Elusive

Most of the proposals to reform the ECOSOC centered around its revitalization, without addressing the basic problem of its role in the present architecture of international economic and financial institutions. There is no doubt that much work had been done by the recent Presidents of the ECOSOC to make it more streamlined, and to revitalize it by making it address topical questions in its domain. There is also little doubt that all this progress did not address its basic shortcoming – that of never being given the chance to function as mandated by the United Nations Charter.[20]

It is true that the ECOSOC is now better off with the introduction of the High-Level Segment, in which Ministers and other high-level officials discuss special topics of interest to the international community. It is also true that it is also better off by fostering

---

[20] de Marco and Bartolo, *op. cit.*, p. 85.

a better dialogue with the Bretton Woods Institutions and by addressing special subjects of topical concern.

On the other hand, no one can deny that the ECOSOC is helpless in its attempts to level the playing field for the majority of the developing countries to participate in the areas of international economics, trade, and finance, and the sooner that this is recognized the better.

Reform of the ECOSOC is at the center of the reform controversy, because a relevant ECOSOC, as foreseen in the United Nations Charter, would never be acceptable to the developed countries. The reason for this is that it would transfer authority to itself, to make decisions of major implication to them, rather than leaving such decisions to the Bretton Woods Institutions, which they control. Therefore, it is hardly surprising that no attempts at reforming the ECOSOC so far have come even close to addressing this concern.

A REFORMED TRUSTEESHIP COUNCIL

To Hold in Trust the Common Values of People

Why is the Secretary-General also having problems with an apparently harmless proposal to make the Trusteeship Council the guardian of the heritage of present and future generations, thus giving it a major role in environment matters and in sustainable development?

Member States are divided on the issue of the Trusteeship Council. This is either because they do not understand some of the good proposals that have been made for giving it a new role, or because they do not realize that a reformed Trusteeship Council may well turn out to be the most cost-effective major organ of the *Better United Nations* of the future.

The original proposal of Malta,[21] that the Trusteeship Council hold in trust the common values of people rather than those of nations, aspiring for independence, is also included in the Secretary-General's comprehensive proposals.[22] Other studies and reports[23] also support a new or reformed Trusteeship Council along the same lines.

So far, little progress or debate has taken place on these proposals. The Secretary-General's proposal on the Trusteeship Council is buried in working groups in the context of the reform of the United Nations Environment Program (UNEP). This matter deserves to be discussed at higher levels and should be included as a major proposal to the Millennium General Assembly.

---

[21] *Ibid.*, p. 69.
[22] See A/51/950, 14 July 1997, p. 27, para. 84 and 85.
[23] See also, The Commission on Global Governance, *Our Global Neighbourhood*, Oxford University Press, 1995 and Kaul. I. et al.(eds), *Global Public Goods*, New York & Oxford, Oxford University Press, 1999.

FROM A UNITED NATIONS TO A UNITED NATIONS SYSTEM

We think that over fifty years of effort to develop the United Nations, as hoped for in the Charter, has not succeeded. The United Nations proper, or the United Nations System, at the dawn of the new millennium is not going to be much different. There is, however, a wealth of ideas and proposals that need to be exploited by insisting that there is no alternative at present to a *Better United Nations* for the new millennium. It is now up to the Millennium General Assembly to play its part and to launch, in a concrete and definite way, a *Better United Nations* for the new millennium – nothing less will do.

We believe that only a relevant and reformed United Nations proper can be the centerpiece of a United Nations System, which can address the needs, priorities and concerns of the majority of the peoples of this world. The next chapter reviews how the present United Nations System works, how it is being reformed, and how its unprecedented body of know-how and expertise can be unleashed and exploited to the fullest in a *Better United Nations* for the new millennium.

CHAPTER 2

THE UNITED NATIONS SYSTEM

SUMMARY

Is this current reformed United Nations and United Nations System adequate to respond to the needs and priorities of Member States? The present relationship of the United Nations to the Specialized Agencies, which is not expected to change too much in the future, is analyzed and commented upon. Specifically, the legal agreements of the various Specialized Agencies with the United Nations are compared, bringing out the significant differences between the more standard agreements and the agreements with the Bretton Woods Institutions.

Most of the Specialized Agencies have also been undergoing some reform. Aspects of this reform, particularly in the International Labour Organization (ILO), the United Nations Educational, Scientific and Cultural Organization (UNESCO), the United Nations Industrial Development Organization (UNIDO), the World Health Organization (WHO), the World Intellectual Property Organization (WIPO), UNCTAD, and one of the Regional Commissions, are discussed. Some conclusions are reached on the seriousness of this reform and on whether it also takes into consideration the reform exercises that are taking place at the United Nations and in other parts of the System.

IS THE PRESENT UNITED NATIONS SYSTEM ADEQUATE TO RESPOND TO THE NEEDS AND PRIORITIES OF MEMBER STATES?

In spite of the best efforts and intentions of the Secretary-General, no real reform has been undertaken which would make the United Nations more relevant according to our yardstick that is spelt out in the next chapter. The reason for this cannot be over-emphasized, namely, that at the United Nations, few things happen unless the most influential of the Member States wants them to happen. It appears that Member States who control the power of the purse and who have been in a privileged position, due to the balance of world power at the time of the creation of the United Nations, are not ready or willing to give up any of their influence in the Organization. As such, these Member States have allowed the Secretary-General and his predecessors to come up with proposals and recommendations for reform, as long as they do not change the controlling influence over the Organization of some of the most influential founding members.

This is evident in the gap that exists between the proposals and recommendations and the implementation of such proposals and recommendations. This fact, added to the fact of the other gaps, dealt with at length in this book, namely the gap between national and global objectives and the gap between words and deeds, could be considered as the main reason for the stalemate in the real reform of the United Nations. To these gaps and apparent contradictions may be added a major historical reason, namely, the contradictions, apparent or real, in the Charter of the United Nations.

Two significant points may be made in this context. The first is that the Charter was changed from the time of Dumbarton Oaks (1944) to the time of San Francisco (1946), in the process also changing somewhat the spirit and high ideals that characterized the earlier meeting. The second is that the final wording, approved in the latter meeting, was interpreted to suit the victors of the war and the most influential of the Member States. This resulted in further contradictions, as a result of the interpretation of some of the Chapters and Articles of the Charter that appears to be different from that intended, when they were approved.

The bottom line is that there is no political will to change the way the most powerful countries influence decisions at the United Nations, in spite of what the Charter says in this regard. As per Article 8 in Chapter III of the Charter, the United Nations shall place no restrictions on the eligibility of men and women to participate in any capacity and under conditions of equality in its principal and subsidiary organs. No significant action has ever been taken to translate this Article into reality. As a result, the United Nations and the United Nations System as a whole can never adequately respond to the needs and priorities of the majority of the Member States. That is why this book attempts to identify the main reasons for the stalemate and why it attempts to propose a different United Nations, which would be a *Better United Nations* to respond adequately to the major concerns of as many people as possible.

Unlike with the United Nations proper, the problem with the Specialized Agencies is not as much one of relevance – due to their specialized nature – but of streamlining and adaptation to the United Nations System at large. No one denies that the Specialized Agencies are far from perfect, and that there has been much duplication and inefficient use of resources. But the point to be made here is that, as we see in this chapter, no stone was left unturned to make the major Specialized Agencies more relevant and more efficient. This was somewhat easier to do than in the United Nations proper, because it was easier to focus the Specialized Agencies on the most important priorities in their area of competence, and to redirect their work accordingly.

As we maintain all through the book, once an entity is relevant it is easier to make it more efficient. To try to make it efficient before that would be a step backwards. No one really wants a more efficient organization that is doing the wrong things. One major factor that facilitated this revolution in the Specialized Agencies was the new crop of Heads of some of the major Specialized Agencies who, because of their experience and vision, did not take long to do wonders with what they had inherited.

THE RELATIONSHIP OF THE UNITED NATIONS PROPER TO THE UNITED NATIONS SPECIALIZED AGENCIES

The Legal Status

While some of the Specialized Agencies have also undergone various levels of reform, as indicated later on in this chapter, the relationship between them and the United Nations proper has not changed much and is not expected to change in the future. It is for this reason that this book devotes a number of chapters to discuss machinery that needs to address this question, and proposes a Policy and Coordination Board (PCB) to replace the ACC.

In the light of the experience of the League of Nations, the founders of the United Nations examined the issue of establishing a single, centralized, global organization with overall responsibility, covering all possible aspects of human endeavor and activity, which might entail systematic cooperation among sovereign States. Some felt that a centralized system was preferable, especially in the areas of economic and social affairs. Others felt that a decentralized system with specialized smaller organizations was, even in theory, the better option. Many felt it was best to proceed with caution and, therefore, to accept the practical reality of the many existing specialized technical intergovernmental institutions such as the IMF, the International Bank for Reconstruction and Development (IBRD) and the International Civil Aviation Organization (ICAO), which were operating in a more objective, and by implication in a less political, environment in their respective deliberative and decision-making organs. The ultimate decision was also influenced by the reservations expressed by the older Organizations, the Universal Postal Union (UPU), the International Telecommunication Union (ITU), and the ILO, regarding an excessively close link with the United Nations.

It followed quite naturally, therefore, that a decentralized network of organizations, with independent legal status, was the only practical solution possible. Hence, the Dumbarton Oaks Conference took a preliminary decision in this regard which resulted in the Charter spelling out the notion of Specialized Agencies and providing for such Specialized Agencies to be brought into relationship with the United Nations (Articles 57 and 63). In this scheme of functional decentralization, the Specialized Agencies have a quasi-independent status. In legal terms, the position of the Specialized Agencies under international law is essentially no different from that of other international organizations, including the United Nations, and sometimes the Member States themselves. Under general international law, the Specialized Agencies are restricted subjects of international law, to the extent that their Member States endow them with an international legal personality. The United Nations, however, enjoys a special position, as it has been recognized by the ICJ as a general subject of international law, even in relation to States that have not recognized it. Therefore, from this perspective, the United Nations is certainly the first among equals.

There are sixteen Specialized Agencies, which have entered into relationship with the United Nations proper through agreements entered into by the ECOSOC, pursuant to Article 63 of the Charter. ILO was among the first Specialized Agencies pursuant to Article 57, whose relationship agreement came into force before the end of 1946.[1] By the end of 1949, ten organizations had entered into formal contractual relationships with the United Nations as Specialized Agencies.[2] By 1961 they had been followed by four more.[3] One Specialized Agency lost its status because of its dissolution, for the International Road Transport Organization (IRO) was terminated in 1952 by agreement between its Member States soon after concluding the relationship agreement. WIPO joined the United Nations System in 1974, International Fund for Agricultural Development (IFAD) in 1977, and, finally, UNIDO in 1985. Many of them also have various types of linkages or cooperation agreements amongst themselves.

The United Nations System

Often this interrelated group of organizations is called the 'United Nations System' or the 'United Nations family', but we prefer to use the former. Looking at the limited interaction that takes place amongst the United Nations and the Specialized Agencies, we feel that the term 'United Nations System' suggests mutual relations that may not be more than the mere exchange of information. For example, the term 'Banking System' in Switzerland, relates to a large number of private banks functioning rather independently of each other and of the major banks, with only a certain amount of information on the services offered being exchanged in an *ad hoc* manner.

The use of the term 'United Nations System' could also be justified on the basis of the variations in the legal agreements, whereby the Specialized Agencies have been brought into relationship with the United Nations. No doubt the basic framework of most of the legal agreements between the United Nations and the Specialized Agencies is quite similar. These agreements form an almost uniform pattern. They contain detailed conditions concerning coordination of the activities of individual Specialized Agencies and of the United Nations as well as the activities of the several Specialized Agencies among each other.[4]

---

[1] Together with FAO and UNESCO.

[2] Besides ILO and the other two agencies referred to in fn. 1, this became true in 1947 for ICAO, IBRD, IMF, in 1948 for UPU, WHO, and IRO, and in 1949 for ITU.

[3] WMO (1951), IFC (1957), International Maritime Organization (IMO) (1957), IDA (1961).

[4] Seidl-Hohenveldern, Ignaz, 'Specialized Agencies', in *United Nations: Law, Policies and Practice, Vol. 2*, Wolfrum, Rüdiger (ed.), Dordrecht-Boston-London, M. Nijhoff, 1955, p. 1204. On inter-agency agreements, see Jenks, Wilfred C., 'Coordination: A New Problem of International Organization', RCADI, 1950 – II, p. 237

Most of the Specialized Agencies agreed to submit all recommendations addressed to them by the Security Council or the General Assembly to their respective decision-making organs. It is interesting to note that, in the case of decisions of the Security Council concerning the maintenance or restoration of international peace and security, they even agreed to render such assistance as the Security Council might request. Most of the Specialized Agencies also agreed to the coordination of their activities, to prevent duplication of administrative and technical services, and recognized the desirability of a single unified international civil service. Above all, most of them also agreed to the full and prompt exchange of information and documents.

Most of the Specialized Agencies also agreed to consult with the United Nations on the preparation of their budgets and to conform, as far as practicable, to standard practices recommended by the United Nations. It may be noted that the International Atomic Energy Agency (IAEA) was not granted the formal status of a Specialized Agency. Instead, it was linked to the General Assembly and the Security Council by a special relationship agreement.[5] Even so, the basic conditions in this agreement are the same as for the Specialized Agencies. Therefore, for all practical purposes it is treated for coordination matters on a par with the Specialized Agencies.

The agreements between the United Nations and most of the Specialized Agencies provide for consultation concerning appropriate arrangements for inclusion of the budgets of the Specialized Agencies within the general budget of the United Nations. However, the resulting consultations have brought forth difficulties in merging the budgets, which were, and still remain, insurmountable.[6] In fact, the core problem revolves around the constitutional limitation on the Specialized Agencies to transfer budget-making powers from their governing organs to the General Assembly. On the practical side, for the United Nations, such a transfer of responsibility would require inclusion of appropriate specialists in delegations. This would also substantially increase the workload of the General Assembly and further lengthen its sessions. In addition, in spite of considerable overlap, there is a sizeable divergence of views in membership at the United Nations and in the Specialized Agencies. Under these circumstances, only some effort has been made to achieve better harmonization of budgetary policies in the United Nations System. It is only in the context of the UNDP funds that a certain amount of consolidation has been achieved, since a fair amount of UNDP funds is channeled through certain Specialized

---

onwards. See also Hüfner, in Wolfrum, *op. cit.*, p. 1365, for whom the relationship agreements are 'in the main identical'. It is recalled that a type of 'model agreement' was established by the agreement between the UN and the ILO, based on a draft version of the ILO; see Jenks, *op. cit.*, p. 205, and Codding, George A., Jr., 'The Relationship of the League and the UN with the Independent Agencies: A comparison', Annals of International Studies 1970, p. 79. For an in-depth analysis of the relations between ILO and the UN, see Tortora, Manuela, *Institution Spécialisée et Organisation Mondiale: Etude des Relations de l'OIT avec la SdN et l'ONU*, Bruxelles, Bruylant (*Organisation internationale et relations internationales* n°12), 1980, pp. 225-317.
[5] This is also due to the opposition of States, in particular the former USSR, which did not want to establish links between the IAEA and the ECOSOC.
[6] Jenks, Wilfred C., *op. cit.*, pp. 228-238 (para. 108). See also UN Documents A/394/Rev. 1; A/404; A/449; A/494; and A/497.

Agencies and generally exceeds the amounts provided for operational activities in their regular budgets.[7]

To meet special situations there are numerous variations in the agreements, with the most important departures being in the agreements of the IMF (the Fund) and IBRD (the World Bank). As Jacques Dagory points out, 'one may divide the agreements into three groups: with most of the Specialized Agencies, agreements were reached on a close relationship, while preserving their legal independence; the relationships with the "old organizations" UPU and ITU are less close; and the relations with the IMF and World Bank Group are relatively loose'.[8]

The Bretton Woods Institutions

Few are familiar, however, with the special and 'loose' relationship of the World Bank and the International Monetary Fund (IMF) to the United Nations. The following quotation manages to pick up the main characteristics of this relationship; 'the IMF and the World Bank are widely, if not generally, seen to be separate from the UN System. In fact, most people would ask whether they are formally part of the System. Although because the answer to this question has to be an unqualified 'yes', the Fund and the Bank are specialized institutions under the Charter and are both members of the ACC,[9] they have, both formally and in practice, only a tenuous relationship to the United Nations System as a whole. There is formal reporting to the ECOSOC each year, but the management of the two institutions clearly believe that they are only answerable to their Boards of Governors, which meet once a year, and to the two full-time boards of executive directors which represent the Governors on the day-to-day approval of policies and operations'.[10]

It does not take long for this relationship to become clear once one starts reading the agreements, which 'provide that the Fund (or Bank) is a specialized agency established

[7] Jackson Report (UN Doc. DP/5), vol. II, pp. 14-15.
[8] For a general analysis of these agreements, see: Jacques Dagory, *Les Rapports entre les Institutions Spécialisées et l'ONU*, RGDIP, 1969-2, pp. 330-377.
[9] 'All of the (relationship) agreements except those with the Fund and the Bank contain a clause whereby the agency affirms its intention of cooperating in whatever further measures may be necessary to make coordination of the activities of the specialized agencies and those of the UN fully effective, and in particular agrees to participate in, and to cooperate with, any body or bodies which the Council may establish for the purpose of facilitating such coordination and to furnish such information as may be required for the carrying out of this purpose. The Fund and Bank agreements include a provision that, to the extent consistent with the provisions of the agreements, the Fund (Bank) will participate in the work of the Coordination Committee and its subsidiary bodies' (Jenks, *op. cit.*, p. 215). In fact, 'the lack of adequate inter-agency coordination remains a common refrain of virtually all evaluations of the UN and Bretton Woods Institutions. Much of the explanation for this inadequacy lies in the fact that the institutions' Member Countries have simply not made coordination a priority. To the contrary, both donor and recipient countries have often acted, for different reasons, to undermine coordination. The institutions have competed for autonomy, resources and turf', Gwin, Catherine, in *The UN and the Bretton Woods Institutions; New Challenges for the 21st Century*, Ul Haq, Mahbub, Richard Jolly, Paul Streeten, and Khadija Haq (eds), New York, St. Martin's Press, 1995.
[10] Douglas, Williams, *The Specialized Agencies and the UN: The System in Crisis*, London, C. Hurst and Company, 1987, p. 160.

by agreement among its Member governments and having wide international responsibilities as defined in its Articles of Agreement in economic and related fields within the meaning of Article 57 of the Charter of the United Nations and that, by reason of the nature of its international responsibilities and the terms of its Articles of Agreement, the Fund (or Bank) is, and is required to function as, an independent international organization'.[11]

The departure from the most standard type of agreement signed by most of the other Specialized Agencies can be, for ease of reference, presented under the following sub-headings.

Representation and Information

The IMF and the World Bank had liberal rights of representation in the United Nations' Bodies, but they did not reciprocate these rights.[12]

As indicated earlier, the relationship agreements generally provide a mutual right for the exchange of information and documents, but in the case of the Bretton Woods Institutions, it was clear that these could withhold information, due to the confidential nature of the loan conditions.[13]

Observance of the Recommendations of United Nations Organs

The relationship agreements provide the United Nations with a right to propose items for inclusion on the agenda, and a commitment of the Specialized Agencies to submit recommendations of the United Nations to its competent organ 'so that the latter may act upon them as well as to support the organs of the United Nations in the exercise of their duties'.[14] In the case of the Bretton Woods Institutions, however, they only undertake to give due consideration to proposals for agenda items.[15]

In fact, in Article 4 of the respective agreements with IMF and the World Bank, the United Nations accepts 'a duty of self-restraint in its relationship' with these two

---

[11] Jenks, *op. cit.*, p. 208.

[12] 'Agreements…established arrangements whereby the IMF and World Bank rights of representation before UN bodies were far more extensive than reciprocal rights of UN institutions'. Gwin, *op. cit.*, p. 113. For more details on the articles dealing with reciprocal representation, see Jenks, *op. cit.*, pp. 208-212.

[13] 'one corner-stone of co-operation in the UN family is the exchange of information and documents. In this respect, the periodical reports of the Specialized Agencies to the UN are particularly important, as is the continuous sharing of information through the regular exchange of documents. This practice is guaranteed in all Specialized Agencies. However, in the constitutions of IMF and the organizations of the World Bank Group there are specific provisions for preserving the confidential nature of loan relationships of these institutions'. From Meng, Werner, in '*The Charter of the United Nations. A Commentary*', Simma, Bruno (ed.), Oxford University Press, 1995, p. 854. This special provision (Article 1.3 of the agreements) says that nothing in the agreement, 'shall be construed to require either of them to furnish any information the furnishing of which would, in its judgement, constitute a violation of the confidence of any of its Members or anyone from whom it shall have received such information, or would otherwise interfere with the orderly conduct of its operations'.

[14] Seidl-Hohenveldern, *op. cit.*, p.1204. Jenks, *op. cit.*, pp. 212-213.

[15] 'the Fund and the Bank only undertake to give "due consideration" to items proposed by the UN' in Jenks, *ibid.*, pp.212-213.

institutions.[16] More specifically, any recommendations have to be agreed by the Bretton Woods Institutions in advance, and matters relating to loan agreements are sacrosanct to their business and the United Nations pledges not to interfere.[17]

Assistance to United Nations Organs (especially to the Security Council)

Most relationship agreements contain provisions concerning assistance to the Security Council (especially as far as enforcement of Chapter VII of the Charter is concerned). However, there are special reservations in Article 6 of the agreements with the Bank and the Fund. The Bretton Woods Institutions only have a duty to provide information to the Security Council in this regard,[18] 'conditioned by the preservation of confidence and the acknowledgement of the Member States' duties towards the Security Council'.[19]

Thus, the duty to cooperate with the Security Council is particularly loose; and it is even looser as far as other United Nations political organs are concerned. For instance, when the General Assembly made declarations that lending to South Africa or to Portugal should cease in the 1960s, the Bretton Woods Institutions only took note of these recommendations and refused to act on them (even though lending to these two countries was phased out for other reasons).[20]

Budgetary Cooperation

The agreements between the United Nations and Specialized Agencies stipulate the duty of the latter to transmit their budgets to the General Assembly, in accordance with Article 17.3 of the Charter.[21] However, the Fund and Bank agreements 'simply provide that the annual reports and quarterly financial statements of the Specialized Agencies will be furnished to the United Nations, which agrees that ... the appropriate authorities of the

---

[16] Meng, *op. cit.*, p. 854.

[17] 'neither organization, nor any of their subsidiary bodies, will present any formal recommendations to the other without reasonable prior consultation with regard thereto'. The Bank agreement contains 'a further clause whereby the UN recognizes that the action to be taken by the Bank on any loan is a matter to be determined by the independent exercise of the Bank's own judgement in accordance with the Bank's Articles of Agreement, and recognizes therefore that it would be sound policy to refrain from making recommendations to the Bank with respect to particular loans or with respect to terms or conditions of financing by the Bank'. From Jenks, *op. cit.*, p. 214. See pp. 213-215, for more details on this point.

[18] For more details, see *ibid.*, pp. 217-218.

[19] Meng, *op. cit.*, p. 854.

[20] Seidl-Hohenveldern, *op. cit.*, pp. 1204-1205: 'Some Specialized Agencies have tried to dissociate themselves from boycott measures which have been recommended by the General Assembly. These agencies claimed that such political measures would counteract the technical interests of the agency concerned ... For these and other reasons the Assembly has established entities such as UNCTAD and UNIDO [which became a specialized agency in 1985] as subsidiary organs without a legal personality distinct from that of the UN. In this way, these entities are under the more direct control of the superior principal organs'.

[21] 'The early relationship agreements go even further than the wording of the UN Charter by mentioning the desirable final goal of a common budget' (Meng, *op. cit.*, p. 855): See, e.g., Article 14 of the agreement with ILO.

Fund and Bank enjoy full autonomy in deciding the form and content of these budgets'.[22] This is so because the Bretton Woods Institutions 'were eager to preserve their financial standing, which could have been undermined if investors had had to presume that decisions would not be made exclusively according to bank standards'.[23]

Civil Service Law and Administrative Procedures

While most Specialized Agencies[24] subscribe to what is known as the Common System, as regards recruitment and conditions of service of staff, the Bretton Woods Institutions agreed only to consult, to come to them as close as possible.[25] This actually means that the Fund and the Bank are totally independent in these areas. For this reason the staff of the Bretton Woods Institutions is better paid and has better conditions of employment than their counterparts in the United Nations and the Specialized Agencies.

Relations with the International Court of Justice (ICJ)

The agreements entitle the Specialized Agencies to request advisory opinions of the ICJ on legal questions, as long as they do not concern the mutual relationship of the agency and the United Nations or other Specialized Agencies.[26] Moreover, Article 34.2 of the ICJ Statute states that 'The Court ... may request of public international organizations information relevant to cases before it, and shall receive such information presented by such organizations on their own initiative'. While most of the Specialized Agencies explicitly accepted a commitment in this regard, the Fund and the Bank refused for reasons of confidentiality.[27]

Revision and Termination of the Agreement

Finally, a significant feature of the Fund and Bank agreements is that these differ from all agreements concluded with Specialized Agencies with respect to their revision and termination conditions.[28] The Fund and Bank agreements are the only ones that

---

[22] Jenks, *op. cit.*, p. 225. For further details on budgetary and financial arrangements, see pp. 225-230, and Schmidt and Koschorreck (in Simma), *op. cit.*, pp. 313-317.

[23] Meng, *op. cit.*, p. 805. 'In addition, they wanted to preserve the confidentiality of their relations with creditors and debtors'.

[24]'All relationship agreements envisage the harmonization of civil service law and administrative procedure, and provide that this harmonization be as far-reaching as possible'. *Ibid.* For more details, see Jenks, *op. cit.*, pp. 221-222. A relative uniformity of staff rules was supposed 'to facilitate an exchange of personnel between the various agencies' (Seidl-Hohenveldern, *op. cit.*, p. 1204).

[25] 'agree to consult from time to time concerning personnel and other administrative matters of mutual interest, with a view to securing as much uniformity in these matters as they shall find practicable'. Jenk, *op. cit.*, pp. 221-222.

[26] Seidl-Hohenveldern, *op. cit.*, p. 1204. For more details, see also Jenks, *op. cit.*, pp. 220-221.

[27] See Article 1.3 of the respective agreements.

[28] 'A review of the relationship agreements was indeed envisaged in the 1970s with the intention of a revision process; however, it came to nothing' (Hüfner, *op. cit.*, p.1365).

(explicitly) envisage the possibility of termination, within a relatively short period of time.[29]

Thus, on the whole, there should be no doubt that the agreements with the Fund and the Bank are not agreements at all. To the extent that these institutions did not agree to give any power to the United Nations, it is even questionable whether they have agreed to collaborate with the United Nations proper at all. In this context, it is easy to understand why no genuine and efficient coordination between the Bretton Woods Institutions and the United Nations is possible, except maybe as a result of the personal disposition and courtesy towards the Secretary-General of the United Nations of the Heads of the Bank and the Fund.[30] In fact, it would not be an exaggeration should one interpret the signing of the agreements with the Fund and the Bank as a statement and a confirmation that the Bretton Woods Institutions have no obligations at all towards the United Nations and its General Assembly, and moreover have no inclination to do so. This state of affairs is certainly not consistent with the idea of the supremacy of the United Nations General Assembly, which is the hallmark of the *Better United Nations*.

How Close a Relationship?

Those who favored centralization had doubted whether the functional decentralization between the United Nations and the Specialized Agencies was the best structure, especially when the tasks of the organizations had become so complex and interlinked that often a dozen or so Specialized Agencies, Funds, Programs, or other entities had to work together as a single team, particularly in the field of development assistance. They favored a unified organization, which might be stronger and more effective.[31]

We feel that there is nothing wrong with the decentralization of the work of the United Nations. In fact, this book makes the case for maximum decentralization. In today's complicated and technologically advanced world, most problems are multi-dimensional in nature and, therefore, require a United Nations with special skills that can be put together and used quickly and efficiently. These skills are certainly not available centrally at the United Nations and it would be unrealistic to expect that they would be available any time in the future. Such skills and specialization are more readily available in the Specialized Agencies. It is for this reason that, later in the book, we propose a new coordination machinery that could bring all this together as needed, by bonding the United Nations proper with the rest of the System, for the benefit of all concerned. This

---

[29] Jenks, *op. cit.*, p. 207. They 'are terminable at six months' written notice, all rights and obligations deriving from them ceasing on the expiry of this time'.

[30] 'The goal of making decisions according to their technical appropriateness and of disregarding political views as far as possible is the reason for the relatively loose relation between the IMF and the organizations of the World Bank Group on the one hand, and the UN on the other' (Meng, *op. cit.*, p. 805). In fact, agreements between the Bretton Woods Institutions and the United Nations 'were designed to put a distance between them because such a configuration was pressed by the major industrial countries, notably the United States, in accordance with their greater voting power in the Bretton Woods Institutions' (Gwin, *op. cit.*, p. 112).

[31] Jackson Report, UN Doc. DP/5, Vol. I, at iv, Vol. II, at 291-292, 298, 301.

would exploit both the special skills found in parts of the System and the leadership of the United Nations proper to ensure quick response, at the lowest cost and without overlapping and duplication.

Sometimes efforts to treat the Specialized Agencies separately from the United Nations, by insulating them apart, did not work. Over the years, various types of political considerations have prevented certain Member States from even participating in the discussions of many Specialized Agencies. For example, South Africa in the period of the apartheid policy was effectively ostracized from most of the Specialized Agencies. However, the vast majority of the arguments for retaining the separate identity of the Specialized Agencies remain valid. In fact, the separate development of each agency over a fairly long period of time has made it impossible to merge them into one organization. When the last comprehensive review of the agreements between the United Nations and the Specialized Agencies was done in 1973 by the ECOSOC, with a view to strengthening the coherence of the system,[32] only a report was prepared[33] and none of the agreements were amended. In general, the executive heads of the Specialized Agencies expressed satisfaction with the *status quo,* which seemed to be based on a policy of non-interference in each other's affairs.

However, it seems that the time has come to make another review of these agreements, so as to make them viable instruments of mutual cooperation for obtaining practical results for the Member States. In particular, the complete independence of the Bretton Woods Institutions would have to be ended, so that financial and monetary policies are brought, so to speak, under the guidance and surveillance of the General Assembly through the ECOSOC. In other words, their agreements with the ECOSOC should be changed to provide for a better relationship between these institutions and the United Nations.

As already indicated, the agreements between the United Nations and the Bretton Woods Institutions are really no agreements at all. They simply put the United Nations on notice that they would never take any advice or instructions from the United Nations General Assembly, its highest organ, or from any other United Nations organ for that matter. A major exercise, therefore, to review all the agency agreements, should be launched immediately. This may not turn out to be an impossible task, as some detractors of a stronger United Nations may want to imply. These agreements should actually be rather simple and standard for all Specialized Agencies including the Bretton Woods Institutions and the WTO. These agreements should give absolute autonomy to the Specialized Agencies in their areas of competence, with the one major proviso that, in recognition of the supremacy of the General Assembly of the United Nations, all Specialized Agencies have to heed the overall guidance and mandates. After all, such guidance and mandates would be subject to the agreement and authority of the Summit level of the United Nations General Assembly. This would have to be the first and necessary, in fact, crucial, ingredient for a really strong and relevant United Nations – anything less than this would not work.

---

[32] ECOSOC Res. 1768 (LIV) V and ECOSOC Res. 1906 (LVII).
[33] UN Doc. E/ 5524.

REFORM IN OTHER PARTS OF THE UNITED NATIONS AND IN SOME OF THE MAJOR SPECIALIZED AGENCIES IN THE SYSTEM

The recent reform efforts in organs such as UNCTAD, and in some of the Specialized Agencies such as ILO, UNIDO, WHO and WIPO, are analyzed to determine their effectiveness and relevance and, more importantly, to see whether the reform efforts took into consideration the reform being undertaken by the United Nations proper. Reform of one of the Regional Commissions is also discussed.

Reforms in UNCTAD

UNCTAD IX, held in Midrand, South Africa, in 1996, adopted a revised mandate for the organization as well as the most far-reaching reforms in its history. Entitled 'A Partnership for Growth and Development', the final document resulted in:

(a) a refined, and more focused, work program;
(b) a streamlined intergovernmental machinery;
(c) a complete restructuring of the secretariat;
(d) a slimmed-down administrative and management structure, and
(e) improved coordination with other organizations.

In tangible terms, this has meant the following:

(a) 25 separate work programs and subprograms were replaced by one program consisting of five subprograms;
(b) the number of intergovernmental bodies was halved; and the number of meetings reduced from 690 in 1992 to 225 in 1997;
(c) in the secretariat, the number of Divisions were reduced from nine to four;
(d) the UNCTAD reforms resulted in financial savings, arising both from intergovernmental action at UNCTAD IX and from measures adopted by the General Assembly and the Secretary-General to streamline the United Nations as a whole. For example, the halving of the number of intergovernmental meeting days generated national savings of some USD2.0 million in 1997 (over the average for 1994-1995). Savings, as part of measures to promote efficiency, include a reduction in established posts of some 22 percent over the 1992-1993 baseline, and underspending in the 1996-1997 biennium of some 13 percent; and
(e) introduction of agreements/arrangements for improved policy and operational coordination with the WTO, the World Bank, UNDP, International Trade Centre (ITC) and UNIDO.

The reforms in UNCTAD were undertaken not as a result of financial constraints, but to ensure the relevance and cost-effectiveness of the organization to the Member States, in terms of the quality of the services to be provided, for strengthening of international cooperation in pursuing its main goal of maximizing the trade, investment and development opportunities of developing countries, and for helping the developing countries to face the challenges arising from globalization in their efforts to integrate into the world economy on an equitable basis.

The need to involve *civil society* — particularly the private enterprise sector — more fully in UNCTAD's work, is a principal aspect of the reform process. In fact, the 'Partnership for Growth and Development' (para.18) mandates UNCTAD to enhance the participation of *civil society* in its activities 'to build a lasting partnership for development between nongovernmental actors and UNCTAD'. The Partners for Development Summit (Lyon, France, November 1998) was considered to be a successful effort at attracting nongovernmental actors, notably the private business sector, to participate in UNCTAD's operational activities. UNCTAD is also considering the possibility of upgrading its existing structured links with the nongovernmental actors.

At the same time, UNCTAD is continuing its efforts to streamline further its central management and support structures, to consolidate the mechanisms for program monitoring and control, and to improve its human resources management policies within the constraints imposed by the fact that UNCTAD is fully a part of the United Nations Secretariat and, therefore, does not have autonomy in matters concerning personnel or budget.

In our opinion, UNCTAD is certainly ready to absorb all economic and development activities of the United Nations Secretariat and to serve as the Secretariat itself to ECOSOC.

Reforms in the International Labour Organization (ILO)

Mr. Juan Somavia joined the ILO as its ninth DirectorGeneral in a special sitting of the Organization's Governing Body in Geneva in March 1999.

In his speech after taking the oath of office, the new DirectorGeneral, the first from the developing world, recognized his special responsibility to ensure that the development dimension colors all the activities of the ILO. He underlined the fact that in spite of economic progress, there was 'inequality between and within countries, with 1.3 billion people living in poverty and 1 billion unemployed or under employed'.[34] He said that global security could not be founded on the instability of so many individuals and families throughout the world and that 'it is truly a tragedy that the century that presided over so much positive social change and unprecedented wealth creation, should end with such high levels of human uncertainty and deprivation'.[35] While urging wide support for the goals of the ILO Declaration on Fundamental Principles and Rights at Work, which was adopted by the International Labour Conference in 1998, Mr. Somavia hoped that it would become a common objective of the multilateral system as a whole, including the Bretton Woods Institutions. 'The ILO should seek to cooperate with all organizations in a

---

[34] ILO press release, March 22 1999, ILO/99/7, p. 1.
[35] *Ibid.*, p. 2.

common endeavor to best implement it. To this end, I would hope that all organizations should play a role. As an absolute minimum, they should undertake not to pursue policies whose practical effect would be to actually ignore these rights in practice.'[36]

Mr. Somavia also emphasized that 'economic outcomes are influenced more by market forces than by legal norms, social institutions or state intervention. The predominance of market-based development is making the enterprise a central architect of social change and the principal source of employment. It is essential for the ILO to engage vigorously and credibly with the community to pursue our goals and promote our values'.[37]

Furthermore, he added that 'social change has led to new and powerful actors of *civil society*, many of whom are organized outside the production process' and that 'social attitudes have changed, leading to greater individualism and narrowing of consensus on collective social responsibility'.[38]

'We must seek to harmonize economic growth with social progress, efficiency with equity, freedom with order and change with stability. We must be inspired by an approach that stresses dialogue and negotiations among autonomous and democratic social organizations representing the interest of all groups in the society', added Mr. Somavia.

In the Program and Budget proposals for 2000-2001,[39] 'the need for strengthening the institutional capacities of the ILO has been highlighted so as to make the ILO more visible, more authoritative and more effective in its action, while at the same time improving its internal efficiency'. The multifaceted approach includes:

(a) actions to reach out to its constituents and the general public through extensive media coverage and dissemination of high quality publications and promotional material, with greater emphasis on video and the Internet;

(b) a proactive approach to policy debates in the ECOSOC and the United Nations System and among the Bretton Woods Institutions and other intergovernmental and nongovernmental organizations, to ensure that its tripartite principles and policies are well known to international policy makers;

(c) a strategic program and budget, the first of its kind, which may, with refinements, become a model for future budgets;

(d) proposed action, based on the Active Partnership Policy, to strengthen managerially and politically the planning process with constituents, and to have a system of regular evaluation of the results achieved from work done in the regions;

(e) a review of the regional organizational structure of the ILO so as to strengthen the capacity of the ILO in economic analysis, and to strengthen and expand its

---

[36] *Ibid.*, p. 2.
[37] *Ibid.*, p. 2.
[38] *Ibid.*, p. 1.
[39] ILO Programme and Budget Proposals for 2000-2001, Strategy and Orientation, GB.274/PFA/9/1, February 1999, p. 50.

statistical functions at the international level in the definition, organization, dissemination, design, and promotion of data and statistics; and

(f) enhancement of the skills and capacities as well as the tools and resources necessary to carry out its work in a changing world.

Reforms in the United Nations Educational, Scientific and Cultural Organization (UNESCO)

The UNESCO's medium-term strategy for 1996–2001 aims at a lean and flexible organization where initiative and creativity prevail over routine. The key principles that guide the functioning of the organization as it moves towards the third millennium are transparency, responsibility, and accountability. The watchword is less bureaucracy and more reflection and action.

The UNESCO of tomorrow hopes to be even more relevant and focused in its activities, even more effective and efficient, even more responsive to rapidly changing circumstances, and to expand even more its presence in the international arena.

Its reform efforts are guided by the following objectives:[40]

(a) continuing the process of maximizing the resources devoted to programs and services of direct benefit to Member States;

(b) improving program delivery, and procedures for evaluating program implementation and performance;

(c) reinforcing cooperation with national and international partners, and creating new partnerships;

(d) consolidating and strengthening the decentralization process;

(e) adapting organizational structures and working methods to an increasingly multi-disciplinary program;

(f) better exploiting the opportunities of modern information technology and telecommunications to achieve greater quality and productivity, while further simplifying related administrative processes; and

(g) improving the performance appraisal and merit recognition systems and other aspects of human resource management.

While formulating strategies, the UNESCO has refocused its original function as an agency that provides inspiration, guidance and encouragement, playing the role of an enabler and a catalyst, but leaving the responsibility for the action itself to its partners – foremost amongst who are its Member States.[41] To perform this role effectively, the UNESCO relies on *greater transdisciplinarity* in its programs, approaches and work methods. The effort and resources for the *benefit of priority groups* (namely, women, young people, Africa and the Least Developed Countries) have been substantially

---

[40] See UNESCO's Website at <http://mirror-us.unesco.org/general/eng/about/mcr/manag/unesco.htm> May 1997.

[41] UNESCO Document 30 C/5, draft Programme and Budget, 2000-2001, Introduction, para. 16, p. xii.

increased in the program and budget for 2000-2001. The UNESCO seeks to promote all approaches for the *alleviation of extreme poverty*, most of them informal and community-based. By capitalizing on the skills and capacities of the poor themselves, these are aimed at helping them to devise their own strategies to rise out of poverty. [42]

In developing *partnerships*, the UNESCO seeks to diversify its relationships further, in order to rally the support of mayors, the media, entrepreneurs, women's and teachers' associations, grassroots movements, religious and secular institutions, nongovernmental organizations and of all those who are in a position to act as intermediaries for their actions at the national and local levels.[43] Above all, the UNESCO seeks to continue its efforts to strengthen complementarity with intergovernmental organizations, primarily the United Nations Specialized Agencies, but also regional organizations such as the Organization for African Unity (OAU), the Organization of American States (OAS), the Association of South East Asian Nations (ASEAN), the Arab League Educational, Cultural and Scientific Organization (ALECSO), the Islamic Educational, Scientific and Cultural Organization (ISESCO), the European Union, the Commonwealth Secretariat and others, taking into account the long-term plans adopted by these organizations that are relevant to UNESCO's field of competence.[44] Therefore, the UNESCO, as a universal organization, while gearing its action to global priorities, also seeks to act in accordance with regional and subregional priorities. To ensure this, the UNESCO seeks to become a decentralized, networked, multipolar organization, creating unity out of its multifarious offshoots and making use of all its national and international partners so as to cover the whole world.[45]

Reforms in the United Nations Industrial Development Organization (UNIDO)

In his opening statement to the 20th Session of the Industrial Development Board in November 1998, Mr. Carlos Magarinos, the Director General of the UNIDO, commented that 'developing countries need a completely new multilateral system, with more integration among its agencies, and stronger links with the private sector and *civil society*'.[46]

Mr. Magarinos felt encouraged to take the challenge to transform the UNIDO to become more focused, leaner, more flexible and much more responsive to changing global needs and the requirements of its clients, as spelt out in the approved 'Business Plan on the Future Role and Functions of UNIDO'. We note that Mr. Magarinos does not consider the transformation of the UNIDO as an end in itself. According to him, the definitive test is whether, as a result of the transformation, the UNIDO can effectively link the interests of developed and developing countries. Further, whether sustainable

---

[42] *Ibid.*, para. 21, p. xiii.
[43] *Ibid.*, para. 22, p. xiv.
[44] *Ibid.*
[45] *Ibid.*, para. 25, p. xiv.
[46] The full statement is available on UNIDO's Website at <http://www.unido.org/doc/who.htmls>, 18 November 1998.

industrial development can be used to fight poverty and unemployment, while, of course, taking care of the environment.

He regards 'a transformed UNIDO as a UNIDO that has a clear idea of its core competencies; an organization that has a clear idea of what it can do best, or its *comparative advantages*; what it cannot do; what it cannot do alone and must do with others if it is to tackle the multifaceted problems of development, and make a sustainable impact'.

The UNIDO also seeks to establish a clear identity in the multilateral system, particularly in the United Nations System. In support of the Secretary-General's reform proposals to achieve greater coherence and effectiveness in the United Nations System, UNIDO has initiated concrete collaboration with a number of agencies. These include, in particular UNCTAD, UNDP, and UNEP, with whom the UNIDO has signed Memoranda of Understanding. The UNIDO has also initiated important new cooperation with the WTO, ITC, UNCTAD, UNDP, the World Bank and the IMF, in the implementation of WTO's 'Integrated Framework of Assistance to LDCs aimed at improving their trade sectors and trade-related activities'.

The UNIDO seeks to actively support integrated approaches at the field level, in tune with the United Nations Development Assistance Framework (UNDAF), the United Nations Development Group (UNDG), common premises such as United Nations Houses and the coordinating role of the United Nations Resident Coordinator System.

Reforms in the World Health Organization (WHO)

The main elements of reform introduced by Dr. Gro Harlem Bruntland, the new Director General of the WHO, who took over in July 1998, include the following.[47]

(a) Introduction of a new structure for governance, with a new senior management team, and with greater transparency in decision-making in a new cabinet form of governance. The cabinet meets on a weekly basis.
(b) Regrouping the 50 ongoing programs into nine clusters, and reducing the number of departments to 35.
(c) Setting up high profile cabinet projects such as 'Roll Back Malaria', the 'Tobacco-Free Initiative' and 'Partnership for Health Sector Development'.
(d) Rethinking management support, with less bureaucracy and more emphasis on performance and results.
(e) Staff mobility and rotation, and an ambitious policy of gender parity.
(f) Forging new and more influential partnerships with external partners and other UN Specialized Agencies.

There is an acute realization in the WHO that the financial resources for health lie overwhelmingly within countries, and that the responsibility for success (or failure) thus lies ultimately with governments. Health spending in low- and middle-income countries

---

[47] Press Release WHO/ 82, 9 November 1998.

totaled about USD250 billion in 1994, of which only USD2 or 3 billion was from development assistance.[48]

It is against this background that Dr. Bruntland seeks to actively promote cooperation and joint efforts with a number of partners – in the United Nations family, in *civil society* and in the private sector,[49] so as to influence the thinking and spending of others concerned with health issues.

In the United Nations System, the WHO is working to strengthen its partnerships with the Joint UN Program on HIV/AIDS (UNAIDS), the World Bank, and the IMF. The WHO has developed working relations with the WTO to make sure that the health dimension of trade and globalization is considered before and during complex negotiations, and not just afterwards.[50]

The WHO is strengthening its work with the OAU and expanding its relations with the European Union. In the last year, the WHO has had a number of round table meetings with industry. The WHO is also working closely with the 'Global Forum on Health Research', in their efforts to catalyze greater public and private sector involvement in developing new products of relevance to the poor.[51]

In February 1999, for the first time ever, the WHO brought together all their country representatives to introduce them to the change process and to learn from their experience.[52]

The WHO has a decentralized structure in the field, with a number of regional offices. However, it is struggling with the task 'to make the whole organization pull together, pursuing a shared corporate strategy'.[53]

Reforms in the World Intellectual Property Organization (WIPO)

A major revamping and reorientation of the WIPO was initiated by the coauthor after he took over as Director General in November 1997.

Earlier, in September 1997, in his acceptance speech delivered in the WIPO General Assembly, he highlighted the unique dual character of the WIPO. It is, on the one hand, an intergovernmental organization serving the needs of the international community of States, and on the other, a global, market-oriented organization serving the interests and needs of a large, dynamic and growing market of users. This led him to stress the principles of accountability and transparency. He also stressed the importance of responsiveness of the organization to technological, social and cultural changes. Above all, he highlighted the significance of the WIPO reaching out to its partners in the United Nations family of organizations and to the WTO to ensure that the expertise and knowledge possessed by the WIPO is also placed at the service of its sister organizations. Finally, he stressed the fact that better internal management, and development of the staff

---

[48] *The World Health Report 1999*, WHO, Message from the Director General, p. xv.
[49] *Ibid.*, p. xvii.
[50] *Ibid.*, p. xvii.
[51] *Ibid.*, p. xviii.
[52] *Ibid.*, p. xix.
[53] *Ibid.*, p. xix.

of the organization, is key to the successful management of the WIPO as an organization for the future.

Rapid developments in technology, the heightened awareness that intellectual property is a resource of unlimited potential, and the increasing importance of intellectual property considerations at the policy-making level, have all had an impact on the scope, volume, and significance of the work of the WIPO. This has led him to define the many challenges that lie ahead for the WIPO, including the following.

(a) *Relevance* – anticipating the priorities of Member States, the private sector, *civil society*, and nongovernmental partners, as well as focusing on problems resulting from new and emerging technologies.

(b) *Governance* – streamlining decision-making processes, working methods, and procedures to make them transparent, cost-effective, customer-focused, and results-oriented.

(c) *Influence* – developing international, harmonized principles and rules through consensus, building institutions that will leave a lasting legacy in developing countries, and harnessing technology for information and knowledge exchange.

(d) *Corporate image* – spreading understanding of the role and importance of intellectual property protection and the work of the WIPO across all segments of society.

(e) *Interdependence* – building linkages in a holistic manner, between intellectual property and international trade and economic, cultural, and technological transformation.

In responding to those challenges and the role of intellectual property in new developments such as the Internet, environmental protection and protection of folklore, WIPO is helping to ensure the creativity, ingenuity, and well-being of generations to come. Some of the concrete steps so far taken by WIPO in this regard are summarized below.

To meet the *challenge of relevance* the WIPO has refocused its activities by creating the Office of Strategic Planning and Policy Development. The purpose of this office is to assist the Director General in fulfilling his oversight responsibilities, and in creating and refining the strategic plan and overall policy concerning the work of the Organization as a whole. In implementing this strategic plan the following new Divisions were created.

(a) The Economic Analysis, Forecast and Research Division to bring a new orientation to the hitherto entirely legal focus of the WIPO, as it looks at the social, cultural, economic, political and technological facets of intellectual property. It does so by scanning the internal and external environment, by commissioning studies and encouraging research. It seeks to predict trends in the use of the intellectual property system. In doing so it seeks to provide a holistic focus to the strategic planning process of the organization. This new focus will help WIPO to respond to problems and opportunities in an objective manner and enhance the global protection of intellectual property rights by making it an effective tool for promoting social, cultural, economic, and technological development of all.

(b) The Global Intellectual Property Issues Division to enhance the understanding of the relationship between the Intellectual Property system and traditional knowledge, biotechnology and biodiversity, folklore and selected aspects of economic, social, cultural and technological development.

(c) The Nongovernmental and Enterprise Affairs Division to oversee relations and cooperation with NGOs and with industry.

(d) The Infrastructure Services and Innovation Promotion Division to promote inventive and innovative activities in developing countries.

(e) The Collective Management Division to promote and assist the collective management of copyright and related rights, so as to further the social, economic and cultural interests of the creators of such works.

(f) The Least Developed Countries Unit to focus on the needs and concerns of the 48 LDCs in deriving real benefit from the Intellectual Property system.

(g) A high-level 'Industry Advisory Commission' and a 'Policy Advisory Commission' have been formed to obtain inputs and feedback from the market sector and from leaders in different walks of life, including political leadership at the highest levels.

The *challenge of governance* has been addressed, *inter alia*, by creating a participatory and team-oriented style of management, and by relying on a results-oriented program and budget. The results-based budget of 2000-2001 seeks to ensure greater accountability and transparency by establishing performance indicators for each of the expected results under every subprogram. At the operational level the following mechanisms are relied upon:

(a) Regular meetings of a new 'Policy Development Group' and a new 'Program Implementation Meeting', in which there is wide representation of senior staff at Director level and above.

(b) Deliberation, decision-making and feedback through a number of Policy Oversight Committees, Task Forces, and Working Groups.

(c) Creation of an Office of Internal Oversight and Productivity.

(d) Creation of a new Division for Performance Evaluation.

(e) Organizing retreats, on a regular basis, on topics of wide relevance to the Secretariat and Member States of the WIPO.

The *challenge of influence* has been met by improving the dialogue with the Member States in a more participatory process through increasing use of informal consultations for the biennial program and budget preparation. The creation of a totally new format for the Program and Budget document, with a clear focus on objectives, key activities, expected results and key performance indicators up to the subprogram level, is a product of this participatory process. The resultant transparency has improved the mutual goodwill and understanding between the Secretariat and the representatives of the Member States.

The WIPO has sought to meet the *challenge of creating a new corporate image* through use of modern information technology to help demystify the concepts of intellectual property and the work of the organization. Through the use of interactive Web sites and multimedia information products, the WIPO reaches vast audiences, which are unattainable by conventional means. Information on the activities of the WIPO is provided in clear, easily understood language in products ranging from films to CD-ROMs to brochures for students, all available via the Internet as well as in traditional form. These products remove intellectual property from an abstract, legalistic context and relate it to everyday life. Interactive exhibitions at the Information Center of WIPO at its Geneva headquarters link intellectual property to the history of human endeavor and progress. Increased contacts with the international media, collaboration with *civil society*, and partnerships with industry all compliment the efforts of the WIPO to project an accessible, understandable 'corporate' image for both intellectual property and the Organization.

The *challenge of interdependence* is sought to be met by improving the cooperation and collaboration between the secretariat of the WIPO and the actors in *civil society* and the market sector, apart from developing closer relationship with relevant organs, bodies and units in the United Nations System, the WTO, and the other Specialized Agencies, notably WHO, UNIDO, UNESCO, and ILO.

Reforms in the Regional Commissions – Example of the Economic Commission for Europe

In 1996, both the General Assembly (50/227) and the Economic and Social Council (1996/41) called for reviews of the regional commissions, with a view to strengthening and enhancing their effectiveness as action-oriented and policy-oriented bodies. All the five Regional Commissions have carried out reforms aimed at achieving greater relevance, efficiency and effectiveness. The individual reviews of these reforms, which were debated by the ECOSOC at its substantive session of 1997, were basically driven by the intergovernmental machinery at the regional level and by the senior levels of their respective secretariats. All of these reforms aimed at improved setting of priorities, rationalization of intergovernmental meetings, efficiency measures and an improved allocation of human and financial resources to produce a relevant work program.

By way of illustration, we look at the reforms undertaken by the Economic Commission for Europe (ECE), which were based on the findings of a detailed questionnaire sent to all member countries and the intensive consultations held thereafter. The commission in February 1997 approved the resultant plan of action and it was formally adopted, together with a political declaration, at the Jubilee session of the commission in April 1997.[54]

---

[54] Official Records of the Economic and Social Council, 1997, Supplement No. 16 (E/1997/36).

At a substantive level, the ECE refocused its activities on strategic areas in which it has recognized expertise and proven advantages, and for which there is widespread support throughout the region. This refocusing has led to a strengthening of activities in the fields of environment, transport, statistics, and trade. The program of work was streamlined accordingly, as was the intergovernmental machinery which was reduced form 14 to 7 principal subsidiary bodies and, at the same time, made more coherent and transparent.

Two mechanisms have been set up, in order to introduce more flexibility in the methods of work: (a) an oversight and adjusting mechanism that will allow existing activities to be terminated and new ones to be initiated in accordance with changing needs and realities; (b) the establishment of a coordinating unit for operational activities which, within the ECE mandate, will organize demand driven seminars and workshops on issues of direct interest to specific groups of countries, primarily countries in transition.

The coordination and cooperation with other regional, subregional as well as global organizations has been strengthened with a two fold objective: (a) to make ECE activities, conventions, norms and standards more widely known and applied; and (b) to promote cooperation and division of labor, on the basis of respective assets and proven advantages. The organizations concerned include the Organization for Security and Cooperation in Europe (OSCE), the Council of Europe, the Organization for Economic Cooperation and Development (OECD), the European Commission, the World Bank, the IMF, the European Bank for Reconstruction and Development (EBRD), the Organization for Black Sea Economic Cooperation, the Central European Initiative, and the Commonwealth of Independent States.

The ECE plan of action also proposes to expand the commission's cooperation with the private sector, by developing activities that address the concerns of the private sector.

THE UNITED NATIONS SYSTEM
AT THE DAWN OF A NEW MILLENNIUM

The recent reform efforts in the Specialized Agencies (ILO, UNESCO, WHO, UNIDO, and WIPO), UNCTAD and in the ECE, indicate a seriousness and commitment of the chief executives of the respective entities to respond to the challenge of relevance and of efficiency. That each of these entities took account of its particular needs and circumstances in fashioning its reform effort was natural and satisfying, to the extent that their respective deliberative and decision-making bodies supported and applauded the measures and actions proposed in the reforms.

A closer look, however, reveals that much of the reform effort was of a reactive rather than a proactive nature. By and large, the reactive effort was conditioned by the immediate concerns of certain key Member States, and, therefore, appears to serve the limited set of interests of a few, rather than the general good of the most needy.

We wish to reiterate, however, that certain major pillars of the United Nations System appear to be in place, and have their capabilities carefully honed to meet some of the challenges of the future. Irrespective of whether the Specialized Agencies were reformed for the reason we put forward, namely to make them more relevant, or for the reason advanced by others, namely to make them cost less, the fact remains that the Specialized Agencies are certainly better today than they were yesterday.

The crucial point now is not to concentrate our resources on creating new machinery to accomplish tasks that are, in the first place, administrative in nature, but to concentrate on tasks which are relevant, in terms of the yardstick of relevance developed in the next chapter.

The issue of strengthened policy coherence and cost-effectiveness of the development cooperation activities of the United Nations System, to give only one example, cannot be satisfactorily addressed by merely creating newer coordinating mechanisms, such as the UNDG, in order to, *inter alia*, oversee the preparations, review and evaluation of the UNDAF. The declared intentions of at least two Specialized Agencies to join this group[55] would lead to a sure prescription for further overlapping and duplication in this already crowded field of the United Nations work. As mentioned in the previous chapter, a measure of success for the newly set up coordination groups, as part of the Secretary-General's comprehensive reform proposals, would be the extent to which these new groups would coordinate the work of the United Nations proper, including its Funds and Programs, so that the United Nations could put forward a consolidated position in meetings of the ACC, without the necessity of numerous representatives from all the United Nations Funds and Programs to be present. For the Specialized Agencies to be moving towards involvement in these newer groups would, therefore, seem illogical, unless of course it is the intention that these new coordination groups should totally replace the ACC.

It is clear that there is an urgent need to improve the substantive coordination of policy at the highest levels in every national capital as well as in the United Nations System, through a reformed ACC as proposed in Chapter 8. Without such reforms, the efforts at field level coordination and collaboration will not result in any substantial improvement in the relevance of the programs, projects and activities.

The crucial point is that, given the enormous magnitude of the challenges to be met in improving the conditions resulting from the suffering and the humiliation of underdevelopment and poverty, and in finding solutions to the ever increasing urgent and destructive regional conflicts, there is urgent need for serious thinking and action to make the United Nations System work as a fully developed system that can mobilize help and assistance in the shortest possible time and with the most effectiveness. This is what this book hopes to contribute to, namely a *Better United Nations*, a *Better United Nations System*, and a better machinery to bring out the best of both.

---

[55] See statement by the Director General of WHO to the fifty-second World Health Assembly, 18 May 1999, and the UNIDO's Website in fn. 46. There should be no confusion that system-wide coordination must be done within a system-wide machinery like the ACC. Before creating new machinery, the present one should be used even if it needs to be completely overhauled.

CHAPTER 3

RELEVANCE
MORE THAN A CLICHÉ

SUMMARY

How does one measure or gauge relevance when it comes to the United Nations proper or the United Nations System? The literature on this aspect of the United Nations debate is more or less nonexistent. Therefore, we give our own yardstick and analysis. In outline, the following aspects of relevance are discussed in some detail.

Primarily, relevance has to be seen in the context of the Charter of the United Nations. The development activities of the United Nations have normally conformed to the neo-classical rules and doctrines of economic theory, namely, following the Ricardian *comparative advantage* theory, which has been shown not to be in the best interest of the developing countries (see Introduction and Annex I). United Nations technical assistance programs were not really as inefficient as most people believed. The problem with these programs was that they were not relevant, that is, that they were headed in the wrong direction and did not help the receiving countries' development. The WTO's globalization efforts seem to follow the same principle, and are, therefore, subject to the same criticism.

What is certainly needed in this area of United Nations activities is a redirection, so that these activities become relevant to the needs of the developing countries and not to the global needs which, as has been shown, leave the poorer countries with only marginal benefits. The crux of the matter is how to achieve such a redirection. This book endeavors to show how such a redirection can be achieved, in this area as well as in other areas of United Nations activities which are not considered to be relevant, and, therefore, do not address the concerns of the majority of the Member States. These areas would certainly include the major areas of concern of the United Nations, including the political and security area.

The most important challenges of relevance have also to be seen from the point of view of the well-being of people: whether this would be in the context of the eradication of poverty, the more equitable distribution of the gains from globalization, or the settlement of political disputes with the least upheaval possible for the populations concerned. The relevance in governance may be seen in the context of lack of coordination, lack of uniform vision and lack of harmonized procedures.

Meeting the challenge of influence could enhance relevance. Education in political affairs should be in all curricula, not only at higher levels of education but also at lower grades. Presenting a good and credible 'corporate' image – an area where some inroads are being made internally at the United Nations could also enhance relevance, but this is still not enough. In its quest towards relevance, the United Nations needs to consider how the business world may increase its interest and investment in the Organization. Relevance may also be increased by meeting the challenge of making the United Nations more global, by integrating into the United Nations System activities of other intergovernmental bodies and organizations like OAU, OECD and EU, among others. Finally, relevance may be enhanced by establishing think tanks (from all agencies, institutions and other sectors of the population) of people with vision and thinkers who do not necessarily represent the views of one organization or another but the aspirations and dreams of people, as reflected in the Charter of the United Nations.

THE MEANING OF RELEVANCE

In the context of the United Nations, it should be very clear that relevance should mean doing as many things as possible for the benefit of as many people as possible. A number of references to relevance can be found in the literature on United Nations reform. The present Secretary-General has used the word quite frequently. Others too have used it quite frequently in the context of United Nations reform. We do not think, however, that the meaning was ever fully explained or developed. Relevance has thus become little more than a cliché in the literature on the reform of the United Nations. For this reason we think that it is worth taking the time to develop its meaning and significance, and to put it in the proper context of the reform of the United Nations.

We have already made the point that the reform of the United Nations was concerned, in the past, more with efficiency than with relevancy. We have also explained why we thought this was the case and why it was so much easier to make the United Nations more efficient rather than more relevant. We had concluded that making the United Nations more efficient before making it more relevant was a step backwards rather than forward. It is for this reason that we endeavor to develop a yardstick of relevance against which all United Nations entities and activities need to be measured before qualifying for a place in the *Better United Nations*.

A YARDSTICK OF RELEVANCE

We, therefore, propose that all United Nations entities and activities be evaluated against the yardstick of relevance as developed here.

First and foremost, to be relevant, the United Nations needs to be in conformity with the Charter. In the spirit of the Preamble, it has to involve and include 'we the peoples' in all its work, operations and benefits. Moreover, as mandated by Chapter III, Article 8 of the Charter, the United Nations must include everyone in its work.

Second, the eradication of poverty should be a major objective of the United Nations, and its work must be primarily directed towards that end.

Third, in the economic and social sectors, the United Nations, and the System, will be relevant when it plays a role in changing the present international and financial architecture to level the playing field, by assisting the developing countries' participation, and by promoting a more equitable sharing of the gains from globalization.

Fourth, in the political and security area, the United Nations will be relevant as long as it reconciles national and global priorities, and in the case of conflicts in such priorities, as long as it finds a peaceful solution.

Fifth, the United Nations must recognize the norms and practices as developed over time and should not ignore the accepted theoretical framework, whether it is the neo-classical theory of trade in its economic programs, or the post Cold War doctrine in its political and security work.

Sixth, the United Nations must ensure that its work is the result of a system of governance reflecting the supremacy of the General Assembly and which has its basis in the democratic process of one-country-one-vote, which is a unique characteristic of the United Nations.

Seventh, the United Nations must see its work as a means for better things rather than as an end in itself.

Eighth, the United Nations must see its objectives as being system-wide, and should allocate its tasks to the entity that can do it best and at the least possible cost.

Ninth, the United Nations must involve, in addition to Governments, the civil society, including the private sector and business, and the parliaments as well.

Tenth, the United Nations must move from concentrating on inputs to considering the outputs and the results of its programs. That is, it should first determine whether the program or task itself is worth keeping or improving, before making efforts to improve efficiency. Therefore, it must attempt to develop a system of result-based budgeting, at first for the United Nations at large, but with the objective of including other regional and subregional organizations, whether governmental or otherwise.

RELEVANCE IN THE CONTEXT
OF THE ACTIVITIES OF THE UNITED NATIONS

The issue of relevance may be dealt with at two levels. The first is the conceptual one, in terms of the need for a neutral, global platform for discussion, dialogue and debate amongst all the countries of the world, on the issues of shared concern for developing a shared vision, mission, objectives and goals. The second level is in terms of the institutional framework created for this platform, in terms of the institutional structures and their functions for active pursuit of the shared vision, mission, objectives and goals.

AT THE CONCEPTUAL LEVEL

The creation and continuing existence of various types of specialized transnational institutional platforms, particularly in the last 150-200 years of human history and especially amongst the sovereign nation States, is tangible proof of their importance and relevance. It is important to note that such transnational institutions, formal or otherwise, have also come into existence in the business world, in terms of transnational corporate entities, as well as amongst the people's organizations under the rubric of *civil society* organizations.

Much of this activity in organization building is directly or indirectly linked to efforts aimed at improving the quality of life of mankind. The growing integration and interdependence of sovereign nation States, the transnational enterprises, the *civil society* organizations, and above all, of the entire system of life on this planet, is becoming more and more tangible with the developments in modern technology. The global reach and impact of local actions, as may happen, for example, in nuclear warfare, or with the unsustainable use of natural resources, or with the live coverage of events by the media through modern information and communication technologies, has indeed accelerated our movement towards the creation of a global village.

The ever increasing speed and ease of travel, communication and the transport of goods, services and ideas, has made this interdependence inevitable and perhaps indispensable. On one side, this interdependence provides a new hope for sharing knowledge and experience to promote human, social, and economic development. On the other side, change, even for the better, can lead to fear and apprehension of the unknown, and the inevitable losses of tradition, culture and the familiar. Managing change for a better tomorrow requires the creation of institutional mechanisms for dealing with the good, the bad and the ugly in a holistic international framework. To make the process of management comprehensible and practical, the issues, concerns and problems need to be dealt with in smaller, cogent frameworks of a relatively homogenous and specialized kind. However, the greater the scattering of such efforts, the greater the need for coordination. It is a reasonable concept that a global platform for discussion, debate and dialogue is required to manage the interdependencies and change in a complex, shrinking and interwoven world. Hence the basic rationale for the United Nations System of organizations.

The Charter of the United Nations

In the aftermath of World War II, when the leaders of the victorious side sat down to develop a conceptual framework, in terms of a Charter, their focus was understandably on preventing another major war, and at the same time, on preserving the *status quo* in terms of the power equations, for the foreseeable future. The bulk of the developing countries, as they exist today, either did not exist then or at least not in their present numbers or as sovereign independent States.

Even so, with the support of some of the smaller developed countries, they were able to negotiate successfully for the inclusion of principles to promote social progress and better standards of living in freedom, and, to this end, 'to employ international machinery for the promotion of the economic and social advancement of all peoples'. That is precisely the reason why Chapters IX and X of the Charter of the United Nations include provisions to deal with international economic and social cooperation, and the Economic and Social Council, respectively. The reasons why things have not developed accordingly are dealt with in other parts of this book.

The economic and social concerns are very much an integral part of the Charter, even though the number of Articles (and chapters) dealing with these concerns is relatively very small. One reason for this limited attention to social and economic concerns, as cited in the preamble to the Charter, was the impact of the two wars during the life of the Founding Fathers of the Charter. Another plausible reason was the predominant focus on foreign policies of national governments, to prevent conflicts from escalating into wars. The military component of power and enforcement of sovereignty was certainly far more pronounced then, unlike the relatively greater weight of economic power in today's world.

Peace and Development

With the changing realities of the real world, should not the conceptual focus of the United Nations also change in the same way, from peace and security to development and underdevelopment? There is a general perception that the United Nations has been more successful in the more visible aspects of international organization activity, in relation to peacekeeping and peacemaking, which because of their greater drama and urgency catch the attention of the media, and, therefore, the public. However, even in this field it has only been able to deliver results when a broad consensus emerged on a certain issue, especially when the more powerful nations were involved; in other words, only when the national and global objectives coincided. The track record of the United Nations and the Specialized Agencies in the myriad other areas of social, cultural, economic, scientific and technological fields is, in general, considered less satisfactory, if not discouraging.

However, to the extent that international organizations make international public policies, the track record of the United Nations and its Specialized Agencies is in general rather impressive. This is especially so if we look at it from a long-term historical perspectives, comparing, say the first half of this century with the second half. But, if the perspective is shifted to the end result, in terms of tangible improvements in the quality of life of the vast majority of poor people, then the picture is indeed dismal. As income inequality between the rich and the poor countries continues to widen, the success and relevance of the United Nations System will have to be judged in the future primarily on the basis of its ability to contribute to an improvement in quality of life, especially of the poor.

One of the biggest stumbling blocks has been how to define the proper role that the United Nations or its Specialized Agencies can play in development. Our position in this respect coincides with the popular view, that the countries themselves are responsible for their own development. But institutions like the United Nations and the System, including the Bretton Woods ones, should facilitate this by creating the right environment, and by helping especially those countries that most need help. It is in this respect that we think that the developing countries, and those least developed among them, were let down because the policies and programs of many of the institutions were not relevant to their concerns. Assuming that there is a consensus on the type of approach that will work, there still is a need to evolve yardsticks and verifiable measures to confirm our arrival at the destination or to measure the extent of our progress towards this goal. In our view, we have to develop institutions that would help to level the playing field, and that would help the weaker players to upgrade their skills and capabilities.

AT THE INSTITUTIONAL FRAMEWORK LEVEL

An institutional framework, however elegant its structure and performance might be, will be meaningful only so long as it facilitates the taking of decisions and actions to achieve desired objectives and goals. In other words, the framework derives its relevance from its usefulness. The core issue is how to define relevance in terms of a verifiable or measurable yardstick of usefulness in the context of the United Nations System.

According to the Charter, the United Nations System was designed, first and foremost, to provide a mechanism for peaceful resolution of disputes and conflicts between States, to enhance security. The sovereign equality of States and their interdependence were seen as two key elements in creating the framework of institutions under the Charter. In spite of the compromises made in the world of *realpolitik* a fair amount of idealism manifested itself in the phraseology of various Articles of the Charter. Even though the institutional architecture of the United Nations System rests on equality of sovereign States, there are obvious elements that detract from its democratic credentials and stand out in sharp relief – most notably the veto power of the permanent members of the Security Council. In practice, the requirement of consensus gives a much bigger role to the powerful States, as does the financial 'veto', when major contributors withhold their assessed contributions, which has the pernicious impact of slowly bleeding the vitality of the organization.

It is paradoxical that an ostensibly democratic edifice may, in reality, be driven by the national agendas of a handful of powerful countries. In a certain sense, the United Nations System has functioned so far in such a way that it could as well be considered an association with limited membership, like the G-7 (G-8). The underlying concern in any examination of its relevance is to determine whether it works for the greatest good of all, and not just a few of its Member States.

At the outset, it must be noted that international organizations are only one of the many channels through which the issues making up international relations flow. International relations continue to be overwhelmingly bilateral in character.

The relevance of the United Nations structures in the field of economic and social relations can be also gauged by the levels at which intergovernmental action is taken. In the ECOSOC and the subsidiary machinery of the General Assembly dealing with budgetary, economic and social matters, the governments are normally represented by officials at lower ranks than, for example, the ministers in charge of economic policy in meetings of the Organization for Economic Cooperation and Development (OECD), or in meetings of other organizations like those of the European Union, or the Heads of States or Governments in the G-7 (G-8) meetings. This question of the level of representation is certainly a matter that must influence our proposals for the *Better United Nations*. This, together with the aspect of wider representation, should figure prominently in any system that is to be considered relevant.

In the increasingly market-oriented development strategies being pursued worldwide, the role of government in national economic management has diminished, and so has the role of intergovernmental organizations in the world economic management, although not to the same degree.

The success of capitalistic, market-oriented, competition-led, technological progress, based on private property rights, has fundamentally altered the balance in favor of the individual versus the State. The reduction in the role of the State is more apparent than real. While more and more economic activity is market driven, the economic environment for the proper functioning of the market system has to be created and sustained by the State. So the capitalist model of development envisages a new, facilitator role for the State as the dominant element. In this new role the State does not wither away, nor does it withdraw from the economic sphere. In fact, it creates new regulations, mechanisms, infrastructures and institutions for dealing with market imperfections and failures.

The Marshall Plan and United Nations Work on Development

Based on the success of the Marshall Plan, in the reconstruction of Europe after World War II, an aid plan was supported by the developed countries in the framework of the United Nations System. The first United Nations Development Decade was the result, and the United Nations Development Programme (UNDP) was created with the former administrator of the Marshall Plan, Paul Hoffman at its head. Part of the enthusiasm for this plan of action was idealism, but part of it was certainly guided by ideological rivalry between capitalism and communism. The failure of the plan had as much to do with inadequate funds, as it had to do with the complete lack of understanding of the conditions and culture of developing countries. Too much was expected with too little funds, inadequate planning and insufficient time to create the enabling environment, and complete disregard of the norms and practices of neoclassical economic thought, predominant at the time.

By the time of the second United Nations Development Decade, the developing countries had begun to approach the development issue from a new perspective. They argued that aid or assistance by itself was not sufficient. There was a concomitant need to alter the colonial structure of economic relations in the world, before any significant improvement in economic performance of developing countries could be expected on a sustained, long-term basis, and hence the slogan 'trade not aid'.

The nature and scope of alterations recommended by the developing countries were very different from those deemed necessary by the developed countries. In addition, changes in the developing countries needed to be complemented by changes in the developed ones. As a result, the second United Nations Development Decade also passed by without much success, in spite of the adoption by the General Assembly in 1974 of the resolution calling for the establishment of a New International Economic Order (NIEO). In fact, the expectations raised by the oil crisis of 1973 in this regard were short-lived, as the bargaining power of the oil producing, developing countries petered out with the decline in oil prices due to the glut in the oil market.

The third United Nations Development Decade was also a lost decade, in which the debt burden of the developing countries made it practically impossible for these countries to make any significant progress, except for a handful of countries in Southeast Asia.

The ongoing fourth United Nations Development Decade is beset by the problems created by the sudden, huge flight of capital, causing economic chaos and social strain in many part of the developing world.

All in all, the United Nations Development Decades have not served any real purpose. In this context, it will also be useful to highlight two main aspects of the question of Overseas Development Assistance (ODA). First, instead of an increase in ODA by the developed countries to reach the target of 0.7 percent of their GNP, as approved by the United Nations General Assembly, it decreased further. In fact, it has never come close to the target. Second, it became clear that governments on a bilateral basis give seventy-five percent of this assistance; about fifteen percent is channeled through the World Bank and other financial institutions, and only about six percent through the United Nations Institutions. This is yet another perspective from which the relevance of the United Nations System needs to be looked at. This scenario would make one wonder whether it is worth financing and supporting the present United Nations Funds and Programs involved in development assistance, to deliver such a minimal percentage of the total ODA, which itself continues to decrease.

The United Nations System – A New Architecture

The United Nations System, for all its shortcomings, is unique and would be difficult to duplicate or re-invent. It is the only available universal system, and if it were to be duplicated or re-invented there would be no guarantee that it would not have the same, if not more, shortcomings. It now has to live up, not only to the demands of governments, but also to the increasing expectations of the peoples of the world. It, therefore, has to adapt itself to the changing world or run the risk of becoming more irrelevant in important fields of human activity.[1] Effective leadership, buoyed by strong political will, will be essential for this transition.

To emphasize the low level of international commitment, supporters of the Organization sometimes point to the fact that the United Nations System's expenditure was only 0.0005 percent of the world's gross product, and only 0.0007 percent of the GDP of 24 industrialized countries. This represented an expenditure of USD1.90 per human being alive in 1992. This would not seem to be exorbitant, they add, in a world whose governments spent about USD150 per human being on military expenditures.[2]

It should be underlined that only a very small number of the critical international issues of the post-World War II era were 'managed' or even influenced by the United Nations. In fact, some insist that the United Nations System will continue to be used by the countries as a forum for debate, dialogue and discussion when other channels are unable to deliver, or when decisions taken elsewhere are to be legitimized and sanctified by the neutral, global United Nations System.

The United Nations System with its dispersed, weak and poorly coordinated structure has played only a minor role in global economic management. For several reasons, industrial countries have not been interested in using the United Nations other than for data collections, studies and policy analysis. First of all, because the United Nations, as an intergovernmental organization, is not based on the values and mechanisms of the market system. Secondly, because the United Nations is a universal organization and developed industrial countries do not want the rest of the world to intervene in their economic policy affairs. Thirdly, because the one-country-one-vote system is not perceived to be compatible with market relations based on economic power.

The architecture of the United Nations System was developed to give primacy to the role of the sovereign national governments. In the real world, the importance and influence of national governments has diminished, while that of the transnational enterprises and *civil society* organizations have increased. As pointed out in Chapter 4, this was more in line with the Covenant of the League of Nations than with the Charter of the United Nations. The Charter gave prominence to 'we the peoples', which was a striking departure from the Covenant of the League. The Covenant was more concerned with the 'High Contracting Parties' and 'relations between nations'.

Looking at the global situation, from the perspective of the developed countries, it seems that the prime problem requiring international attention is that of human insecurity, arising out of conflicts and wars. Looking at it from the viewpoint of the developing countries, the major concern continues to be mere survival, as they are insecure in terms of food, shelter, clothing, and many other basic needs which they cannot even think of at present – except perhaps as luxuries.

---

[1] Urquhart, Brian and Erskine Childers, *A World in Need of Leadership: Tomorrow's United Nations,* Dag Hammarskjold Foundation, Uppsala, Sweden, 1990, p. 9.
[2] Childers, E. and Brian Urquhart, *Renewing the United Nations,* Uppsala, Sweden, 1994, p. 143.

A Special Commission on the Economic and Social Work

In 1987, the ECOSOC, by its Decision 1987/112, established the Special Commission of the Economic and Social Council to undertake an in-depth study of the United Nations intergovernmental structure and functions in the economic and social fields. From the outset, the objectives of the Special Commission raised controversy. Most of the industrialized countries agreed that the purpose of the exercise was to agree on the principles or direction of reform, with a view to obtaining administrative and financial efficiency before settling down to the details of the intergovernmental structure. For them, the reform process should have aimed at improving the cost-effectiveness and efficiency of the United Nations' structure and functions in the economic and social fields. On the other hand, the Group of 77 argued that the purpose of reform was to make the United Nations more relevant in international economic cooperation and development, and in promoting economic-social progress.[3]

It has also to be acknowledged that what some perceive as major accomplishments, appear to others as peripheral matters. While applauding the United Nations' peacekeeping successes, and appreciating the positions of the superpowers and the efforts of the middle powers, many third world governments are concerned about the perceived redirection of the world diplomatic agenda away from global equity and economic development. For these governments and their peoples, debilitating internal poverty and constraining external dependence remain the crucial problems. Confronting these problems remains the top priority of both their domestic and foreign policies.[4]

Although the structure of development activities of the United Nations has changed considerably, the premise behind such activities has not. The present structure was referred to in the Introduction. It was shown that the problem with the technical cooperation activities of the United Nations was not that these were inefficient, but that they were not relevant, and as such were part of the problem rather than part of the solution.[5]

Technical cooperation, being the main thrust of the development activities of the United Nations, is still given on the basis of assisting the developing countries to develop within a set structure, namely the present international economic order. The debate on the new international economic order and the various United Nations development decades and strategies are just that – debates and very little else!

Comparative advantage, as a doctrine of free trade and gains from such trade, has not worked for most of the developing countries. Still, although there is ample proof that economic relations on such a basis do not appear to assist developing countries, the United Nations has not changed. The term *comparative advantage* is explained in some detail in Annex I.

---

[3] Saksena, K. P., Demand for Reform: Subsequent Developments, *Reforming the United Nations: The Challenge of Relevance*, Newbury Park, Sage Publications, 1993, pp. 128-130.

[4] Puchala, Donald J., and Roger A. Coate, *The Challenge of Relevance: The United Nations in a Changing Word Environment*, The Academic Council on the United Nations System, Reports and Papers, 1989-5, pp. 28-29.

[5] See Ph D dissertation, Bartolo, *op. cit.*

The role of the United Nations development activities must be seen in this context, and so must the role of other organizations, including the Bretton Woods Institutions and the WTO. This is certainly of interest and concern in the work of the WTO, and the problem of relevance reappears in the context of the drive towards globalization and liberalization, and the resulting marginalization of the developing countries. The United Nations would only become relevant to the majority of the peoples if it addresses this problem.

Relevance of the United Nations is also better served by using scarce resources more diligently, by avoiding duplication of effort through better coordination within the System and, as importantly, outside it. The United Nations System should not duplicate the efforts even of other intergovernmental institutions, whether these are global or regional or subregional. Governments themselves have the major responsibility here, to speak with one voice. This voice should be one at the United Nations, at the various Specialized Agencies of the United Nations System and also outside it, for example at the OAU, OECD, European Union (EU), and all the other institutions, whether global or regional.

RELEVANCE OF CIVIL SOCIETY

The United Nations has to be primarily relevant to the people, by responding to the needs and concerns of governments and the *civil society*, the latter being sometimes a better safety net for the people's urgent needs and emergencies. As implied in the previous part, the definite emphasis in the Charter of the United Nations to the people, in contrast to the Covenant of the League of Nations, did not significantly change the primacy given to the sovereign Member States. This gave rise to the polemic whether Member States really represented their people, and whether the United Nations and other organizations were being exploited for the benefit of the populations that the Member States represented. Without getting involved in this polemic, the questions raised could not be ignored particularly when the great majority of the Member States were not represented by democratically elected governments. In spite of the Covenant having a less democratic quality than the Charter of the United Nations, the League did not ignore the *civil society* completely.

The League of Nations and Civil Society

In a considerable number of cases, the League tried to act and influence governments through public opinion, which necessitated increasing the importance of the 'Information Department' of the League's Secretariat. In fact, it can be said that the League could gain influence or credibility only by acting as an organ of the 'international community', notwithstanding the interests of particular States.[6]

---

[6] Ray, Jean, *Commentaire du Pacte de la Société des Nations Selon la Politique et la Jurisprudence des Organes de la Société*, Paris, Sirey, 1930, p. 70.

Article 24 of the Covenant included the mandate to place all international bureaus under the direction of the League. Although this appeared to have the intention of developing close relationships and collaboration between the League and the international NGOs, the Council of the League, in fact, decided, as early as 1923, to exclude these private organizations from the scope of Article 24. This collaboration was, therefore, never institutionalized. In spite of Article 25[7] of the Covenant encouraging closer cooperation with the national Red Cross organizations, the International Committee of the Red Cross (ICRC), for example, was only recognized internationally with the Geneva Convention of 1949 and its protocols (1977).

In contrast to the emphasis later given to the human rights of the individual, the protection of particular groups of *civil society* was not uncommon during the time of the League of Nations. This was evident in the relationship of the International Labour Organization (ILO)[8] to the League, the international supervision and protection of minorities after the First World War, and the obligations of the members towards the inhabitants of the colonies or 'mandates' as these were known then.

During the time of the League of Nations, *civil society* was considered to be synonymous with public opinion. Therefore, in that era, when the international society largely relied on only one actor, namely the State, the attempts to give access to non-State actors in intergovernmental forums must not only be seen as progressive but also as a harbinger of things to come. This situation must have had some influence on the drafters of the Charter of the United Nations, when they grappled with the role of NGOs in the United Nations. The question is, though, how much of an influence?

The United Nations and Civil Society

In sharp contrast to the Covenant of the League of Nations, the Charter of the United Nations, right from its Preamble, strikes an innovative chord by giving prominence to 'we the peoples' rather than to the Member States or the Governments. Needless to state, this prominence was not sustained in the Charter and it faded in places to the 'nations' and 'members'. On the other hand, the concern as to whether the 'peoples' were adequately represented at the United Nations did not fade and, in fact, continues to be a major challenge facing the world community and those involved in reforming it.

This topic, in fact, figured prominently in the work of the recent series of *ad hoc* Working Groups organized by the recent Presidents of the General Assembly of the United Nations, referred to in some detail in Chapter 1. However, as in other areas dealt

---

[7] Article 25 stated that, 'The Members of the League agree to encourage and promote the establishment and cooperation of duly authorized voluntary national Red Cross organizations having as purpose the improvement of health, the prevention of disease and the mitigation of suffering throughout the world'.

[8] The ILO, with its tripartite representation, was founded in 1919 on the basis of a provision in the Treaty of Versailles (Article 329) that called it a constituent part of the organization of the League. Membership in the ILO was acquired automatically together with League membership.

with by the various Working Groups, no concrete decisions were reached.[9] There seemed to be, however, a consensus that the United Nations would benefit from increased inter-action with the *civil society*. On most other points, like funding for participation by the *civil society* in meetings and work of the Organization, and the establishment of links between them and the General Assembly, no consensus could be reached.

Once, it was decided that the relevance of the United Nations and the System has to be seen first and foremost in the context of the people, the major emphasis given in this book to the *civil society* and parliaments should not come as a surprise to anyone. Our concern is that the *Better United Nations* has to ensure full and complete representation of all the peoples of the world. By *civil society* we mean all nongovernmental and other organizations and institutions, including the businesses and the private sector. We also include parliaments, to reflect the points of view, that in certain democracies, wishes and concerns of particular peoples may not be reflected in the views of their legitimate governments. This is the only area where the *Better United Nations* would tolerate some overlapping, because we believe that valid, fair and just representation can never be over-emphasized, particularly in a system that is biased towards the *status quo*.

RELEVANCE AS THE SOLE JUSTIFICATION FOR THE WORK OF THE UNITED NATIONS

The question of efficiency is a distraction in United Nations reform. The views and priorities of the 188[10] Member States should not be used to mandate activities, unless these activities conform to the relevance guide developed above or to some other appropriate one. Only thereafter should we be concerned with efficiency.

The yardstick of relevance developed above should serve as the basis for the *Better United Nations*, and the historical and theoretical developments referred to in the Introduction should serve as a methodological framework for the discussion on reform that follows.

---

[9] For a synthesis of the proposals and observations made on this topic by Member States, United Nations Organs, independent commissions and experts on the increased involvement of the *civil society* (and parliaments) in the work of the United Nations, see WGUNS/CRP: 3/Add.4.

[10] With the admission of Kiribati, the Republic of Nauru and the Kingdom of Tonga, there are now 188 Member States of the United Nations as of 14 September, 1999.

CHAPTER 4

THE CHARTER
OF THE UNITED NATIONS
ON COORDINATION AND REFORM

SUMMARY

The Charter of the United Nations reflects the Founding Fathers' dreams and hopes for the Organization. What can we still learn from this solemn declaration when it comes to reform and the lead role of the United Nations when it comes to coordination? In fact, this chapter even analyzes the questions of coordination and reform during the League of Nations. Although there were not as many agencies, how was coordination dealt with at that time? Did it have time to reform? This analysis of the situation before the United Nations was founded should throw some insight on how coordination and reform, so much a part of our life now, were considered then.

On the matter of coordination, some Articles of the Charter are analyzed and reviewed [Articles 17 (paragraph 3), 57, 58, 60, 63 (particularly paragraph 2), and 64].

In the context of reforms, we have studied and analyzed Chapter XVIII of the Charter on amendments and the few amendments approved since the founding of the United Nations. We have drawn some conclusions about how the Founding Fathers saw the possible changes to the Charter and to the United Nations in the future. Is it significant that it was made so difficult to change the Charter?

It does not take long for one to discover the richness of the research and scholarship available on the Charter of the United Nations, as concerns the questions of coordination and reform. Maximum use was made of this, and great pains were taken to credit the eminent scholars and authors for their ideas and insights. For this reason, it was often preferred to use direct quotes extensively.

COORDINATION UNDER THE LEAGUE OF NATIONS

The League of Nations System

One always refers to the League of Nations as the predecessor of the United Nations, with little or no knowledge that other international organizations also existed at the time. In fact, about twenty other organizations, somewhat technical, already existed at that time.[1] While the Covenant of the League relied on the constitutions of some of those organizations, it also attempted to bring them within the sphere of activity of the League.[2] Article 24 of the Covenant referred to the fact that 'international bureaus' already existing should be placed under the direction of the League, with their consent.[3]

Thus started the first attempts at coordination between the League and the group of international organizations that existed soon after World War I. In fact, the original intention of the framers of the Covenant was to go much further, by assuming central control over the financing of all international activities for the League.[4] This was far more ambitious as compared with anything in this regard in the United Nations Charter, as one can see later in this chapter.

The initial aim of Article 24 was that it should be applied to all, or almost all, the international administrative unions.[5] This was also seen as an effort by the League to get involved with economic and social matters, in spite of the fact that such matters were, in general, left out of the final draft of the Covenant.[6] In fact, Article 24 was never implemented and most of the existing agencies remained independent.[7] In the end only

---

[1] Simma, Bruno (ed.), *The Charter of the United Nations: A Commentary*, Oxford University Press, 1995, pp. 69-70.

[2] *Ibid.*, p. 66.

[3] The 'matters of international interest' concerned were enumerated by Article 23: 'fair and humane conditions of labor'; 'just treatment of the native inhabitants of territories under the control of members'; 'traffic in women and children, and traffic in opium and other dangerous drugs'; 'trade in arms and ammunition'; 'freedom of communication and of transit and equitable treatment for the commerce'; and, finally, 'prevention and control of disease'. For an in-depth analysis of Article 23, see: Ray, Jean, *Commentaire du Pacte de la Société des Nations Selon la Politique et la Jurisprudence des Organes de la Société*, Paris, Sirey, 1930, pp. 652-660, and Yepes, J. M., and Pereira da Silva, *Commentaire Théorique et Pratique du Pacte de la Société des Nations et des Statuts de l'Union Panamericaine*, t.111, Paris, Pédone, 1939, pp. 245-256.

[4] Goodrich, Leland M., Edvard Hambro and Anne Patricia Simmons, *Charter of the United Nations. Commentary and Documents*, New York and London, Columbia University Press, 1969, p. 165. However, 'this was never achieved to any great extent' (*ibid.*).

[5] Codding, George A., Jr., 'The Relationship of the League and the UN with Independent Agencies: A Comparison', *Annals of International Studies*, 1970, p. 70. See also Yepes, J.M., and P. da Silva (*op. cit.*, p. 277): '*Le but poursuivi par les auteurs du Pacte était visiblement de faire de la Société une sorte de clearing house de la vie internationale*'; for Walters, Francis P., (*A History of the League of Nations*, Westport, Greenwood Press, 1952, p. 60). Article 24 was inserted 'in the expectation that the international offices in question ... would be merged in the organization of the League and managed in the future by the League Secretariat'.

[6] Codding, *op. cit.*, p. 71.

[7] Siotis, Jean, 'The Institutions of the League of Nations' in *The League of Nations in Retrospect*, Boston-New York, Walter de Gruyter, 1983, p. 28.

six organizations associated themselves with the League, and these were not even the major ones.[8]

Some leading scholars of the League of Nations give three reasons for this. The first and foremost was the fact that the United States did not become a member of the League, and objected to any agency of which it was a member having any affiliation with the League.[9] Second, the spirit of autonomy of most of these agencies was much stronger than the framers of the Covenant thought.[10] Thirdly, the genuine concern of some of the agencies that the League would not survive, and that this would affect their own existence.[11]

It is, therefore, clear that conscious efforts at coordination by the League failed miserably.[12] Maybe the only lesson that one could learn from all this was that no organization should attempt to control or coordinate others before its own house is first put in order.

REFORM OF THE LEAGUE OF NATIONS

Reform According to Article 26 of the Covenant

Since the beginning of the League of Nations there were frequent efforts to amend the Covenant, to make it easier to enforce or to make it compatible with other pacts and treaties.[13] This was not always successful. The League could be 'reformed' either by applying Article 26 of the Covenant,[14] by concluding new treaties outside the Covenant framework, with the intention of complementing it or improving it.[15]

---

[8] The list of these organizations and their dates of affiliation are quoted in Codding, *op. cit.*, p. 73.

[9] Codding, *op. cit.*, p. 73. See also Jenks, Wilfred C., 'Amendment of the Covenant', *British Yearbook of International Law,* 1937, vol. 18, p. 159, p. 171: after 'the decision of the United States not to become a member of the League … it became clear that the League of Nations would not become a universal organization and a tendency developed to create new machinery outside the framework of the League. As the inter-war period ran its course the tendency to create new organizations outside the League framework became more pronounced'. Therefore, for this author, the League experience ' has left virtually no heritage of organizational complications' (*ibid.*, p. 170).

[10] Ranshoffen–Wertheimer, Egon F., The International Secretariat, Washington, DC, Carnegie Endowment, 1943, p. 84. See also Codding, *ibid.*, p. 73: 'The secretariats feared the possible encroachment of the larger body on their freedom of action'.

[11] *Ibid.*, p. 74. For this author: 'If the League had been able to implement Article 24, …the fall of the League could well have had disastrous consequences for the affiliated organizations' (p. 86). See also Simma, *op. cit.*, p. 803, who emphasizes the consequences 'of the negative developments in the League in the 1930s' on the (non-) application of Article 24.

[12] Ranshoffen–Wertheimer, *op. cit.*, p. 85. For more details, see Ray, *op. cit.*, pp. 671-672, and Yepes, J.M., and P. da Silva, *op. cit.*, pp. 2777-2791.

[13] *The Aims Methods and Activity of the League of Nations*, Secretariat of the League, Geneva, 1938, p. 52.

[14] It stated: '1. Amendments to this Covenant will take effect when ratified by the Members of the League whose Representatives compose the Council and by a majority of the Members of the League whose Representatives compose the Assembly. 2. No such amendments shall bind any Member of the League which signifies its dissent therefrom, but in that case it shall cease to be a Member of the League'. On the origins of

Our interest here is in the first approach; namely, on how the Covenant could be changed or amended. This could be done in two ways. One, by undertaking a *technical legal reform* whereby the provisions of the Covenant are amended so as make them compatible with the technical requirements of a treaty or a piece of legislation. Two, through a *politico-legal reform*, meaning to amend the Covenant to bring it in line with the political realities of the period.[16]

Politico-Legal Reform

Concerning the *politico-legal reform*, the Secretariat of the League was cautiously considering, in 1938, that the organization was in a crisis due to the inability of the League to intervene effectively in the first Sino-Japanese war (1931-1932) and later in the Italo-Ethiopian war (1935-1936). It appeared obvious that the League could not come to the rescue of a weaker Member State in case of a conflict, and, therefore, seriously considered amending the Covenant to remedy this.[17] More precisely, the Special Assembly of the League of Nations decided, in July 1936, to abandon further efforts to resist the Italian conquest of Ethiopia by economic sanctions. This brought about a long and arduous process to reform the League of Nations.[18] Although this was not the first time that the League was unable to prevent or contain a conflict, it was the first time that it realized that it needed to take joint action against an aggressor. We know that this did not succeed.

It was, however, a signal for the League to both ensure and guarantee adherence to the obligations in the Covenant or else to relax or change these obligations. It was clearly the right time to either defend the objectives and obligations of the Covenant or to change them.[19] As in any debate, the members of the League were divided into two sides. One side was in favor of increasing the power of the League by enabling it to intervene in conflicts without the agreement of a Member State which was party to a dispute, and by making sanctions compulsory. The other side was in favor of a more pragmatic approach

---

Article 26, see Ray, *op. cit.*, pp. 685-687, and Yepes, J.M., and P. da Silva, *op. cit.*, pp. 306-309; on the (procedure leading to the vote of the amendments): *ibid.*, pp. 309-318.

[15] The following examples can be given: the Treaty of Mutual Assistance; the Geneva Protocol of 1924; the Kellog Pact; the Treaty for Improving the Means of Preventing War; the Treaty for Financial Assistance to the Victims of Aggression, etc. 'These schemes ... might rightly have been counted as proposals for reform' (Walters, *op. cit.*, p. 710).

[16] Guggenheim, Paul, 'Legal and political conflicts in the League of Nations. A contribution to the reform of the League', in *The World Crisis*, by the Professors of the Graduate Institute of International Studies, London-New York-Toronto, Longmans, Green and Co., 1938, p. 200.

[17] *ibid.*, p. 184 and p. 201.

[18] Walters, *op. cit.*, p. 709. In fact, the concept of League 'reform' was first brought into the debate by Mussolini in 1933: 'The Fascist Grand Council announced (12 December 1933) that Italy would withdraw unless there were a radical reform. There was nothing to show what changes were demanded ... Except in Germany, the Italian initiative was coldly received', and Mussolini 'soon dropped his campaign...But the movement had been started' (*ibid.*, p. 711).

[19] *Ibid.*, p. 687.

that would recognize the circumstances, which sometimes made sanctions impractical and impossible to enforce.[20]

Finally, the Assembly invited all Member States to send their observations and suggestions to strengthen the Covenant in this respect.[21] Although a committee set up by the Assembly in 1936 further discussed the matter, the two sides could not reconcile their differences and the discussion led to no significant progress.[22]

Technical Legal Reform

As far as the *technical legal reform* of the League is concerned, it was underlined above that the League had been unable to apply any effective coordination in terms of Article 24 of its Covenant. On the other hand, it established specialized bodies with responsibilities in education, health, housing, emigration, nutrition, and cultural and scientific activities and in areas of international economic and financial cooperation. Neither the League's Council nor the Assembly, under whose authority they were established, could keep such diverse activities regulated. [23] This led to a further effort at establishing machinery to regulate and improve these various technical agencies.[24]

The Council appointed the Bruce Committee to do this in May 1939 and it submitted its report to the Assembly at the end of August 1939.[25] The Bruce Committee's report recommended the establishment of a Central Committee for Economic and Social Questions, to coordinate all League bodies engaged in economic and social activities. This new Committee was to have the same authority as the Council did in the area of political and collective security.[26] This Economic and Social Committee never had the chance to function within the League's framework, but scholars of the League of Nations

---

[20] Jenks, *op. cit.*, p. 159.

[21] Walters, *op. cit.*, p. 688.

[22] *Ibid.*, p. 713. 'Sanctions or no sanctions, a coercive League or a consultative League – this was the question that reappeared at every turn of the debate. It was a debate which could not be settled by voting, and which never looked likely to be settled by compromise' (*ibid.*, pp. 714-715).

[23] Siotis, *op. cit.*, p. 28. Walters seems to be of a different opinion: for him, the League's institutions 'had learned much about the interdependence of the activities which they had hitherto carried on in separate compartments. Connexions of the League organs with one another, with the ILO, and with outside agencies, had been multiplied, in particular during the years when the League was progressively losing its power to control or influence the great issues of peace and war' (*op. cit.*, pp. 756-757). This author thinks that the main problem lies elsewhere, namely, in the subordination of the agencies to the League's Council: indeed, this institution which 'controlled them at every turn was rarely capable of giving them help or guidance... A further weakness in the established system was that while the United States was taking a full share in the activities of all the expert organizations, effective decisions still rested with a body in which American representatives had no place' (*ibid.*, pp. 758-759).

[24] *Ibid.*, p. 759.

[25] That is, only a few days before the German invasion of Poland. Therefore, it 'could never really be examined within the League's framework. The Report did, however, have a great influence on the elaboration of the UN Charter' (Siotis, *op. cit.*, p. 28). Bruce was the Australian delegate at the Council and the Assembly.

[26] *Ibid.* For that purpose, it seems that it was to be made up of Ministers of Commerce, Finance, Transport, or Health, to give its deliberations an increased authority. However, the 'civil society' was also to be represented: indeed, this institution 'would be allowed to co-opt a few individual experts to sit side by side with the delegates of governments' (Walters, *op. cit.*, p. 762).

seem to agree that this was the forerunner of the Economic and Social Council of the United Nations, which was established some years later.[27]

It is not difficult to conclude that League reform was a rare occurrence, whether *politico-legal* or *technical legal,* in spite of the various efforts to achieve this. Indeed, apart from a few purely formal amendments to the Covenant, no substantial or overall reform was ever possible.[28] This was both because the proposals were too confrontational, and could never gather a consensus, or because the process itself was too lengthy and cumbersome.

COORDINATION ACCORDING TO THE CHARTER OF THE UNITED NATIONS

Articles 57 and 58 of the United Nations Charter

Neither coordination nor reform was easy under the League of Nations. Whether some lessons could have been learnt from these first real experiments with a multifaceted international institution would be difficult to say. One thing is sure, however: attempts at coordination and reform have not been any easier in the United Nations than they were for the League of Nations.

Two different sets of reasons are usually given for the need for effective coordination in the United Nations. The first is the increase of the number of Specialized Agencies and the resulting increase in demands on the System. The second is the rampant overlapping and duplication of activities, as a result of an ever expanding United Nations, that seems to have been exacerbated by the lack of the development of effective coordination machinery.[29]

These two reasons need to be analyzed in the context of the Charter of the United Nations. The first relates to the expected relationship of the United Nations proper to the Specialized Agencies, particularly in the context of Article 58 on coordination. The second refers to whether the lack of adequate machinery to prevent this overlapping and duplication can be traced back to the Charter itself. Indeed, one will see that there remains a basic ambiguity in the respective roles of the General Assembly and the ECOSOC as far as coordination is concerned. It was never clear which one of these two organs had the primary responsibility in this area. In the circumstances, not only was some overlapping unavoidable but, more importantly, no coordination was done at all.

Concerning the first reason, Articles 57 and 58 of the Charter provide the basic principles governing this relationship. Article 57 states that the Specialized Agencies

---

[27] See *ibid.,* and Siotis, *op. cit.,* pp. 28-29. This second author notes, however, that 'the UN system remains much more decentralized than the one envisaged in the Bruce Committee Report'.

[28] For more details on the amendments voted by the Assembly, and on those actually accepted by Member States, see: Ray, *op. cit.,* pp. 687-694, and Yepes, J.M., and P. da Silva, *op. cit.,* pp. 318-321.

[29] Dicke, Klaus, 'Reform of the UN', in *United Nations: Law, Policies and Practice,* vol. 2, Wolfrum, Rüdiger (ed.), Dordrecht–Boston–London, M. Nijhoff, 1995, pp. 1013-1014. For a history of coordination reform (proposals) within the UN System, see pp. 1014-1019.

'shall be brought into relation with the United Nations', but without defining the precise meaning of this relationship. However, Article 58 immediately fills this gap by indicating that the Specialized Agencies shall 'coordinate' their 'policies and activities' with the United Nations.[30]

Agency Agreements

What is the meaning of coordination in this context? Does it imply a vertical or a horizontal relationship between the Specialized Agencies and the United Nations proper? Moreover, what are the normal channels for coordination? The answer to the last question is given by Article 63.1, namely, that the primary channel to reach that goal shall be 'agreements' freely entered into by the United Nations and the agencies.[31] Therefore, 'the degree of a Specialized Agency's dependence on the United Nations in terms of law is only a question of the terms of the relationship agreement'.[32]

The Charter does not stipulate either the nature or the content of the agreements to be entered into with the Specialized Agencies. It accords great freedom in this regard to the General Assembly, the ECOSOC, and the Specialized Agencies concerned. It shows no intention of controlling or subordinating them legally, as befits the nature of the agreements between sovereign equals. This is clearly stated in the *Report to the President on the Results of the San Francisco Conference* by the American Secretary of State.[33]

Moreover, using methods involving the sharing of information, discussion and persuasion in order to achieve coordination, the agreements do not confer upon the United Nations any control over budgets or programs, but underline the independent and decisive autonomy of the Specialized Agencies in these matters.[34]

---

[30] The precise wording of Article 58 is the following: 'the Organization shall make recommendations for the coordination of the policies and activities of the Specialized Agencies'. To quote Meng, Werner, (in Simma, *op. cit.*, p. 817): 'The agencies are under no obligation under the UN Charter ... to do more than study those recommendations and to report on the consequences they wish to draw'.

[31] The whole situation is summed up by Goodrich et al., (*op. cit.*, p. 383): 'in the economic and social fields the objectives of the general international organization should in large measure be achieved through autonomous specialized organizations created by inter-governmental agreement and brought into relation with the UN by agreements freely entered into on both sides'.

[32] Meng, *op. cit.*, p. 805.

[33] 'The Charter has little to say about their nature and content ... The design is clear; the specialized agencies are to be accorded the greatest measure of freedom and initiative compatible with purposeful and coordinated action on the part of the General Assembly, the ECOSOC and the agencies and organizations brought into relationship with them ... the agreements do not have the effect of subjecting the Specialized Agencies to effective United Nations control or of placing them in a subordinate legal position. They are in the nature of agreements between sovereign equals'. Quoted by Jenks, Wilfred C., 'Coordination: A New Problem of International Organization', RCADI, 1950-II, p. 180.

[34] They 'rely upon methods of information, discussion, and persuasion for achieving coordination. They do not give the United Nations organs control over budgets and programmes of the Specialized Agencies; rather they treat the Specialized Agencies as equals in their power to take independent decisions regarding policies and programmes', *ibid.*, p. 396. Thus: 'Autonomy for the agencies was the pattern that evolved' (Codding, George A. Jr., 'The relationship of the League and the UN with the independent agencies: A comparison', *Annals of International Studies,* 1970, p. 82). This author explains this matter of fact because the very first agreement concluded by the UN in accordance with Article 63 of the Charter was negotiated with ILO; this agreement of

The Charter itself is also very clear on the autonomy of the Specialized Agencies. For example, Article 17.3 states that the Specialized Agencies shall submit their budgets to the General Assembly,[35] but does not confer on the General Assembly any specific financial power of control over the budgets of the Specialized Agencies.[36] As indicated in Chapter 2, where some of the agreements were analyzed, the agencies 'enjoy full autonomy in deciding the form and content of such budget'.[37] One can say, therefore, that for the Specialized Agencies, budget policy remains an internal matter.[38]

Moreover, the Specialized Agencies' annual reporting to the ECOSOC does not change their complete autonomy one bit. Article 64 reflects the independence of the Specialized Agencies in areas of their competence, under their mandates, comparable to that of Member States.[39] Indeed Article 64.1 seems to put Specialized Agencies and Member States on the same level when it states that the ECOSOC 'may make arrangements with members of the United Nations and with the Specialized Agencies to obtain reports'.

Primary Responsibility for Coordination — Is it of the General Assembly or of the ECOSOC?

As far as the second of the reasons is concerned, namely the rampant overlapping and duplication, the Charter does not state clearly whether it is the ECOSOC or the General Assembly that has the primary responsibility in the area of coordination. In fact, its Articles are contradictory on this point. This ambiguity has thus triggered some uncertainty, or at least some overlapping in this area, since both the General Assembly and the ECOSOC have created subsidiary machinery to coordinate the work of the United Nations proper with that of the Specialized Agencies.

This ambiguity is revealed in Articles 60 and 63.2 of the Charter. Article 60 states, 'Responsibility for the discharge of the functions of the Organization set forth in this Chapter shall be vested in the General Assembly and, under the authority of the General

---

association 'gave the ILO all the autonomy and authority, in the fields of labor, that he could have hoped for ... (This first agreement) set the standard for all the negotiations that followed. Each agency quickly developed what might be called a 'most favored agency' policy, and requested that if a privilege were granted to one it had to be granted to all ... Some agencies ... were able to get by with substantially fewer responsibilities to UN organs than those assumed by the ILO' (*ibid.*, p. 79).

[35] The precise wording is the following: 'The General Assembly shall consider and approve any financial and budgetary arrangements with specialized agencies referred to in Article 57 and shall examine the administrative budgets of such specialized agencies with a view to making recommendations to the agencies concerned'.

[36] 'does not confer on the General Assembly any special financial power for controlling the specialized agencies' Schmidt, Rudolf, and Wilfried Koschorreck, in Simma, *op. cit.*, p. 313. For more details on the practical application of Article 17.3 (arrangements in the relationships agreements, budgetary and financial procedures, common system of salaries and allowances), see *ibid.*, pp. 313-317.

[37] Quoted by Goodrich et al., *op. cit*, p. 424.

[38] 'the adoption of their budgets was and still is an internal matter'. Hüfner, 'UN System', in Wolfrum, (ed.), *op. cit.*, p. 1366.

[39] 'reflects the principle that the Specialized Agencies, within the areas of their competence under their respective charters, enjoy a measure of autonomy which requires respect for their independence comparable to that shown for Member States'. Goodrich, et al., *op. cit.*, pp. 426-427.

Assembly, in the Economic and Social Council'. However, Article 63.2 states that the ECOSOC, 'may coordinate the activities of the specialized agencies'.

This relatively subtle difference did, however, elicit some commentary from the experts on the subject. W. Meng points out that Article 63, while defining the predominant role played by the ECOSOC in initiating relationships and in coordinating activities of the Specialized Agencies, does not, with Article 60, specify its primary role in that area. He also points out that, although it is a main organ of the United Nations and not subordinate to the General Assembly, the ECOSOC remains actively under the guidance and mandate of the General Assembly.[40] Meng explains this fact historically, as the ECOSOC having been conceived as a subsidiary organ of the General Assembly during the Dumbarton Oaks Conference; while, at the San Francisco Conference, it was vested with additional tasks and became a principal organ of the United Nations, the wording of Article 60 was not altered, resulting in the surprising situation of one principal organ being controlled by another in an important field of activities.[41]

Whatever the explanation, this situation has created a major problem for the United Nations, as the Charter does not clearly attribute ultimate responsibility for the actions in question. The General Assembly's assuming these activities, in conformity with Article 60, would invalidate Article 63.2, except for the ECOSOC's allocation of its own work. However, since Article 63 attributed a predominant role to the ECOSOC, Article 60 only implies supervision on the part of the General Assembly.[42] It is Meng's view that 'although history seems to favor the latter opinion, the practice of the Organization conforms with the former'.[43]

According to Codding, certain time-consuming practices were abandoned in 1952, like the supervision of the activities of the Specialized Agencies by the General Assembly, the joint sessions of the Second and Third Committees of the General Assembly devoted to considering the ECOSOC's report on relations with the Specialized Agencies, their joining up with the Fifth Committee to review reports of the Advisory

---

[40] 'Article 63 states in principle the predominant role of the ECOSOC in launching the relationship with Specialized Agencies and in coordinating their activities. But this rule, taken together with Article 60, does not say that the ECOSOC has the primary role in that area. It is always active under the guidance and the order of the General Assembly. This is curious, given the fact that the ECOSOC is a principal organ of the United Nations and, within the organization of the United Nations, is not subordinated to the General Assembly', *ibid.*, p. 858.

[41] *Ibid.*, p. 821.

[42] 'a major problem for the organization of the United Nations. The Charter does not make it clear who should be ultimately responsible for the actions in question. On the one hand, one could assume that the General Assembly could take over these activities in conformity with Article 60. This would practically invalidate Article 63.2 beyond the level of the ECOSOC's internal distribution of responsibilities. But one could also say that Article 63 expressly gave the ECOSOC the predominant role, and that therefore Article 60 means only that the ECOSOC is under the surveillance of the Assembly', *ibid.*, p. 858. This author seems to favor the former solution because he states elsewhere that 'The scope of independent activities by the ECOSOC under Article 63 is ... dependent on the decision of the General Assembly. Article 63 is consequently only important within the limits of Article 60' (*ibid.*, pp. 821-822). However, on the other hand, one should note that whereas the UN Charter 'does not define in detail how the Assembly is to discharge its general responsibility' under Article 60, it 'is more specific in its enumeration of the ECOSOC's powers', (Goodrich et al., *op. cit.*, pp. 395-396). This fact would lead one to a different conclusion.

[43] Meng, *op. cit.*, p. 858.

Committee on Administrative and Budgetary Questions (ACABQ) on the budgets of the Specialized Agencies and administrative coordination.[44] For Codding, the move by the General Assembly away from the consideration of inter-agency matters leaves the ECOSOC as the sole major United Nations organ to be so involved.[45]

According to Meng, however, the General Assembly conferred considerable freedom upon the ECOSOC, just after the founding of the United Nations, by making basic political decisions and mandating the ECOSOC to execute them through resolutions addressed to Specialized Agencies, thus transforming the General Assembly decisions into concrete actions. The ECOSOC mediated between the Assembly and the Specialized Agencies, while making important executive decisions. Consequently, the ECOSOC lost its important position concerning United Nations coordination to the General Assembly.[46] He concludes that, from then on, the ECOSOC played only a subordinate role in the coordination of the United Nations System, subordinate to the Committees of the General Assembly.

He supports his view by pointing out that the newly admitted Member States considered that the General Assembly was certainly more representative than the limited membership of the ECOSOC, and felt that these countries did not want the ECOSOC to supervise the Specialized Agencies consisting of more Member States than the ECOSOC itself.[47]

Whichever point of view one takes, the fact remains that whether one believed that the General Assembly or the ECOSOC had the leading role in coordination, the ambiguities referred to earlier resulted in parallel and overlapping activities in this area. The end result of this was very little, if any, effective coordination at all.

---

[44] 'In the beginning the General Assembly devoted a great deal of attention to the problem of review of the activities of the Specialized Agencies. For a while the Assembly's Second and Third Committees went in joint sessions to consider the annual ECOSOC report on relations with the Specialized Agencies and they joined the Fifth Committee to consider the reports of the ACABQ on the budgets of the Specialized Agencies and the problems of administrative coordination. These practices were abandoned in 1952 because of the demands they made on the General Assembly's time', Codding, *op. cit.*, p. 83. On this evolution, see Hill, Martin, 'The ACC', in *The Evolution of International Organizations*, Luard, Evan (ed.), New York, Praeger, 1966, p. 127. This is certainly one of the most authoritative articles on the topic of inter-agency coordination, as seen in the chapters on ACC.

[45] Codding, *op. cit.*

[46] 'Immediately after the foundation of the United Nations, the Assembly gave the ECOSOC considerable freedom. It made the basic political decisions and gave the mandate to the ECOSOC to execute them. The ECOSOC then made resolutions, addressed to the Specialized Agencies ... Which transformed the decisions of the General Assembly into concrete actions. Thus, the ECOSOC was the intermediary between the Assembly and the Specialized Agencies, but an intermediary that made independent decisions on execution. Later on, the position of the ECOSOC concerning the coordination of the United Nations System lost importance in favor of the General Assembly'. Meng, *op. cit.*, p. 857. More precisely, it is in the 1950s that 'the power shifted from the ECOSOC to the General Assembly and its committees' (p. 859).

[47] *Ibid.*, pp. 858-859. 'An improvement of this situation is not likely unless the ECOSOC is expanded to global membership ... But the political will for such a change ... is apparently not available at present' (p. 859).

The Transformed Administrative Committee on Coordination (ACC) – A Natural Solution

For precisely this reason it is felt that the ACC, transformed as the Policy and Coordination Board (PCB), would be more effective in the *de facto* coordination of the United Nations System, leaving the role of the major organs, whether it is that of the ECOSOC or of the General Assembly, exclusively for reporting. The actual coordination and the control of duplication can best be left at the working level, namely, for the transformed ACC (PCB).

There is no doubt that the Charter gave emphasis to the role of the United Nations proper in fostering coordination and cooperation among the United Nations entities. It seems, however, that the Charter never intended either to relegate the status of the Specialized Agencies as inferior to the United Nations proper, or to challenge the autonomy or independence of the Specialized Agencies.

It should not be difficult to conclude that the failure of the ECOSOC in the area of coordination could have been due to the ambiguity in the Charter. And this failure is so great that some have been encouraged to call for its abolishment. We are not yet ready, though, to support this, since we believe that before such a drastic move, the ECOSOC should be given a chance to exercise its authority, considering its relationship to the General Assembly and more importantly to the transformed ACC. The ECOSOC has not yet been given this chance, as mentioned clearly in Chapter 1.

The Charter of the United Nations does not refer to the role of coordination of the United Nations Secretariat. It does not even mention the ACC, which was only established by the ECOSOC. Can the Secretariat or the Secretary-General and ACC invoke some authority from the Charter for their role in coordination? As seen earlier, the ambiguity concerning the roles of the ECOSOC and the General Assembly should place the onus of such a task on machinery that is different from either the ECOSOC or the General Assembly. It is in this context that the ACC should establish itself as the natural machinery that could be entrusted with such a task, reporting to the General Assembly and to the ECOSOC, as necessary.

THE CHARTER OF THE UNITED NATIONS ON REFORM

Articles 108 and 109 of the United Nations Charter

Although the Charter of the United Nations does not deal with United Nations reform as we know it today, it has a clear and strong message that the reform (or amendment) of the Charter itself was never intended to be easy. Should this be taken as a message that United Nations reform should also be difficult to accomplish? We do not think so. We still think, however, that it is useful to discuss the various levels of reform in the context of the Charter. Some scholars thought that the Charter was intended to be a rigid and unalterable document or constitution.

We agree with the view that this instrument is a rather rigid one, whether we take into account Article 108 or Article 109, or even the *de facto* (or informal) amendment procedure. Indeed, as Klaus Dicke points out, this question of focus on the Charter reform should not hide the fact that reform at the United Nations has a long history and that this rigidity did not prevent the proliferation of reforms below the level of the Charter. He criticizes though, the reform capability of the United Nations and the serious shortcomings that include misled, incomplete and uncontrolled reforms creating structures upon structures, particularly in the area of coordination of the United Nations System.[48]

The Theory and Practice

The Charter of the United Nations could, in theory, be amended in two ways. According to Karl and Mützelburg, Articles 108 and 109 of the Charter provide two distinct procedures for constitutional amendment, the former dealing with ordinary amendment procedures for single provisions, requiring no special meeting or conference, and the latter for more complex changes, requiring the convening of Member States to a conference for the purpose. The difference between them is limited to the procedure, and in substance there is no difference.[49]

The first feature of Chapter XVIII of the Charter is, therefore, that the methods of amendment under Article 108 and Article 109 differ in procedure but not in substance.[50] The second feature is that of rigidity. Meinhard Schröder points out that 'the Charter was intended to be a rigid, that is basically unalterable, constitution for the community of nations'.[51] This rigidity is confirmed by the extent of the majority required under both Articles, namely two-thirds, and most importantly by requiring also the unanimity of the permanent members of the Security Council.

---

[48] 'focus on a Charter reform … should not hide the fact that reform has a long history in the United Nations and that the United Nations' capability to initiate reform process below the level of Charter amendments is one of the most interesting characteristics of the United Nations System … On the other hand, however, there have been serious shortcomings in the United Nations' reform capability. Misled, incomplete or uncontrolled reform measures have led to organizational structures which in turn have called for new structural adjustments; this has been particularly true with regard to the coordination of the units of the United Nations System', Dicke, *op. cit.*, p. 1012. For him, it is the question of coordination of the UN system 'which has given UN reform the character of a never-ending clock-spring' (*ibid.*).

[49] 'The Charter provides two distinct procedures of constitutional amendment and devotes to each of them a separate Article (108 and 109). Article 108 deals with the ordinary amendment procedure aimed at the change of any single provision and requiring no special administrative arrangement. Article 109, on the other hand, refers to a revision of the Charter; i.e., to a large-scale project to be prepared by a conference of Member States especially convened for the purpose. However, the difference between the ordinary amendment procedure under Article 108 and the extraordinary (review) procedure under Article 109 is limited to their initial stages, while the material prerequisites and legal effects are basically the same', Karl, Wolfram, and Bernd Mützelburg, in Simma, *op. cit.*, p. 1165.

[50] Willson, Carolyn L., 'Changing the Charter: The UN Prepares for the 21st Century', *American Journal of International Law,* 1996-1, p. 116.

[51] Schröder, Meinhard, 'Amendment to and Revision of the Charter', in Wolfrum (ed.), *op. cit.*, p. 21. To which he adds: 'The *de facto* amendment constitutes an effort, at least in part, to overcome this rigidity'.

A formal amendment[52] to the Charter can be introduced either through Article 108 or Article 109 (the two Articles constituting Chapter XVIII of the Charter). Karl and Mützelburg state that the difference between the two Articles lies in their scope that, in the case of Article 109, allows a comprehensive review of the Charter.[53] Schröder thinks that, since the terminology of the two Articles varies, Article 108 covers a particular provision while Article 109 has far-reaching implications, possibly even a general review.[54] On the other hand, Zacklin believes that the use of different terminology in different Articles of the Charter to describe the same act is somewhat confusing, since amendments and alterations do not appear to convey fundamentally different notions.[55] He concludes that a review procedure could lead to merely insignificant changes in the text, but adds that there is no impediment to seeking comprehensive and drastic changes by way of the ordinary amendment procedure.[56]

Karl and Mützelburg argue that the importance of Article 109 was merely historical, 'its significance has always been restricted to the political-psychological sphere, as it was a major factor in overcoming the resistance of many small- and medium-sized States in San Francisco to the "Yalta formula" (the right to veto). The prospect of a review conference in the foreseeable future, when the cards would be reshuffled gave them consolation and hope'.[57] The same authors add that, therefore, 'most of their efforts went into a provision, which would ensure and facilitate the holding of such a conference. This resulted in a facilitated convocation procedure, to be initiated automatically if no such conference had been held before the 10th annual session of the General Assembly'.[58] Zacklin points out that the special conditions for calling such a conference, if no such

---

[52] In contrast, there are informal or *de facto* amendments, that is, amendments introduced through UN practice or custom. 'There are two methods applied by Member States if they wish to amend the Charter by way of *de facto* amendment. The provisions of the Charter are either extended beyond their scope by tacit agreement between Member States and this agreement becomes established practice, or they are, according to a widely held opinion, constantly disregarded' (*ibid.*, p. 24). We know that the International Court of Justice had the opportunity to recognize the validity of such a *de facto* amendment, first in the Namibia case (*ICJ Reports*, 1971, pp. 16-22: with regard to Article 27.3 of the Charter).

[53] Karl and Mützelburg, *op. cit.*, p. 1179. 'Such a review could hardly be carried out within the framework of a regular session of the General Assembly without affecting its ongoing work. Hence a special procedure was established for this purpose, namely a General Conference of the members of the UN. In contrast to the ordinary procedure according to Article 108 based on the annual sessions of the General Assembly, Article 109 provides for an extraordinary procedure for amendments requiring particular measures' (*ibid.*).

[54] Schröder, *op. cit.*, p. 21. Indeed, Article 108 speaks about 'amendments', whereas Article 109 deals with 'alterations' of the Charter.

[55] Zacklin, Ralph, *The Amendment of the Constitutive Instrument of the United Nations and Specialized Agencies*, Leyden, Sijthoff, 1968, p. 111. To the same extent, 'the differences in wording between the English and French texts (amendment/amendment in Article 108; alteration/modification in Article 109.2) have no legal significance' (Karl and Mützelburg, *op. cit.*, p. 1180).

[56] See, also Zacklin, *ibid:* 'there seem to be no legal or constitutional barrier which would prevent a comprehensive revision of the Charter from being undertaken under the procedure of Article 108'.

[57] Karl and Mützelburg, *op. cit.*, p. 1180. For more details, see Goodrich et al., *op. cit.*, p. 643: 'The decision to include specific provision for a general conference to review the Charter stemmed largely from the desire to assure those who were dissatisfied with certain provisions that there would be an opportunity for reconsidering the document at some future time'.

[58] Karl and Mützelburg, *ibid.* On the (non-) application of Article 109.3, see *ibid.*, p. 1184. Today, 'there is no doubt that Article 109.3 has become obsolete' and that it is 'a mere historical reminiscence' (*ibid.*).

conference had been held by the 10th session of the Assembly, were contained in Article 109, as distinguished from Article 108.[59]

As emphasized by other scholars, it was important to note that any alteration of the Charter recommended by a General Conference could come into force only when ratified by all the permanent members of the Security Council. So, whether amendments were voted in the General Assembly in accordance with Article 108 or 109, the process was substantially the same to the extent that the two Articles require an equally rigid procedure.[60]

The Charter of the United Nations as a Very Rigid Instrument

It appears very clear from the above analysis that the Charter of the United Nations was supposed to be a very rigid and inflexible instrument. This objective was clearly achieved. Both under the ordinary (Article 108) and the extraordinary (Article 109) procedures, amendments had to follow a two-step process.

First, the amendment must be adopted by a two-thirds vote of the members of either the Assembly (Article 108) or a General Conference called to review the Charter (Article 109). At this stage, it should be noted that while the General Assembly can adopt resolutions on important matters by a two-thirds majority of the members present and voting (Article 18), approval by two-thirds of all the Member States is required for the adoption of amendments to the Charter.[61] This is supposed to reinforce the integrity of the Charter, by making amendments more democratic and difficult,[62] by giving a dissenting minority the power to block Charter amendments [63] and by the fact that even a two-thirds majority does not make the amendment legally binding, since at that stage it is only a recommendation.[64]

Second, Charter amendments adopted by the General Assembly (and by the Conference, for that matter) come into force only when ratified, according to Article 108 and Article109.2, by two-thirds of the members, including all the permanent members of the Security Council. In other words, abstention (that is, nonratification) on an amendment by one of the permanent members of the Security Council amounts to a veto.[65]

Schröder defends this provision, despite the risks of nonratification of an amendment, on the basis that it recognizes the superpowers as the guardians of international peace and

---

[59] Zacklin, *op. cit.*, p. 117.

[60] Goodrich et al., *op. cit.*, p. 644.

[61] *Ibid.*, p. 638, and Karl and Mützelburg, *op. cit.*, p. 1168. This remark 'applies to the adoption requirement by the General Assembly and the Conference, since the States involved are by and large the same' (*ibid.*, p. 1180).

[62] *Ibid.*, pp. 1168-1169.

[63] *Ibid.*, p. 1174. These two authors see this rule as a 'small compensation for the smaller States': on the one hand, the Security Council permanent members have a veto power as far as amendments are concerned; but, on the other hand, 'the major powers cannot impose Charter amendments on small States'.

[64] *Ibid.*, p. 1169.

[65] Indeed, 'abstaining from ratifying an amendment means that no valid ratification takes place' (Schröder, *op. cit.*, p. 23), in contrast to the practice developed under Article 27.3 (Karl and Mützelburg, *op. cit.*, p. 1174).

security, preventing shifts in responsibility if they are overruled.[66] Others, understandably consider this privilege accorded to the permanent members, which provoked greater opposition at the San Franscisco Conference than the Charter provision of the right of veto in the Security Council (Article 24.1), as extending their dominance to all other Charter matters which may require desirable and justified amendments in the future.[67]

The rigidity of the Charter is reinforced by the 'constitutional' nature of this document. No reservations to the Charter, or to its amendments, are allowed. This is confirmed by the fact that Charter amendments also bind the members who did not vote for them.[68] However, these members have the option to withdraw from the organization should they wish to, if the amendments infringe on their rights and obligations as members. They would not be able to withdraw, however, for a mere organizational or minor change in provisions.[69]

Therefore, the United Nations Charter has proved to be a rigid document both in theory and in practice.[70] Efforts to amend the Charter in accordance with either Article 108 or Article 109 have not been too successful.[71] To reinforce what was stated earlier, on the historical and political-psychological interest, Article 109 has so far never been applied. On the other hand, there have been only three cases where Article 108 has been successfully applied up to now. All these cases dealt with the enlargement of the Security Council and the ECOSOC.[72] Even these harmless and *prima facie* consensual amendments had to overcome important obstacles. In fact, in two of the three cases, the consensus of the permanent members of the Security Council was obtained only in the second phase of the procedure.[73]

---

[66] 'Despite greatly jeopardizing the possible ratification of an amendment, this provision corresponds with the intention of the Charter that superpowers be entitled with the task of maintaining international peace and security and of preventing any shifts in responsibility brought about by over-ruling', Schröder, *ibid.*

[67] 'this privileged position of the permanent members met with even stronger opposition at the San Francisco Conference than the Charter provision conferring a right of veto on permanent members within the Security Council. For it did not only permit the perpetuation of the special role assumed by permanent members within the United Nations System for the maintenance of international peace and security (Article 24.1), but extended this dominance to all other Charter matters in which future amendments seemed to be desirable', Karl and Mützelburg, *op. cit.*, p. 1174. This remark can be extended, of course, to virtual amendments to Articles 108 and 109 themselves: indeed, legally speaking, 'all Articles of the Charter are open to review'; it can hardly be expected that the formal review of the Charter will ever be made any easier because of this regulation (Schröder, *op. cit.*, pp. 22-23).

[68] Karl and Mützelburg, *op. cit.*, p. 1172.

[69] *Ibid.*, p. 1176.

[70] *Ibid.*, p. 1165. See also Zacklin, *op. cit.*, p. 114.

[71] Schröder, *op. cit.*, p. 23. This remark can be extended to the *de facto* 'procedure': actually, '*de facto* amendment does not seem to be very different from formal review' (*ibid.*, p. 26).

[72] 'These amendments responded to a perceived need to reflect the changing composition of the Organization's membership in those two bodies' (Willson, *op. cit.*, p. 117), and took into account 'the dramatic growth of the UN membership resulting from decolonization' (Karl and Mützelburg, *op. cit.* p. 1177). For more details on the three Charter amendments through Article 108 (1963-5; 1965-8; 1971-3), see *ibid.*, pp. 1177-1178.

[73] *Ibid.*, p. 1177. See also Zacklin, *op. cit.*, pp. 116-129. This explains that this second phase 'extends over a longer period of time … The process of ratification could (or : happened to) last 20 or even 30 months'. (*Ibid.*, p. 1173). In fact, 'the principal obstacle to any amendment to the Charter was the position taken by the members of the Soviet group to the effect that, since modification of the Charter required the approval of all five

In the light of this analysis, one can easily understand that the formal procedure to amend the United Nations Charter, spelt out in Article 108 and Article 109, is not likely to be applied in cases where in-depth or profound changes are envisaged. Therefore, it is not difficult for one to conclude that any reform proposals that require a substantial Charter amendment are bound to be nonstarters. The only hope to change the Charter of the United Nations in substance is through the informal or *ad hoc* procedure. This also appears unlikely to happen if any significant changes are sought to be made. The only window of opportunity is thus for relatively minor changes in the Charter, like the ones that may be needed for the *Better United Nations*. This will, of course, require political will, firstly, to accept the proposed changes, and, secondly, to do this without the procedural constraints of Chapter XVIII of the Charter.

A PRAGMATIC WAY FORWARD

The Charter can be used as an excuse to stall reform, and it is being used exactly for this reason by some. We argue all along, that the *Better United Nations* would not require any basic changes in the Charter for this reason. The transformed United Nations referred to in Annex III certainly does. It is mainly due to this fact that we put forward *A Better United Nations for the New Millennium*, as a more realistic alternative to a fully transformed United Nations, whose time admittedly has still not come.

---

permanent members, they would oppose any amendments until the People's Republic of China was represented in the Organization' (Goodrich et al., *op. cit.*, p. 642).

CHAPTER 5

THE ADMINISTRATIVE COMMITTEE
ON COORDINATION
THE HISTORY

SUMMARY

The history and development of the ACC, and a summary of the more important literature on it and its subsidiary machinery, is reviewed and analyzed.

The ACC was established by the ECOSOC resolution 13 (III) (1946). It was composed of the Secretary-General of the United Nations and the executive heads of the Specialized Agencies and the IAEA. Participation in the ACC now includes the executive heads of other United Nations Funds and Programs, including the UNCTAD, UNDP, UNEP, United Nations Population Fund (UNFPA), UNICEF, World Food Programme (WFP), United Nations International Drug Control Programme (UNDCP), United Nations High Commissioner for Refugees (UNHCR), and United Nations Relief and Works Agency for Palestine Refugees in the Near East (UNRWA).

Its existence was strengthened somewhat by resolution 32/197 on the 'Restructuring of the Economic and Social Sectors of the United Nations System'. Resolution 40/177 on 'Coordination in the United Nations and the United Nations System' is considered to be another important stage in the development of the ACC.

Like other parts and machinery of the United Nations, the ACC went through various attempts at reform, the highlights of which are referred to in this chapter. The above mentioned resolutions and other reform efforts, like the one in 1992 and the present one, are analyzed, in this and the following chapters, in a comprehensive manner to bring out any significant developments or departure from its implied role in the Charter and its founding resolution.

This chapter concludes with an analysis of how the present machinery of the ACC developed. At present, the ACC has five committees and a number of subcommittees, whose work is discussed in the next chapter. The machinery of ACC is also presented in graphical form.

THE HISTORY AND DEVELOPMENT OF THE ADMINISTRATIVE COMMITTEE ON COORDINATION (ACC)

As seen in the previous chapter, the Charter of the United Nations was not too clear on the exact roles of the General Assembly and of the ECOSOC in coordinating the work of the Specialized Agencies and, therefore, of the system at large. This ambiguity, together with the sometimes tentative nature of the relationship agreements of the Specialized Agencies with the United Nations, did not augur well for a smooth functioning of coordination machinery like the ACC. Moreover, the establishment of coordination machinery by both the General Assembly and the ECOSOC did not make matters of coordination any easier. Considering, however, the initiative of the ECOSOC to establish the ACC soon after the creation of the United Nations, one may need to accept ACC as the natural mechanism for coordination in the United Nations, despite all the legislative and constitutional uncertainties referred to earlier.

Coordination mechanisms set up later by the General Assembly were bound to duplicate the work of the ACC, or the work that the ACC was supposed to do. No matter what artificial differences there were between the two sets of mechanisms, as for example between the ACC and the Committee on Programme Coordination (CPC), the problem was not solved by joint meetings of the two Committees (which rarely take place any more). The justification usually given for the existence of both Committees, namely, that in the ACC it was the Specialized Agencies themselves that coordinated their own work, and that in the CPC it was the Member States that coordinated the programs of the Specialized Agencies, is not only simplistic but hits a nerve that may unravel the whole mystery of why the United Nations could never get a handle on this relatively simple task. The proposals on coordination for the *Better United Nations* take this into consideration and suggest that this task be handled exclusively by the ACC, with the active and comprehensive participation of the Member States at the level of the ECOSOC, but certainly not at the level of the CPC or the Fifth Committee of the General Assembly. Their mandates should not include any substantive discussions, particularly on social and economic matters.

This does not mean that we are taking the side of the ECOSOC in this controversy. We consider the General Assembly to be the supreme organ of the United Nations and there should be no doubt about this, but in the context of coordination it is felt that the ECOSOC should have the lead role, with the understanding that it would be under the overall guidance of the General Assembly. It is primarily for this reason that so much emphasis is being given to the ACC, since a relevant and efficient ACC would make the task of the ECOSOC in this regard so much easier.

History of the ACC – The Founding Resolution

In 1946, the Economic and Social Council resolution[1] established the ACC as a standing committee of administrative officers consisting of the Secretary-General and the corresponding officers of the Specialized Agencies 'for the purpose of taking all appropriate steps, under the leadership of the Secretary-General, to insure the fullest and most effective implementation of the agreements entered into between the United Nations and the Specialized Agencies'.

According to the resolution, the Council 'being desirous of discharging effectively its responsibility under the Charter of the United Nations to coordinate the activities of the Specialized Agencies, undertakes after reference if necessary to an appropriate commission or to an *ad hoc* committee, to consider and to make recommendations or decisions ... regarding matters referred to it by the Secretary-General from the Committee ... and matters arising outside the area of the agreements between the United Nations and the Specialized Agencies which are or may become the subject of difference of view between the Specialized Agencies and the United Nations or between the Specialized Agencies, or between the Specialized Agencies and commissions or other subsidiary organs of the Council, and to make recommendations concerning ways and means of improving relations between these bodies'

In Chapter 2, it was pointed out that the relationships established between the various Specialized Agencies and the United Nations through intergovernmental agreements, and the wide international responsibilities in the economic, social, cultural, educational, health, and related fields, were provided for in Article 57 of the Charter. Coordination was provided for in Articles 58 and 63, in which specific authorization was implicitly given to the Council to initiate studies and reports, make recommendations, call international conferences, and set up commissions on matters within its competence.[2]

It is, therefore, hardly necessary to mention the important significance of these agreements, which were negotiated by the Council and major intergovernmental institutions between 1946 and 1951. One must, therefore, reemphasize the important features of the agreements, which include the following: United Nations representation at all agency meetings (except those of the Bretton Woods Institutions), agency representation at the ECOSOC's commissions, committees, including main committees of the General Assembly, and such participation of the Specialized Agencies without any right to vote. All agreements, except those involving the Bretton Woods Institutions, contain a clause authorizing agency participation in the ACC as well as in other coordinating machinery which was expected to be created at a later time by either the ECOSOC or the General Assembly. Agreements with the ILO, Food and Agriculture Organization (FAO), UNESCO, WHO, ICAO and World Meteorological Organization (WMO) provided for consultations between the Secretary-General and the Directors General of the Specialized Agencies concerning preparation of the agencies' budgets. Finally, the agreements between the Specialized Agencies and the United Nations

---

[1] Resolution 13 (III) of 21 September 1946.
[2] See Chapter 4.

recognized the need for a single, unified international civil service. This need resulted in the setting up of an International Civil Service Commission whose function is to advise on the means of ensuring common standards of recruitment and conditions of work.

Martin Hill on Coordination of the Economic and Social Work of the United Nations

Martin Hill[3] traced the reasons for the highly decentralized nature of the economic and social work of the United Nations to the establishment of the ECOSOC, more specifically to Chapters IX and X of the United Nations Charter, which is influenced by the experience of the League of Nations and of the reforms proposed by the Bruce Committee. The majority of Member States not in favor of centralization argued, as they did during the League of Nations, that autonomous international organizations could survive political conflicts even if the United Nations did not. Another reason given was that, by the time the San Francisco Conference convened, several essential parts of the new international economic and social organizations already existed, or were being established, as autonomous international entities, such as the ILO, the IMF, and the World Bank.

He defined coordination in the system, not as an end in itself, but as a means towards promoting human freedom and dignity, greater economic security, equality of opportunity, and banishing fear and want.[4] He then described some of the main criticisms of the ACC, including those concerning issues such as: (a) unresolved differences of views regarding respective competence of different Specialized Agencies in regard to action at regional levels, (b) lack of cooperation among organizations and their staff, (c) failure to consult, (d) divergence of objectives, (e) proliferation of intergovernmental organs of unmanageable size and overlapping mandates, (f) proliferation of independent voluntary funds for non priority purposes, (g) soaring budgets for tasks not well considered from a standpoint of cost/benefit or coordination, (h) the near impossibility of comparing and thus coordinating future plans of different Specialized Agencies, (i) the involvement of many agencies in almost every undertaking, and (j) independent public information.[5]

Absence of coordination at the international level, he added, led to overlapping mandates and competencies, parallel activity or deliberate duplication, which was reflected at national and regional level.[6] This also manifested itself in the area of fund-raising, resulting in uncoordinated simultaneous trips of high officials, each working independently and often unaware of the plans and efforts of their colleagues.[7]

---

[3] Former Assistant Secretary-General for Inter-Agency Affairs and author of a study entitled: *The United Nations System: Coordinating its Economic and Social Work,* Cambridge University Press, Cambridge, England, 1978.

[4] Hill, *ibid.,* p. 1.

[5] Hill, *ibid.,* p. 2.

[6] Hill, *ibid.,* p. 3.

[7] Hill, *ibid.,* p. 51.

Program coordination, he stated, was an area in need of order, coherence and clarity, a task which occupies much of the time of the ACC machinery in its search for agreements on concepts, sorting out of functions and the establishment of criteria and guidelines in respect of closely related activities of different organizations.[8]

Though practical minor results were achieved through regular efforts made to solve individual coordination problems, a broader set of problems concerning policy coordination and structure moved into focus, namely, the concern about the fragmented character of the system, both institutional and budgetary, and the possibility of further fragmentation.[9]

Attitudes have shifted since the San Francisco conference in 1945, from excessive concern about protecting the autonomy and independence of the Specialized Agencies, to seeking greater unity and leadership in the System. There is growing recognition that only the United Nations can provide policy coordination throughout the entire System, with a framework to ensure that the policy decisions of different Specialized Agencies in different sectors are consistent and mutually supporting, if related, and that it alone can mobilize the political will and take the political decisions, so that the Specialized Agencies contribute effectively to the solution of major world problems.[10]

Hill refers to the Group of 25 which, although it is now only of historical significance, played a role in the attempts to strengthen coordination in the economic and social sectors of the United Nations System, by proposing a new post of Director General in the United Nations proper. This, together with a new Advisory Committee on Economic Cooperation and Development, to be chaired by the newly proposed Director General, never gathered enough steam to be of any significance to either the coordination of economic and social activities of the United Nations System or to the ACC itself.[11]

Development of the ACC – A Major Step by the General Assembly

The General Assembly resolution 32/197[12] was a landmark resolution in setting up a restructuring of the economic and social sectors of the United Nations. The resolution had a major section on the ACC, not too well known, but still significant in the development of the ACC.

Adopted by the General Assembly on 20 December 1977, resolution 32/197 approved for implementation many of the proposals referred to earlier, notably the new post of Director General who, under the direction of the Secretary-General, was to ensure 'the provision of effective leadership to the various components of the UN system in the field of development and international economic cooperation and exercise overall coordination within the system, to ensure a multi-disciplinary approach to the problems of development on a system-wide basis'.

---

[8] For specific examples of the related activities, see E/4744 of 1969 and E/5389 of 1972/73.
[9] Hill, *op. cit.*, p. 19.
[10] Hill, *ibid.*
[11] Hill, *ibid.*, pp. 162-170.
[12] A/RES/32/197 of 20 December 1977.

He was also to ensure 'within the UN, the coherence, coordination and efficient management of all activities in the economic and social fields financed by the regular budget or by extra-budgetary resources'. Appointed for a period of four years, he was entrusted with other tasks related to the *ensemble* of the economic and social activities of the United Nations and was to be provided with the necessary support and resources.

The Secretary-General was to appoint a Director General for Development and International Economic Cooperation during the first quarter of 1978, to implement the recommendations in assisting the organs, organizations and bodies involved in the restructuring process, to report to the General Assembly at its 33rd session, and to submit a report to the ECOSOC at its 64th session, with details on his plans for implementing the recommendations.

This first major readjustment initiated by the General Assembly emphasized the need for inter-agency coordination to be centered on the ACC, under the leadership of the Secretary-General and 'streamlined and reduced to a minimum, and except where the discharge of permanent functions necessitates the retention of continuing machinery, the maximum use of flexible *ad hoc* arrangements'. The ACC was to adjust its agenda, functioning and reporting systems in order to 'respond fully and promptly to the priority concerns, specific requirements and program of work of the General Assembly and the ECOSOC'.

The General Assembly Acts Again on ACC – A Further Development

General Assembly resolution 40/177[13] was the next action of some significance on the ACC. The resolution recalled relevant parts of Articles 6, 15, 17, 57, 58, and 63 of the United Nations Charter and reaffirmed resolution 32/197 and resolution 1926 of July 1985. It stressed the need for effective and improved coordination in the United Nations System as laid down in the Charter and the agreements between the Specialized Agencies and the United Nations.

The Secretary-General was requested by the General Assembly, in consultation with the executive heads of the Specialized Agencies, to reexamine critically and constructively all aspects of the question of coordination and to submit to the General Assembly at its 42nd session, through the ECOSOC, a comprehensive analysis of current mechanisms and procedure with recommendations for improving coordination. He was also to report orally to the ECOSOC at its 2nd session in 1986 and submit a progress report at the 41st session of the General Assembly.

The Secretary-General's report in 1987, in response to this resolution, devoted considerable attention to the functioning of the ACC and to inter-secretariat coordination. While positive achievements were acknowledged, it was admitted that the restructured machinery had not 'altogether fulfilled the original expectations'. Executive heads were burdened with too many questions of varying degrees of importance and of a very diverse nature. A need was felt for increasing secretariat support and for improving the quality of documentation.

---

[13] A/RES/40/177 of 17 December 1985.

The Next Stage of Development – The Blanchard Reports

Following an ACC request to Mr. Francis Blanchard[14] to review its role and functioning, and the structure and functioning of its subsidiary machinery, a preliminary report was submitted in 1992 and a supplementary report in 1993. These reports came to be known as the Blanchard reports.

The main purpose of the preliminary report was to identify areas in which reforms were pertinent and necessary in order to improve the functioning of the ACC. It contained three sections, the first dealing with the mandate and working methods of the ACC and its subsidiary bodies, the second with a better division of labor and access to resources for improved implementation of statutory and operational activities, and the third with data collection and the dissemination of information.

Blanchard maintained that improving the working methods alone was insufficient. Other difficulties stemming from 'a lack of transparency in the system, an unclear division of labor, unequal access to budgetary and extra-budgetary resources and inadequacies in the dissemination of information' had to be resolved as well.

The Specialized Agencies have lacked conviction in coordination due to the inability of governments to set clear global objectives and their tendency to formulate these objectives in a way which is difficult to implement.

A new definition should be given to the ACC's mandate, in terms of restriction rather than expansion. Its administrative function should increase in importance and complexity from a management standpoint and that of sensitive issues relating to the international civil service. Its political function should acquire special significance. In the light of the new international context, agreements between the United Nations and the Specialized Agencies should be reviewed and supplemented. Though they contain useful provisions concerning exchange of information and mutual representation, there are no sufficiently clear commitments with respect to coordination.

The ACC is not a think tank. It must concentrate on developing concrete measures on a small number of major issues that require the cooperation of agencies or institutions. The ACC must also express a political will, serving as a forum to work out measures for implementing decisions of the ECOSOC. The executive heads of the Specialized Agencies should communicate the proposals or programs worked out by the Secretary-General to their deliberative bodies.

The ACC should be selective in its choice of agenda and pragmatic in its operation, favoring action but without ruling out reflection or exchange of views. With the help of outside experts, who could appear before the ACC, short and impeccably researched background documents should be prepared, containing specific proposals and alternative solutions. Although the rule of consensus is to be recommended, expression of opposing views should be allowed. There should be no imposing of vetoes. The ACC debates should result in decisions, or a summary by the Secretary-General with his conclusions.

---

[14] Former Director General of the ILO and a long time member of the ACC.

These rules should be codified in a form supplementing the existing agreements and be put into practice. This would place increased responsibility on the subsidiary bodies.

Blanchard recommends two committees instead of four, becoming the key components of the ACC responsible for identifying issues calling for technical consultations between Specialized Agencies. After this, only those issues on which no settlement has been reached at committee level would be submitted to the ACC. The Specialized Agencies making up the ACC should appoint high-level staff to participate in the work of the committees.

The secretariats of the subsidiary bodies, be they permanent or fixed term, should be adequate in both size and quality. The staff, currently dispersed, should be consolidated into two cores, the first to service the committee responsible for management and personnel questions, and the second assigned to the committee responsible for development issues. It would also service the organizational committee. The office of chairman of the bodies should be entrusted to senior officials for a minimum term of two years.

The organizational committee whose role is to contribute to the successful working of the ACC by any means – intellectual, administrative or material – should also ensure that the subsidiary bodies follow up the conclusions and decisions of the ACC. Given the need for high caliber support services, the executive heads could in certain cases appoint 'Sherpas', chosen for their competence in the subject area under discussion in the ACC, to undertake the necessary preparations. The organizational committee's composition should correspond exactly to that of the ACC, and its chairman should serve as secretary of the ACC.

Following discussions in New York on 21 October 1992, Blanchard was asked to finalize his report to enable the ACC to agree on a position with regard to both mechanical problems and coordination issues of a general nature. The proposals in the supplementary report cover the mandate, the working methods, the reform of the subsidiary bodies, the division of labor and access to resources and information sharing.[15]

Reform of the ACC is a Never Ending Process

Reform of the ACC is continuing, and has featured in nearly every one of its agendas since the present Secretary-General took office. The ACC continued reviewing some of the reorganization approved as a result of the Blanchard recommendations. A number of broad objectives were identified by the ACC in 1996, which included increasing the System's capacity to cope with the effects of globalization and the post Cold War conflicts and with poverty eradication. In 1997, there were efforts to distinguish issues requiring concerted actions by parts of the System and the need to strengthen the secretariat support of ACC. As recently as 1998, the ACC approved further changes to

---

[15] For more details of the proposals one may see ACC/1993/CRP.1 of 29 March 1993, and for more information on the preliminary report, ACC/1992/CRP.7 of 15 October 1992.

the methods of work and the machinery of the ACC[16] was recognized. The Office of Inter-Agency Affairs was created as part of the comprehensive reform proposals of the Secretary-General.

Some of the ideas and recommendations in this book are also being discussed by the ACC, in spite of their drastic and revolutionary character. The emphasis of the ideas in this book is on relevance first, and streamlining and efficiency later. The details are given in Chapter 8.

PARTICIPATION IN THE ACC

The ACC is the only forum bringing together the executive heads of all organizations of the system. The participation in the ACC with full membership includes, besides the United Nations, 14 Specialized Agencies (FAO, IBRD, ICAO, IFAD, ILO, IMF, IMO, ITU, UNESCO, UNIDO, UPU, WHO, WIPO, WMO), the IAEA, the WTO and nine UN Programs and Funds (UNCTAD, UNDP, UNDCP, UNEP, UNFPA, UNHCR, UNICEF, UNRWA, and WFP). High-level officials from UNITAR, United Nations University (UNU) and the Regional Commissions participate as and when required.

As pointed out in the next chapter, a number of departments and divisions of the United Nations Secretariat also attend meetings of the ACC. This was not always looked upon positively by the Specialized Agencies.

It should be pointed out that the ACC is exclusively a forum of the United Nations Secretariat and the secretariats of the Specialized Agencies of the United Nations System. The Member States are completely out of this arrangement. Coordination of the Specialized Agencies' work by the Member States is usually conducted within the coordination machinery set up by the General Assembly and its Committees, primarily but not exclusively by the Committee on Programme Coordination (CPC) of the Fifth Committee of the General Assembly. Meetings of the two elements, so important for overall coordination, were never really a success.

MACHINERY OF THE ACC

Diagram 5 shows the ACC as it has developed over the years and as it is functioning at the present time. The substantive work is done by four main committees: the Consultative Committee on Administrative Questions (CCAQ), the Consultative Committee on Program and Operational Questions (CCPOQ), the Inter-Agency Committee on Sustainable Development (IACSD), and the Inter-Agency Committee on Women and Gender Equality (IACWGE). The last two are the most recent additions. The

---

[16] See the JIU report on the Review of the Administrative Committee and Coordination and its Machinery, JIU/REP/1999/1, for details. This report seems also to reflect some of the views in the book, particularly on relevance, although it stops short of making any significant new recommendations.

Diagram 5. Organigram of ACC and its subsidiary bodies

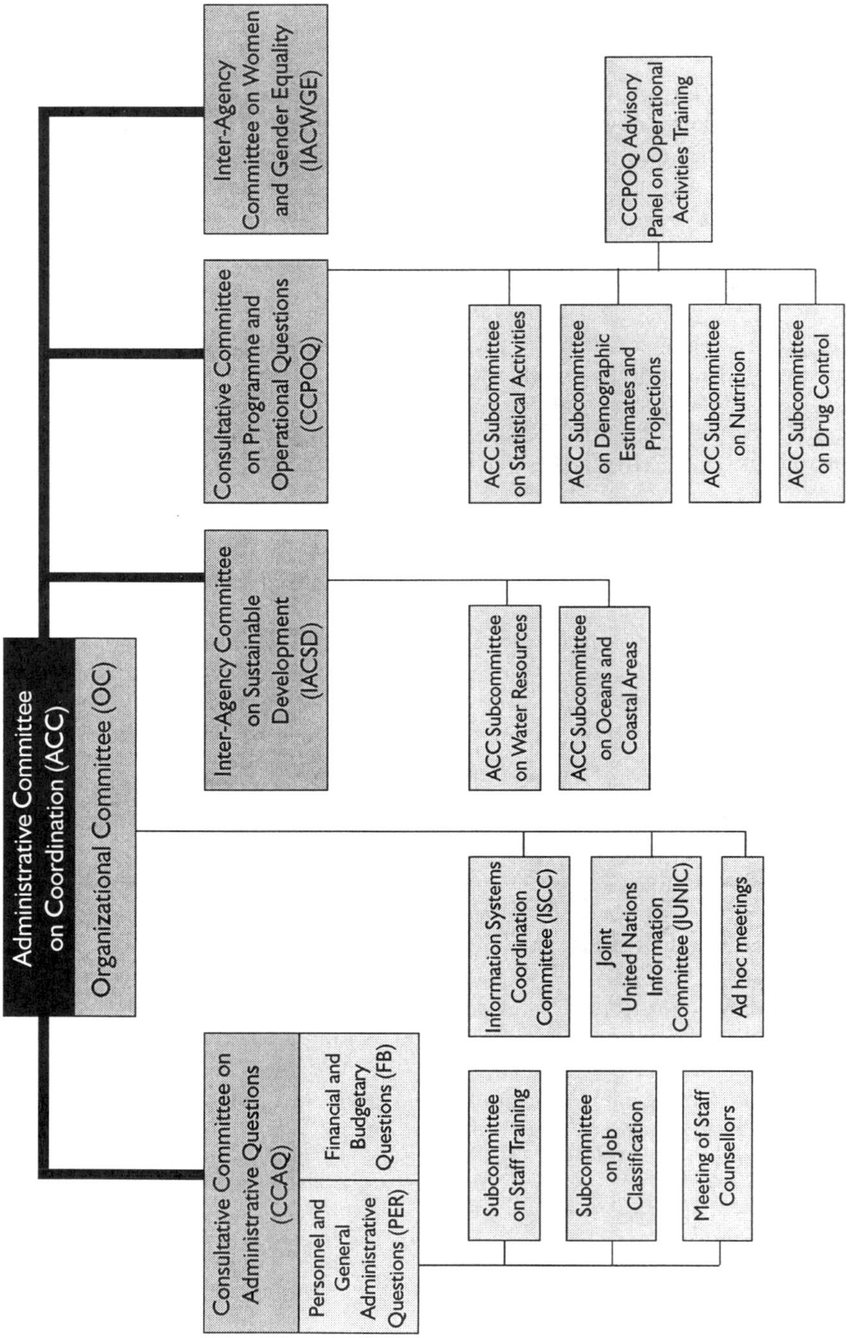

Administrative Committee on Coordination (ACC)

Organizational Committee (OC)

Inter-Agency Committee on Women and Gender Equality (IACWGE)

Consultative Committee on Programme and Operational Questions (CCPOQ)

CCPOQ Advisory Panel on Operational Activities Training

ACC Subcommittee on Statistical Activities

ACC Subcommittee on Demographic Estimates and Projections

ACC Subcommittee on Nutrition

ACC Subcommittee on Drug Control

Inter-Agency Committee on Sustainable Development (IACSD)

ACC Subcommittee on Water Resources

ACC Subcommittee on Oceans and Coastal Areas

Information Systems Coordination Committee (ISCC)

Joint United Nations Information Committee (JUNIC)

Ad hoc meetings

Consultative Committee on Administrative Questions (CCAQ)

Personnel and General Administrative Questions (PER)

Financial and Budgetary Questions (FB)

Subcommittee on Staff Training

Subcommittee on Job Classification

Meeting of Staff Counsellors

Organizational Committee (OC) and the Office for Inter-Agency Affairs are responsible for the preparation of the meetings of the ACC. As can be seen from the diagram, the above committees are divided into a number of subcommittees. Other working groups and panels are set up, as and when it is necessary to do so.

The present machinery has developed over the 50 years or so that the United Nations has existed. The resolutions, reports and proposals referred to above must all have had some influence in one way or the other on how the ACC finds itself today. The present Secretary-General has particularly made it one of his major objectives to make the ACC work better.

The history and the development of the ACC given in this chapter serve as a necessary background to the ensuing chapters on ACC, particularly to the chapter on the better ACC for the future.

CHAPTER 6

THE ADMINISTRATIVE COMMITTEE
ON COORDINATION
THE PRESENT

SUMMARY

This chapter starts with an explanation of how the present ACC and its subsidiary machinery work and with a review of the status of the ongoing reform. A reference is made to some personal anecdotes on the ACC, to underscore its shaky reputation.

The heads of Specialized Agencies have always looked at the ACC with skepticism. Since the General Assembly had little or no influence on the legislative bodies of the Specialized Agencies, therefore, few could understand how the Secretary-General could influence the work of the Agencies. So, what was the real impact of the ACC on the Specialized Agencies? What is it now, and is it any different from before?

Some heads of the Specialized Agencies do not attend regularly the meetings of the ACC. Some of them have even gone directly against its directives in an area where the ACC is said to be the most effective, that is, in the area of the 'common system' of personnel and conditions of service.

The ACC could not even prevent the UNDP (a sort of a junior partner) from establishing an operational arm within the UNDP, namely, the Office of Project Execution (OPE), later, Office of Project Services (OPS). This operational arm took away projects and, therefore, income from the Specialized Agencies, in spite of the fact that the Specialized Agencies were unanimously against the UNDP in this regard.

The Specialized Agencies were also against the presence of so many Funds and Programs in the ACC that were strictly represented by the Secretary-General. Yet, even on this, no action was taken.

THE PRESENT ACC AND ITS SUBSIDIARY MACHINERY

Up to the present time, the ECOSOC continues to struggle to find its niche in the United Nations, as mandated by the Charter, with regard to coordination of the United Nations activities that fall within its areas of competence, and with regard to other matters as well. Our concern in this chapter is with the former, namely, coordination.

As seen in the previous chapter, it did not take the ECOSOC much time to establish the ACC. It was significant that the founding resolution emphasized the main objective as being to ensure the most effective and fullest implementation of the agreements entered into between the United Nations and the Specialized Agencies. As seen earlier, these were agreements that were, at best, tentative, and, at worst, controversial and varied.

Despite efforts to bring the ACC in line with the current priorities of the United Nations,[1] it has failed to live up to its expectations. This was mainly due to two reasons. First, because it inherited the vague and tentative characteristics of its parent organ, the ECOSOC. Second, because most of the priorities of the United Nations were themselves unfocused and, as maintained throughout this book, not relevant to the concerns of the majority of the world's peoples.

Diagram 5, on the ACC and its subsidiary machinery, shows the present number of committees, subcommittees and panels. The Organizational Committee (OC) is central to the ACC and, some critics maintain, even more important than the ACC itself. The Organizational Committee meets frequently to prepare the agenda for the two annual sessions, one usually in Geneva in the spring and the other in New York in the fall. In addition, it also prepares and drafts decisions for the ACC, most often as a result of inputs and reports from one or more of the subsidiary bodies.

The members of the ACC (OC), as the Organizational Committee is commonly known, are senior staff members of the United Nations and the Specialized Agencies, who are considered to be more familiar with the details of the work than their principals. Any decisions prepared by these senior officials usually only require the rubber stamp of approval from the ACC itself. In fact, this has been the case during most of the life of the ACC, and it was very rare indeed that the ACC disagreed or asked the ACC (OC) to reconsider the matter. This is how it was up to very recently, when the ACC had come under increased criticism and its work had, therefore, been under close scrutiny. The new Secretary-General has made special efforts to increase the credibility of the ACC, and efforts to reform it have recently been high on its agenda. Some, however, suggested that more needs to be done and that the past practice of relying on the ACC (OC) for improvement did not work, and had to stop. Some, in fact, suggested that the ACC (OC) was not part of the solution, but part of the problem.

Since the members of the ACC (OC) were normally generalists, they had attracted the contempt of the more specialized parts of the subsidiary machinery of the ACC which, in spite of some excellent work, found that their work was hardly recognized or endorsed by the ACC itself. One such specialist body is the Consultative Committee on Administrative Questions (CCAQ).

---

[1] See General Assembly resolutions 32/197, 20 December 1977, and 40/177, 17 December 1985.

The CCAQ is generally concerned with two broad areas, namely, Personnel and General Administrative Questions (PER), and Financial and Budgetary Questions (FB). These two broad areas were further divided into other subcommittees and panels.

When one looks carefully at the work of CCAQ and its output, it becomes clear that the United Nations System requires such contributions, if for nothing else, to standardize the administrative and financial rules and regulations for such a large and varied system as the United Nations. In addition, some lesser-known work of CCAQ needs stronger endorsement from the ACC and a more action-oriented consideration by the ECOSOC. One such piece of work is the report and analysis by CCAQ of the programs and resources of the United Nations System, which is usually prepared for each biennium.[2]

This report presents a wealth of information on the budgets of the various Specialized Agencies of the United Nations System. It does not take too much time to see the overlapping and duplication among the work of the Specialized Agencies, something that so many people criticize and about which so little is done. This report makes its way through the system, from CCAQ to ACC (OC) and then to the ECOSOC with hardly a ripple of interest or debate. Of course, one may say that since the report is published as an ECOSOC document, it is for the Member States to consider and discuss. This is certainly one way of looking at it. But a relevant United Nations System would ensure that the Member States in the ECOSOC would be expected to discuss such a report, after the ACC had identified the overlapping and duplication, and had made recommendations on how to remedy it and prevent it from occurring again in the future.

Another important part of the ACC subsidiary machinery is the Consultative Committee on Program and Operational Questions (CCPOQ), a sensible amalgamation of the two Consultative Committees on Substantive Questions, one dealing with program matters and the other with operational activities. As can be seen from the diagram of ACC, CCPOQ has a number of subcommittees dealing with topics like training and job classification. This committee attempts to coordinate the operational activities of the United Nations System, including technical cooperation. There is concern, however, that CCPOQ overlaps with the two most recent additions to the ACC subsidiary machinery, namely the Inter-Agency Committee on Sustainable Development (IACSD) and the Inter-Agency Committee on Women and Gender Equality (IACWGE).

A recent addition to the ACC machinery is the Office for Inter-Agency Affairs, headed by a senior United Nations staff member, who chairs the ACC (OC) and is also secretary of the ACC. This is one of the innovations introduced by Kofi Annan as part of his efforts to reform the ACC.

Other committees of the ACC have permanent chairpersons and some have chairpersons that are selected by rotation from senior staff of the United Nations System. Similarly the staff of the ACC machinery are mostly permanent, supplemented by other staff as needed.

Cooperation of the ACC with intergovernmental bodies has been rather erratic. Meetings held jointly between the ACC and the Committee on Programme Coordination (CPC) of the Fifth Committee of the General Assembly seem to have been discontinued.

---

[2] E/1995/64, 18 May 1995.

The ACC reports regularly to the ECOSOC, and sometimes, as referred to earlier, more substantive reports are put on the agenda of the ECOSOC. This hardly ever results in any serious debate or concrete action.

SOME INSIGHTS AND ANECDOTES

One characteristic of the United Nations is its propensity to expand and grow. If something does not work, it is easier to create something else rather than try to change the ineffective part or entity. *Apropos* of the ACC, one can give some examples in the area of operational activities. The ACC was never very effective in this area. As a result of this, the United Nations System experimented with other modalities, some of them rather successful. Old hands at the United Nations speak with a degree of nostalgia, for example, about a coordination mechanism within the United Nations Development Program (UNDP) that worked well, at least up to a certain point. The Inter-Agency Task Force (IATF) in UNDP was indeed very effective, in spite of the fact that it duplicated, to a large extent, the work of CCSQ (OPS), the predecessor of CCPOQ.

This full-time arrangement, housed within UNDP headquarters and staffed by a few of the best people in the business from the major Specialized Agencies, worked well for a number of years. Its main objective was to bring the Specialized Agencies that were the main executing arms of UNDP closer to the UNDP itself, to settle major problems like the amount of overheads to be paid to them and other principal concerns. One such concern was the matter of *'self-execution'* of projects by UNDP itself, and later by UNDP's own Office of Project Execution (OPE), now known as the United Nations Office of Project Services (UN/OPS).

This matter was never resolved, in spite of constant efforts for a number of years by the ACC and the IATF. Some think that this friction between UNDP and the Specialized Agencies was the main reason for the demise of the IATF.

Another parallel mechanism with the ACC that also seemed to be more successful than the ACC itself, was the Joint Consultative Group on Policy (JCGP) which, although it had limited permanent membership, allowed other interested organizations to participate. The JCGP consisted of the International Fund for Agricultural Development (IFAD), the United Nations Development Program (UNDP), the United Nations Population Fund (UNFPA), and the United Nations Children's Fund (UNICEF). The United Nations High Commissioner for Refugees (UNHCR), the United Nations International Drug Control Program (UNDCP), and the United Nations also participated, especially when the JCGP discussed matters of wider interest like the triennial policy review of the United Nations operational activities.

This arrangement worked very well and brought some order and coordination to the bulk of United Nations operational activities funded from 'extra-budgetary sources'.[3]

---

[3] According to the United Nations terminology, this means activities funded from voluntary funds allocated for such activities over and above the Regular Budgets (assessed contributions) of the United Nations and the Agencies.

This group was chaired by one of the members on a basis of rotation, and was considered to be fair and democratic. The JCGP, despite its effectiveness, was discontinued and its functions were absorbed in the United Nations Development Group (UNDG) which was established as part of the Secretary-General's comprehensive reform referred to earlier, in Chapter 1. It may be recalled that the Secretary-General established the executive committee formats to coordinate the work of the United Nations' Funds and Programs in their various areas of competence.

The major distinction between this type of machinery and that of the ACC, is that the Executive Committees included only the United Nations' Funds and Programs, in contrast to the ACC machinery which included the entire United Nations System. This distinction allayed the concern of duplication and overlapping with the ACC and its subsidiary machinery.

As stated in Chapter 1, the executive committees were expected to involve only the United Nations and its Funds and Programs and should, as a result, be represented at the ACC by the Secretary-General of the United Nations or his representative. This would respond to a long-standing criticism by the Specialized Agencies that the United Nations should cut down the number of its representatives in meetings of the ACC and its subsidiary machinery. The 'over-crowding' of the ACC and its subsidiary machinery by the representatives of the United Nations has always been a bone of contention, and probably one of the reasons why the Specialized Agencies looked at the ACC with some concern and cynicism.

It was not unusual in some ACC meetings to find that about a third of the persons attending were representing various parts of the United Nations. For example, before the post of the Director General for International Economic Cooperation was abolished, the Director General regularly attended the ACC together with the two Under Secretaries-General of the economic and social departments, and other senior officials from various other parts of the United Nations. The senior officials of the United Nations also met regularly and separately, under the chairmanship of the Secretary-General, to coordinate the work of the United Nations proper. In fact, some wondered why, in spite of this, the United Nations still had to be represented in force at the ACC. Since no decisions were taken by vote in the ACC, this fact should not have been of much concern. The Specialized Agencies, however, saw it from the point of view that, since the majority of those participating in ACC meetings represented the United Nations, it must certainly have an effect on the discussions, especially when there was a disagreement (which happened quite often).

It was not difficult for persons familiar with the ACC to detect a degree of animosity or at least some uneasiness among the members of the ACC at the lead role of the United Nations. No one objected to, or had any problem with, the leadership role of the Secretary-General *per se* – this was clearly in the ECOSOC mandate. Some, however, were uneasy with the attitude of the United Nations proper in taking this matter for granted, and in the way the chairmanship of some of the subsidiary machinery including ACC (OC) were selected, and how some were permanently retained.

There were other events that demonstrated this unease. Some observers of the ACC recall, for example, an incident when a Secretary-General needed to leave the ACC meeting and proposed his recently appointed Director General for International Economic Cooperation to take the chair, against the protestations of some of the most senior heads of Specialized Agencies.[4] The Specialized Agencies had always accepted that, in the absence of the Secretary-General, the senior most of the heads of the Specialized Agencies would take over the chairmanship of the ACC. The members of the ACC demonstrated in no uncertain terms that the United Nations, in the absence of the Secretary-General, did not have a monopoly of the ACC.

Some of the members of the ACC did not understand why, if the General Assembly of the United Nations had little or no influence on the legislative bodies of the Specialized Agencies, the Secretary-General would be any different when it came to the heads of these Specialized Agencies in the ACC. Some feel that the atmosphere of camaraderie created by the present Secretary-General helped in changing the attitude of some of the members of the ACC, and there seems to be more willingness on the part of the Specialized Agencies to cooperate.

THE SPECIALIZED AGENCIES DID NOT SEE MUCH ADVANTAGE IN SPENDING TIME AND RESOURCES ON THE ACC

The Specialized Agencies felt that they were not getting much return on the substantial investment they were making in the ACC in time and resources, both financial and human.

In one of their most trying moments, when the Specialized Agencies wanted to stop the United Nations Development Programme (UNDP) from usurping their technical cooperation role, the ACC let them down. The ACC could not stop UNDP from taking technical cooperation projects away from the Specialized Agencies, in spite of the fact that the founding resolution specifically mandated it to find solutions to exactly this type of disagreement or dispute. Although UNDP was not considered a full member of the ACC (being a United Nations' Program), it was represented regularly in the ACC, but nothing could be done to stop it from jeopardizing the participating and executing agency role of the Specialized Agencies.

With the failure of the Inter-Agency Task Force in UNDP to stop the creation of the Office of Project Execution (OPE), and its eventual expansion at the expense of the Specialized Agencies, the role of the ACC in this matter became crucial. One of UNDP's original aims was to be a funding agency that would use the capabilities and expertise of the Specialized Agencies of the United Nations System, to execute and implement technical cooperation projects on behalf of the governments receiving the funds.

---

[4] This was not a casual or a spontaneous proposal by the Secretary-General. The Group of 25, referred to earlier, which originally recommended the establishment of the Director General post, did, in fact, recommend that the Director General would also deputize for the Secretary-General when he chaired the ACC (see Gardner Report, *op. cit.*). This, of course, was never accepted by the Agencies and the efforts of the Secretary-General to force the issue failed and was never attempted again.

Using the justification that the Specialized Agencies were inefficient and expensive,[5] the UNDP established its own executing arm, namely, the Office of Project Execution (OPE), later to be known as the Office of Project Services (OPS). This, of course, had a terribly adverse effect on the work of all the Specialized Agencies of the United Nations, most of which were, at that time, participating and executing agencies of UNDP.

Generally, in addition to their regular budgets (assessed contributions of Member States), the Specialized Agencies relied on the 13 percent overhead, paid to them by UNDP, to maintain and upgrade their expertise, to enable them to better serve the countries receiving technical assistance. The entry of UNDP into the operational area was, of course, a great setback for the Specialized Agencies, and their troubles mounted with the increase of OPE's business, which expanded very quickly. It was regularly receiving a greater percentage of UNDP funds, at the expense of the Specialized Agencies.

The ACC was helpless when all this was happening. The United Nations Development Program (UNDP), through OPE, was soon executing and implementing[6] technical cooperation projects in the areas of competence of most of the Specialized Agencies, and overlapping and duplication was, therefore, more rampant in the United Nations than ever before. No one can suggest that this was the exception rather than the rule. It was clearly the order of the day. In spite of this, the ultimate machinery that the Charter of the United Nations and the ECOSOC established to deal with matters like this could not do anything and failed to live up to the expectations of the United Nations System.

How something like this could be allowed to happen in the United Nations still baffled the most ardent supporters and followers of the Organization, not to mention the Specialized Agencies themselves. How a relatively recently established organization like the UNDP could do such a thing still left some seeking an answer.

A prevalent view was that, since the UNDP had failed in one of its major objectives, namely, to ensure adequate funds for technical cooperation for the developing countries, especially the least developed of them, it had to create OPE for its own survival. This was considered a particularly credible view since, with the introduction of 'Government Execution' in the early 1990s, the other major objective of UNDP was no longer valid. To respond to this criticism, UNDP arranged for OPE to obtain an autonomous status, but very few were convinced.

---

[5] Agencies originally received 13 percent of the project budgets as overhead costs from UNDP for the projects they executed.

[6] Originally, the words 'execution and implementation' of projects were used interchangeably at the United Nations and more or less meant the same thing. With the advent in the early 1990s of 'Government Execution', however, a difference started to develop. Since the GA resolution in 1990 on this matter made it clear that from then on, no United Nations agencies (including UNDP and OPE) could execute projects, a change in the meaning of the word 'execute' could justify the continuing participation of the United Nations. Thus UNDP, or OPE, or an agency, could execute the project while the government would implement it. With the new meanings, UNDP or an agency would be responsible for the overall management or 'execution' while the Government would be responsible for the day-to-day management or 'implementation'. This was considered by some to be an ingenious way of going around the General Assembly mandate, to continue the involvement of the United Nations.

On the other hand, it satisfied UNDP's major donors, since OPE's rules and regulations on procurement and recruitment were less stringent as compared with those of the Specialized Agencies. This facilitated faster implementation and delivery of project inputs, and a greater share of the donor's money going back to these countries in the form of contracts, procurement, and recruitment.

THE REFORM OF ACC: WHAT DOES IT DO NOW THAT IT DID NOT DO BEFORE? IS THE ACC ANY BETTER AFTER SO MUCH EFFORT AT REFORM?

The ACC, as seen in the previous chapter, has undergone a number of reforms. Its machinery had changed, thanks to proposals like those of Blanchard[7], and efforts like those of Secretary-General Kofi Annan and others before him. In spite of all this, it is not believed that even today, the ACC could have helped the Specialized Agencies in preventing the creation of UNDP/OPE; probably not even stalling it. More importantly, it could not have prevented the result of this, namely the duplication and overlapping. This is even more unbelievable when one considers that the formal resolution concerning the ACC, referred to so many times earlier, mandated that the ACC would prevent such conflicts between the Specialized Agencies and other entities from going unresolved. According to some critics, this failure was sufficient justification to warrant its abolishment.

Like reform in other parts of the United Nations, reform in the ACC was mainly concerned with its administrative machinery rather than with its agenda or relevance, as will be seen in the next two chapters.

Even so, in the area of efficiency, the ACC still leaves a lot to be desired. The ACC machinery continues to be too large and constrained by permanent entities that are sometimes obliged to look for tasks since they cannot always be kept fully occupied. For example, simply amalgamating CCSQ (OPS) and CCSQ (Prog) into CCPOQ did not solve the problem of lack of focus and relevance in the areas of programs and operational activities of the United Nations. It might have made CCPOQ more efficient, by reducing the number of meetings and possibly the staff involved, but the question of substance remained relatively unchanged.

In the area of CCAQ there appeared to be more success. This was mainly due to the recent streamlining, but again, although the results were better than in other areas, they were not enough to increase the credibility of the ACC and its work.

After all the efforts made so far to streamline the machinery of the ACC, it is still too cumbersome, perhaps slightly more efficient, but hardly any more relevant. The recent creation of the Office of Inter-Agency Affairs, as part of the Secretary-General's reform efforts of the ACC, seems to have created more overlapping and duplication, particularly with ACC(OC), although, in principle, it seems a good first move. It is, therefore,

---

[7] Blanchard, *op. cit.*

necessary to consider how to solve this endemic problem in the United Nations, namely, the tendency to create something new without abolishing what it was supposed to replace. One may borrow an analogy from space exploration and compare this phenomenon to the new satellites launched into space while the old ones they replace are left there to self-destruct. Unfortunately, at the United Nations, the useless entities self-destruct very slowly, if at all.

The ACC and its subsidiary machinery continue to meet more often than is necessary. Also, it does not seem to be making full use of proposals made for the optimal use of the Internet and other advances in information technology.[8]

THE IMPACT OF REFORM

The reform efforts, particularly in the last two years, have had some impact on the ACC machinery, but no real progress has been made to make it more relevant by dealing effectively with the matters that are of most importance to the peoples of the world, or by coordinating the work of the Organization to safeguard the relevance of the Specialized Agencies. What is required is something much more drastic than changing the names of some of the subsidiary machinery, while leaving them with more or less the same tasks.

The ACC needs to be seen, therefore, as the bond between the United Nations and the Specialized Agencies and the bridge with the outside world at various levels. The effective use of this bridge could lead to a better dialogue with the legislative bodies, the secretariats of the United Nations System, and the people at large.

---

[8] See de Marco and Bartolo, *op. cit.*, p. 112.

CHAPTER 7

THE ADMINISTRATIVE COMMITTEE ON COORDINATION THE THEORY AND PRACTICE

SUMMARY

As in other parts of the United Nations, the ACC has undergone some reform (see Chapter 5). The present stage of the ACC reform is referred to in Chapter 6. The various legislative mandates by the General Assembly and the ECOSOC on ACC, from the very beginning of the ACC until now, and the various proposals and recommendations that were put forth by various commentators and experts, whether from inside or outside the United Nations System, are examined. In particular, we examine whether the present ACC is functioning as foreseen by the drafters of the United Nations Charter and the founding resolution.

Can it be said, as in the case of the United Nations reform in general, that the point of relevance was largely missed and that the best that could be done was a number of proposals to make the ACC more efficient, while forgetting the most important point of why the ACC was established in the first place? In other words, we try to show how far the theory is from reality when it comes to the role and practice of the ACC.

If, by the United Nations, one means more than the United Nations Secretariat and the United Nations Funds and Programs, then reform of the United Nations must begin with the reform of the ACC.

Since 1946, the international institutions have witnessed an extraordinary evolution in the areas of humanitarian, political, social, and economic development within the framework of the United Nations. This was, and still is, the main reason for the strength and independence of the United Nations Specialized Agencies in their respective specialized fields. However, as stated in Chapter 4, the Charter of the United Nations underscored the need for coordination of the activities of the United Nations and those of the Specialized Agencies. Coordination was necessary to ensure long-term cooperation and policy alignment, and to prevent duplication and overlap.

With the increasing demands being made on the organization, the pace of technological change, the ambitious programs of various United Nations Specialized Agencies, the emergence of a new leadership culture, and the impact of information technology, the concept and logic of coordination becomes both vital and complex, albeit also controversial. On the threshold of the third millennium, a collective vision is needed to address this crucial question. A vision that is politically sound, objective, realistic, cost-effective and oriented towards obtaining results – a vision of commitment towards future generations. Without this, the United Nations is bound to face the risk of becoming irrelevant and would be in danger of being phased out in the next century.

The ACC is the body entrusted with the task of coordination. In this context, it faces five major challenges, namely, those of relevance, governance, interdependence, influence, and 'corporate' image. These challenges are dealt with in some detail.

Developments in information and communication technology and sophisticated institutional management techniques have rendered unworkable and ineffective, a body which was established more than 50 years ago to meet the simpler *ad hoc* coordination needs of a United Nations very different from that of today. Although the ACC could have worked to some extent, when most of the United Nations bodies were in the early stages of development and the demands on the United Nations System somewhat less complicated than today, the present needs in the areas of intellectual research, peacemaking and peacekeeping techniques, human rights protection, economic development, humanitarian matters, social dynamics, and the streamlining of global agendas, pose challenges that are far more complex. This complexity requires a new ACC.

THE THEORY AND PRACTICE OF THE ACC

'A new system-wide culture must emerge, based on systematic policy consultations, effective decentralization, full respect of each other's mandates and competencies, and a common appreciation of the challenges ahead and of the respective strengths of the various organizations of the system in meeting them.'[1]

On paper, the ACC had very clear objectives, as seen in most of the resolutions and reports referred to in Chapters 5 and 6. How did the ACC develop differently from the theory and why? How far is the theory from reality, when it comes to the role and practice of the ACC?

---

[1] Annan, Kofi, in the ACC's Annual Report of 1996.

One of the reasons cited[2] for discrepancies between theory and practice is incomplete adherence to the guiding principles (prior consultations, leadership role of the Secretary-General, division of labor, and teamwork among the Specialized Agencies). Another reason appears to be related to the result of the ACC meetings where specific objectives or targets are aimed at, but without the roles of the governing bodies and their secretariats being clearly stipulated. As a result, most of the conclusions remain generous intentions, which cannot be implemented in practice.

ECOSOC Resolutions and Other Legislative Mandates

The founding resolution 13 (III) of 1946 envisaged the ACC as a standing committee, chaired by the Secretary-General and made up of the heads of the Specialized Agencies. However, the ACC grew too large and heterogeneous. Soon after it was created, suggestions were made that it should itself deal only with key issues and subjects, while other matters requiring cooperation should be dealt with at a lower level, by the Specialized Agencies directly concerned. Very little was done in this respect and the ACC is still struggling with this matter, with little success. As to the results and impact of its meetings, even when the ACC considers major issues, and statements on these are unanimously approved, there is usually no major impact because the statements are not sufficiently action-oriented. As the mandate of the ACC continued to expand beyond the usual administrative matters to include some issues of policy and strategic planning, the question of a new name for the ACC came up and was discussed, but again no action was taken.

ECOSOC resolution 259(ix)[3] called for the concentration of effort and available resources, reconciling the autonomy and technical expertise of the Specialized Agencies with the general responsibilities of the United Nations, reconciling its role of coordinator with its role of governing organ of a wide spectrum of activities, the recognition of the role of the United Nations in providing policy coordination, (a framework within which the individual policy decisions of the different Specialized Agencies would be coherent for the whole United Nations System), and mobilizing the political will and decisions of the different Specialized Agencies. Functional decentralization, while being a source of strength and vitality, has unfortunately also led to a proliferation of activities and overlapping.

The setting up in 1947 of the Regional Commissions {Economic Commission for Europe (ECE) and Economic Commission for Asia and the Far East (ECAFE)}, with very wide mandates covering vast areas of economic and social development, has had conflicting results. The mandates overlapped those of the Specialized Agencies and provoked a closed attitude and the setting up of parallel networks. Elaborate measures were introduced to counteract this effect with little success and high costs.[4]

---

[2] JIU Report 1999, *op. cit.*, p. iv.
[3] Hill, Martin, *op. cit.*, p. 18-19.
[4] *Ibid.*, p. 26.

The search for priorities, to exploit limited resources with maximum efficiency, led to the ECOSOC elaborating six major program priorities in 1952. This had little impact, as evidenced by the General Assembly, in 1973,[5] calling on the Council to indicate priorities. The success of positive coordination depends on the willingness of all the organizations concerned to participate and on the United Nations Secretariat to develop central decision-making.

The new orientations set forth in the proceedings of the 6th and 7th Special Sessions of the General Assembly and the Declaration on the Economic Rights and Duties of States[6] were to affect central issues of policy directly, such as the regime of international trade, the transfer of real resources to finance the development of developing countries, international monetary reform, the transfer of technology, the application of science and technology for development, industrialization, and food and agriculture, in order that far reaching structural reforms could advance the new international economic order.[7]

Other proposals included placing the United Nations funds under the control of thirdworld countries, linking the then General Agreement on Tariffs and Trade (GATT) for trade negotiation with UNCTAD, and bringing everything under the control of the General Assembly. In practice, as every one knows, very little changed.

Recommendations made by Martin Hill prior to 1977, concerning increased responsibility of secretariats in implementing certain activities, are reiterated by the JIU report of 1999, which also recommends the designation of an official vice-chairman of the ACC. Both Hill and the JIU report stress the need for increased cooperation and coordinating responsibility on the part of executive heads. They strongly recommend one regular ACC session per year, complemented, if required, by extraordinary sessions concerning specific issues. This recommendation is also included in our proposed transformation of the ACC.

General Assembly resolution 32/197 of 1977 set some standards for the ACC, which were more or less adopted. Thus, one can say that this resolution redirected the ACC within the larger context of the restructuring of the economic and social sectors of the United Nations, and that the modern ACC became a reality. This redirection of its priorities and the streamlining of its procedures brought it in tune with the requirements and the program of work of the United Nations. In practice, this was a major step for the ACC, bringing it, in theory, as close as was possible to implementing its mandates to date, with great expectations that it would launch itself into the 'golden age' of coordination of the economic and social activities of the United Nations at large. It did not take long, however, for these expectations again to lead to more disappointments, highlighted by the General Assembly resolution 40/177 of 1985 and the outcome of the years that followed.

---

[5] *Ibid.*, resolution 3199 (xxvi), p. 54.
[6] Resolution 3201 (S-vi) at 6th Special Session of the General Assembly, in Hill, *op. cit.*, p. 153.
[7] *Ibid.*, p. 99.

More Recent Reform Initiatives

Reform initiatives from the 1990s onwards, with their emphasis on strengthening secretariat support for the ACC and its machinery, improving the decision-making process, and promoting a symbiotic relationship among standing committees, subsidiary bodies of the ACC and the participating organizations,[8] had already been preoccupations in the Hill report.

The Blanchard reports of 1992 and 1993 emphasized the need for modifying the ACC's functions from administrative coordination to policy coordination and for providing impetus and effective direction under the authority of the Secretary-General.[9] They also recall that the Chairman and the members of the ACC should abide by the guiding principles. The 1993 report highlighted the fact that the ACC had a constant concern for consensus and an excessive preoccupation with unanimity, as it could not take a position detrimental to the interests of any one agency or stand in opposition to its executive head. Some of the other reasons put forward in explaining the inefficiency of the ACC were the differing attitudes and approaches of its members, the negative connotation of coordination amounting to overcentralization, the ineffective decision-making process of the ACC and its subsidiary bodies, insufficient policy consultations and information communication, and an ineffective follow-up and monitoring mechanism.

In spite of some progress, the impact of the ACC on coordination has been low and has left a lot to be desired. Critics believe that most of the proposed solutions were cosmetic, did not provide the correct answers, and that the most prominent effect was the proliferation of the ACC machinery. We believe that, as the right questions were not asked, the answers could not have been right either.

The long history of attempts at developing and reforming the ACC does not seem to have equipped it with the necessary tools to undertake its tasks of coordination effectively. The various efforts at streamlining were not enough to enable it to find its niche in the United Nations. As with reform in other parts of the United Nations, the trend was to concentrate on efficiency at the risk of forgetting relevance. This produced the same results as in other parts of the United Nations, namely, of going around in circles in an effort to show changes, the end result being an ACC which is certainly not better, and probably worse, than before.

It can easily be said that the point of relevance was missed in most efforts to reform the ACC. This could be attributed, possibly, to the fact, that the weak original mandate was never adequately corrected, since almost immediately after its creation, the main preoccupation became streamlining, without ever focusing on what the committee had really to accomplish beyond reviewing and reporting on the obligations of the Specialized Agencies in accordance with their agreements with the United Nations. One can say that, in theory, it was not realistically expected to do more than ensure that the relationship agreements were complied with, and that it could, therefore, never rise to the expectations

---

[8] JIU report 1999, *op. cit.*, p. iv.
[9] Supplementary report by Mr. Francis Blanchard, 1993, para. 25.

of those who looked towards the ACC to guide and lead the United Nations System to making an impact on major developments in the world. The more important mandates, written or implied, like the ensuring of the orderly implementation of some of the noble objectives of the Charter in the area of economic and social affairs and the area of settling disputes among the Specialized Agencies themselves, were simply ignored.

As a result, the evolution of the ACC, which occurred mainly within the context of the wider roles and responsibilities of the United Nations, primarily in the economic and social sectors, never fully expressed the deep and ardent concern reflected in the Charter of the United Nations from which it was insulated by the founding resolution. The fact that the Charter was also rather tentative on whether to assign the important task of coordination to the General Assembly or the ECOSOC did not help matters.

REFORM IN THE UNITED NATIONS
SHOULD START WITH REFORM OF THE ACC

If, by the United Nations, one means more than the Secretariat and the Funds and Programs, reform of the United Nations System should start with a significant reform of the ACC. This reform has to be different from what we have seen in the past, and different from what we are seeing now.

One cannot, therefore, treat the reform of the ACC independently from the reform of the United Nations System. In the past such compartmentalization prevented the presentation of a clear vision of the ACC and of its objectives. The ACC has to be seen as something more than a committee to keep the Specialized Agencies in line. The natural niche for the ACC, to bring out the best of both the United Nations proper and the United Nations System was difficult to find. The main reason was that no part of the United Nations System wanted to lose any of the work that was traditionally its own. No one planned for creating a mechanism for dealing with turf battles in the business of managing the United Nations System. Whenever these battles occurred unexpectedly, as in the case of the UNDP and the OPE, the ACC did not know how to deal with the matter, and, therefore, did not.

Coordination was seen by most as a threat of being forced to give up parts of their work that was duplicated elsewhere. In the respective areas of competence, the distrust was quasi absolute, and certainly no Specialized Agency or the United Nations, for that matter, was willing to give anyone else any authority to decide on such matters.

The task of the ACC needs to be seen from a perspective that predates the founding resolution, namely, the perspective of the Charter of the United Nations, also keeping in mind the lessons of the Covenant of the League of Nations in this respect. For this reason, the further reform of the ACC has to be of a different kind from what we have seen in the past, and different from what we are seeing now. In our view, reform in the United Nations should start with the reform of the ACC. Such is the vision of this book.

THE ACC DID NOT KEEP UP WITH THE PROGRESS AND DEVELOPMENT IN OTHER PARTS OF THE SYSTEM

Since the beginning of the United Nations, the international institutions have made extraordinary progress in their respective fields and we believe that the ACC did not make commensurate improvements to meet the challenges that the Charter envisaged with respect to coordination. The ACC failed to coordinate, which is necessary to ensure long-term cooperation and policy alignment and to prevent duplication. The ECOSOC also shares in this failure but, as pointed out already, the political constraints of the ECOSOC did not apply to the ACC. With the increasing demands being made on the United Nations System, on the threshold of the new millennium, a reformed and effective ACC could be a part of the vision of promise and hope for future generations.

In spite of the undisputed leadership of the Secretary-General of the United Nations in the ACC, its work, reform, and development should not be the sole and exclusive responsibility of the United Nations proper. The Specialized Agencies, for reasons stated earlier, did not consider the ACC to be their own since they did not have any ownership of it. As a result, the ACC missed being an active partner in the progress achieved by some of the Specialized Agencies and missed profiting from the advances in information and communication technologies, unlike some of the Specialized Agencies. The ACC could only be part of the sluggish development of the United Nations proper, with all its political constraints, experienced by some of the major organs, primarily the ECOSOC. The Specialized Agencies, therefore, cannot be fully absolved of their responsibility for leaving the ACC out of the progress that some of them have experienced. The Specialized Agencies now have another chance to claim ownership (or at least part-ownership), by taking advantage of the new open-minded leadership of the United Nations, so as to profit from the opportunities and timing of the moment. At this auspicious time of reassessment and rededication, auguring a better start to the new millennium, the ACC deserves a new, stronger ownership, better investment, and a pivotal place in the *Better United Nations* of the future.

THE ACC FACES FIVE MAJOR CHALLENGES TO BE PART OF SUCH A VISION

It would not be easy to break from the past, but rising to the challenges of relevance, governance, interdependence, influence, and 'corporate' image would facilitate the transition to a new and better ACC.

The Challenge or the Test of Relevance

There are many pressing global issues that would benefit from a thorough analysis and policy guidance from the leadership of the United Nations. The level of use of communication and information technology, and the proper use of the vast experience of the United Nations in international affairs, are critical elements in determining its role and effectiveness in, and contribution to, global governance. The ACC would become relevant if it spearheads such a leadership role of the United Nations.

In the next century, within the framework of a new United Nations System, the ACC should lead the support for executive decision-making and responsibilities. This is inevitable in view of the critical mass of experience of the United Nations and the Specialized Agencies, on one hand, and the Regional Commissions and related bodies, on the other. In spite of an abundance of documentation at the United Nations that refers to coordination, there is still no consensus on its real meaning and significance. Coordination, to be relevant, must allow the United Nations to focus on its mission with vision, and without duplication and waste of resources. In this role, coordination is not simply a mechanism to prevent duplication and to streamline working methods and procedures. It is more than that; it is a means of enhancing international cooperation. It is a catalyst to enable the United Nations System to deliver what the Member States need, with positive impact and at the least possible cost.

For the ACC to be a successful catalyst, first, it is indispensable to make coordination a crucial element in global relations, and to carefully assess its impact on the contribution made by the United Nations System to international peace and security. Second, it is essential to distinguish between two levels of coordination. One is related to the United Nations proper and to its Funds and Programs, and the other is related to the Specialized Agencies. Only then can one look at the broader picture of coordination of the United Nations at large. Coordination then becomes a basic ingredient of the modern international system and of contemporary public international law.

In this regard, the agenda of the ACC itself is critical and should be reviewed seriously. It should be of a global character and should address issues that are of interest to the entire United Nations System and the international community. No agenda of the ACC should be considered serious if it does not include items such as the reform of the United Nations System, and proposals for strategic budgeting of all bodies and Specialized Agencies of the United Nations System. Strategic budgeting is essential to the simplification and streamlining of the working methods and procedures of the entire United Nations System. It would not only have an impact on resource allocation and the accrued savings, but would also have a long-term substantive and political impact on the United Nations at large as well as on the Member States themselves. This is, perhaps, the only nonsubstantive item that may be included on the agenda of the ACC itself, for which the permanent Secretariat would prepare all the ground work (so that the executive heads would spend as little time as possible on discussion, to allow them to concentrate on items of more global concern). Only in this way would the ACC measure up against the yardstick of relevance developed in Chapter 3. Only in this way would the ACC rise to the challenge and the test of relevance.

A Model of Governance

A project for the basic review of the working methods and procedures of the ACC is particularly timely, especially in view of the emerging challenges that the new century will pose for international cooperation and the urgent need to establish concrete methods of policy coordination, both at the international and the national levels. For this reason, this matter will be dealt with, in some detail, in the next chapter. The ACC, in whatever form it survives, should be the fulcrum of a *Better United Nations* for the new millennium.

Interdependence: A Necessary Ingredient

No reform of the United Nations would be complete unless the relationship between the United Nations proper and the Specialized Agencies is scrutinized with the objective of making the whole system interdependent. The focus on efficiency of the work of the whole United Nations becomes more urgent as the overall task becomes more complex and difficult, and as the resources become scarcer. This aspect in the Secretary-General's comprehensive reform proposal figures only as a reference to future work and is, therefore, not dealt with adequately.

In this context, the relationship between the ACC and the ECOSOC needs to be examined carefully, keeping in mind that the ECOSOC itself faces basic problems of reform and revitalization. In fact, the ECOSOC, with its broad mandate and limited membership, may not be the best organ to oversee the work of the ACC. As stated earlier, it would make more sense to relate the ACC directly to the General Assembly and its General Committee, reporting to the ECOSOC only on matters dealing with the agreements of the Specialized Agencies with the United Nations, and, of course, other matters of an economic and social nature, as necessary.

The global priorities, as identified by the Member States, and the best contribution that the United Nations could make to dealing with such priorities, should be the major criteria for including items in the agenda of the ACC. The importance of the ACC would always bring it to center stage since the problems faced by the world today are most often, if not always, multifaceted and interdisciplinary, and, therefore, no agency on its own would have a chance to succeed. This has to be the single most important element that qualifies the ACC for that permanent and most essential niche in *A Better United Nations for the New Millennium*.

A Matter of Influence

Two obvious prerequisites are to be met if the issue of coordination is to be dealt with seriously. The first is that Member States should establish global parameters for coordination at the level of the General Assembly. The reason for this is that coordination should be handled at the highest political level, at least until there is an unmistakable political will to support a lower-level coordinating mechanism, which would extract the best from the system with the least possible cost. This should be followed, secondly, by a decision to review coordination issues within all the legislative bodies of the Specialized Agencies, so that the respective constituencies of these Specialized Agencies, at the highest level, deal with all matters of importance concerning coordination. We cannot afford to continue to deal with such important matters as these in an *ad hoc* manner, as has been done so far. Moreover, national level policy coordination should be taken seriously by the Member States themselves, who should ensure consistent positions, whatever the forum in which such positions are presented.

An important step forward would be for the ACC to establish a system that takes into account important feedback from Member States; only then would it have a greater impact at the national level. The ACC should issue policy statements that could guide both the United Nations System and the national governments. These elements are central to our proposals for the transformation of the ACC into a Policy and Coordination Board (PCB).

The Question of 'Corporate' Image

The ACC was established by the ECOSOC resolution 13 (III), 1946, with a rather vague mandate. It is a little known body because so far its image in the United Nations System or, for that matter, in the Member States is not very well identified.

The Charter of the United Nations does not define the ACC, as an entity. However, there is no doubt that it has its roots in the Charter. The impression that the ACC was created by the ECOSOC as one of its subsidiary bodies is, in our view, wrong. It is true that resolution 13 (III) established it and that the ACC reports to the ECOSOC, but that does not mean that it necessarily fits solely into the activities of the ECOSOC or merely supplements its activities. The Charter of the United Nations, we think, gives more scope to the ACC than that mandated by the ECOSOC to coordinate the work of the Specialized Agencies. The ACC should also exploit its potential as a forum to bring together the organizations of the United Nations System at the highest executive level, uniting an impressive array of know-how and technology that needs to be put to work for the good of mankind – becoming a unique engine of development for the new millennium.

In such a role, the ACC faces the managerial challenge of exploring the potential and defining the strengths of the various components of the United Nations System. First and foremost, therefore, the ACC has to address its 'corporate' image, as it were, by becoming the ultimate example of efficiency which others could follow. This is also a basic theme in our proposals for the transformation of the ACC into the PCB.

THE PRESENT CIRCUMSTANCES AND COMPLEXITY REQUIRE A NEW ACC – A BETTER ACC

The failure to benefit from developments in information and communication technologies and the absence of sophisticated institutional managerial techniques (as are followed in the corporate world) has rendered the present ACC unworkable and ineffective. This is understandable since the ACC was established 50 years ago to meet the simpler *ad hoc* needs of a United Nations that were very different from those of today.

Although the ACC could have worked when most of the Specialized Agencies were in the early stages of development, the present needs in the areas of intellectual research, peacekeeping and peacemaking techniques, human rights protection, economic development, humanitarian matters, social dynamics, and the streamlining of global agendas, pose challenges that are far more complex than this committee can ever hope to meet successfully in its present form. Hence the need for a new ACC – a better ACC.

CHAPTER 8

THE ADMINISTRATIVE COMMITTEE ON COORDINATION A BETTER ACC FOR THE FUTURE

SUMMARY

Only a relevant and effective ACC would have a role in the United Nations System for the new millennium. If it cannot be so, then what can replace it? Various options are analyzed, ranging from a streamlined ACC mechanism that is not too dissimilar from the present one to a quasi 'chat room' on the Internet, which would be on for 24 hours a day, requiring no travel or other expenses, except possibly brief interventions 'on line' for certain decisions to be taken by the executive heads of the Specialized Agencies.

The solution we propose is somewhere between the two options mentioned above, that is, a completely transformed ACC to be called the Policy and Coordination Board (PCB) with a permanent secretariat headed by a Secretary of the PCB.

The recent establishment of the Office for Inter-Agency Affairs at the United Nations headquarters is a perfect example of the lack of purposeful orientation that is common in United Nations reform. Not only does this office seem to duplicate most of the work of the Organizational Committee of the ACC, but it is also in the wrong part of the Secretariat. A solution in this case would be to put this office directly under the Secretary-General and to make it absorb the Organizational Committee of the ACC, and the rest of the subsidiary machinery of the ACC. The head of this office should be a senior official from the United Nations System, to be appointed on a rotation basis.

This chapter attempts to develop a transformed ACC (to be called the PCB) using the analysis in earlier chapters, by proposing a detailed outline of the new machinery. Two diagrams are also included. The transformed ACC (PCB) will have a very clear objective of developing policy statements and of coordination. It would be in continuous contact with all the parties and would meet only rarely under the chairmanship of the Secretary-General, or the head of a Specialized Agency designated by him, depending on the subject matter to be coordinated. Such meetings would also have to be coordinated with the legislative meetings, so that coordination would be comprehensive and transparent. This should not disturb the Member States, whose foremost prerogative is to make policy, since the PCB would only develop policy with the objective of facilitating the mission of the United Nations System to use expertise with the utmost clarity and purpose for relevance, and at the least possible cost to achieve efficiency.

A clear relationship of the PCB to the ECOSOC and to the General Assembly would have to be defined and perfected so that the PCB finds its rightful place in a *Better United Nations* for the new millennium. If the PCB fails to do this, it fails to justify its role and, therefore, an alternative to it will have to be found, since its role should enable the United Nations to deal with problems in an integrated manner. In our modern and complex world, problems usually require the expertise and action of more than one agency.

ACC LIKE OTHER UNITED NATIONS ENTITIES SHOULD ALSO PASS THE TEST OF RELEVANCE TO SURVIVE IN THE BETTER UNITED NATIONS

A Test of Relevance for the ACC

It should by now be clear what 'to be relevant' means in the context of the United Nations. This meaning was developed from the earliest parts of the book. We saw how the United Nations and the System can be relevant, and also that it is easier for the Specialized Agencies themselves than for the United Nations proper to be relevant. This is mainly due to the specialized nature of most of the Agencies. Once this specialized mission is aimed in the right direction the Agencies will pass the test of relevance. This is more difficult for the United Nations proper, with its many different Funds and Programs.

Generally, one may suggest that the ACC would be relevant only if it could integrate the implementation of what the Specialized Agencies do best in their area of specialization with clear vision and purpose. This can only be done if the ACC deals mainly with appropriate subjects, that are well prepared substantively and that can be developed in policy statements, in conjunction with the specific roles and tasks of the various Specialized Agencies. There should be coordination to accomplish the objectives of the stated policy, preferably within a set time limit. The relevance of the ACC has also to be seen and tested against the yardstick of relevance developed in Chapter 3.

A Flexible ACC

The ACC must have the flexibility to do the above, whether it is in the context of humanitarian or other objectives, for example, in the Balkans or in the eradication of poverty in Africa and in other parts of the world. It is, therefore, important that the ACC first helps to choose the appropriate area of action, and second delivers the best that the System can offer to solve, or attempt to solve, problems with the greatest clarity of vision and purpose.

It must come as no surprise that the ACC is presently not equipped to do this. In spite of a number of reforms already undertaken to improve its machinery, the ACC still has to be overhauled and transformed. It has to move away from relying on generalists to plan and organize its work, towards more rational and professional methods. It follows that, once this rationalization of work of the ACC is accepted, the ACC machinery as described in the previous chapters would need to be overhauled completely. Since the Office of Inter-Agency Affairs has already been established, it can be the center of the ACC, while it is being transformed into the PCB. This office would have the immediate task of directing and facilitating such a transformation, even within the present structure. General guidelines for this task have already been made available to the ACC itself during its sessions of 1998 and 1999, and will be developed further, later on in this chapter.

VARIOUS OPTIONS CONSIDERED AND DISCUSSED

An ACC that Must Come of Age

The chapter on the history of the ACC is useful to help trace the origins and, more importantly, to help to see the development of the ACC. Items concerning reforming the ACC continue to occupy a place in its current agendas. This could have only one implication, that the numerous reforms in the last 50 years or so have not yet solved the problems of the ACC. Different justifications and explanations for this, such as that the reforms were necessary only to bring the ACC up-to-date with current problems, are not convincing, since it is clear that the ACC is still not facing up to its task as mandated in the founding resolution or as later modified. The creation of the ACC some 50 years ago was influenced by the circumstances and events of that period, as was the case with other organs and entities of the United Nations. Very few, if any, of the organs and entities reflect the problems and circumstances of the world today. The ACC is no exception.

There is general agreement that the main objective for the creation of the ACC was to ensure that the Specialized Agencies live up to the agreements that they signed with the United Nations. Today the role of ACC is seen rather differently. The ACC must also respond to other tasks, which concern timely and effective action in cases of appeals and emergencies by a much larger and more complicated United Nations System. In other words, the ACC should no longer be seen simply as a watchdog ensuring that the

Specialized Agencies live up to the promises they made in the agreements with the United Nations. The ACC today should certainly become an important and irreplaceable bond between the United Nations and the wider system to ensure a consolidated response to whatever it is called to do for the benefit of those most in need. The sooner the agenda is unencumbered with reform matters, to make way for more important subjects the better. In other words, the sooner the ACC is transformed and redirected to relevant work, the better it is for those for whom the United Nations was primarily created.[1]

In the same spirit seen throughout this book, no criticism is aimed at any one person or organization for that matter. The objective continues to be a frank and realistic attempt to present our view of the situation as we see it and as we think it should become. In this endeavor we will not hide behind the niceties of diplomatic language. This, in our view, would only make things more difficult, since it would tend to hide rather than to expose the problem. We are determined to resist the temptation of falling into this trap, at the risk maybe, of making a few people unhappy.

The ACC as a Means to Facilitate the Attainment of the Aspirations of the Majority

The reform and development of the ACC, referred to earlier, do not make the ACC more relevant even though it might have made it somewhat more efficient. The streamlining of the ACC machinery was more often than not a response to pressure for change, and in such circumstances it was not surprising that change came only as an *end* rather than as a *means* to improved delivery.

Bringing the ACC into line with modern technology as proposed in *A Second Generation United Nations*[2] by using, for example, modern information technology, was a step in the right direction, but did not go far enough. In the present world, where everything can be available through a terminal and keyboard at the office or at home, the functioning of the ACC should become more 'electronic'. One may shudder at the idea of an ACC as a *quasi* 'chat room' on a permanent basis, in spite of its attractiveness, and the advantages that it could bring. Few may realize that, for some people, long lines at the bank and conferences with bank managers to transfer money from one country to another are things of the past. These facilities are available at their fingertips at the office or at home. Is it Utopian to see some of the meetings of the ACC or its machinery as things of the past, for the same reason? We do not think so, but we admit that maybe the time for this revolution may not have come yet. In the meantime, therefore, we would stay on a more conventional plane and propose the transformation of the ACC into the PCB.

---

[1] Reference should be made to the Preamble of the Charter of the United Nations and Chapter III, Article 8.
[2] de Marco and Bartolo, *op. cit*, pp. 111-112.

THE RATIONAL ALTERNATIVE FOR A BETTER ACC

The signing of the United Nations Charter, on 26 June 1945, marked the birth of an indispensable organization, the United Nations, to maintain international peace and security and to ensure the well-being of mankind. This was seen as a less costly alternative to the production and accumulation of armaments as a means to achieve similar aims. The organizational structure of the United Nations has developed and grown to such an extent that coordination has become a key issue. It is, therefore, crucial to have a mechanism to bring out the best in the organization and its component parts. The ACC, once it is adequately reformed, can fulfill this task.

The management of this organization, with clear objectives in view, is critical, whether it is at the level of the United Nations proper or at the level of the United Nations System. Several initiatives taken for better coordination of the whole United Nations System have either partly succeeded or failed completely.

The attempt to reform the coordination machinery of the United Nations should not be abandoned. It is clear that an experiment as noble as the United Nations, created by the will of the peoples of the world, should not be allowed to fail for the lack of the right multilateral coordination machinery. We believe that the machinery of the ACC can be so transformed as to effectively achieve the desired objectives.

As shown in Diagram 6, a better ACC may be transformed into a Policy and Coordination Board (PCB), with the heads of Specialized Agencies and other institutions as Directors and the United Nations Secretary-General as President. The President would report to and receive mandates from the United Nations General Assembly, while the Directors would report to and receive mandates from their respective legislative bodies.

The PCB would develop policy statements with the help of its permanent secretariat, which could serve as a policy think tank. Through the permanent secretariat of the PCB, a permanent bridge would thus be built, by involving all the legislative bodies and all the secretariats of the United Nations System. The secretariat of the PCB will monitor the implementation of agreed policy. This bridge would also be extended to the Member States, who in most instances should be the beneficiaries of the policy statements, as the PCB, through its secretariat, would direct its actions to the level of 'all the peoples'. Such actions could also be monitored at the country level, through the existing network of Resident Coordinators, which would have to be modified for the role of representing the United Nations System and not one particular organization. The present membership of the ACC could easily be adjusted for the transition to the PCB.

The newly established Office of Inter-Agency Affairs could be upgraded to form the permanent secretariat of the PCB, to be headed by a senior staff member from the United Nations System (preferably by rotation for a period of up to three years). This secretariat, besides acting as a think tank, would also replace the present Organizational Committee (OC) and all the other subsidiary machinery of the ACC. This could be implemented immediately, since even in its present form, the ACC would benefit from such a move.

Diagram 6. Policy and Coordination Board (PCB)*

Member States

Origin of Policies

President

Directors**
(Heads of Specialized Agencies, IAEA, World Trade Organization, Bretton Woods Institutions, Regional Commissions, and Funds and Programs)

Secretary of the PCB

Policy and Coordination Board (PCB)

Permanent Secretariat of PCB

Issuance of policy statements (for public at large)

Proposals to General Assembly, ECOSOC and Governing Bodies of Specialized Agencies, IAEA, World Trade Organization, Bretton Woods Institutions, Regional Commissions, and Funds and Programs

Issuance of UN System-wide guidelines

Interpretation and Development of Policies

Coordination of Action and Implementation

Ad hoc Task Forces*** or subgroups, as necessary

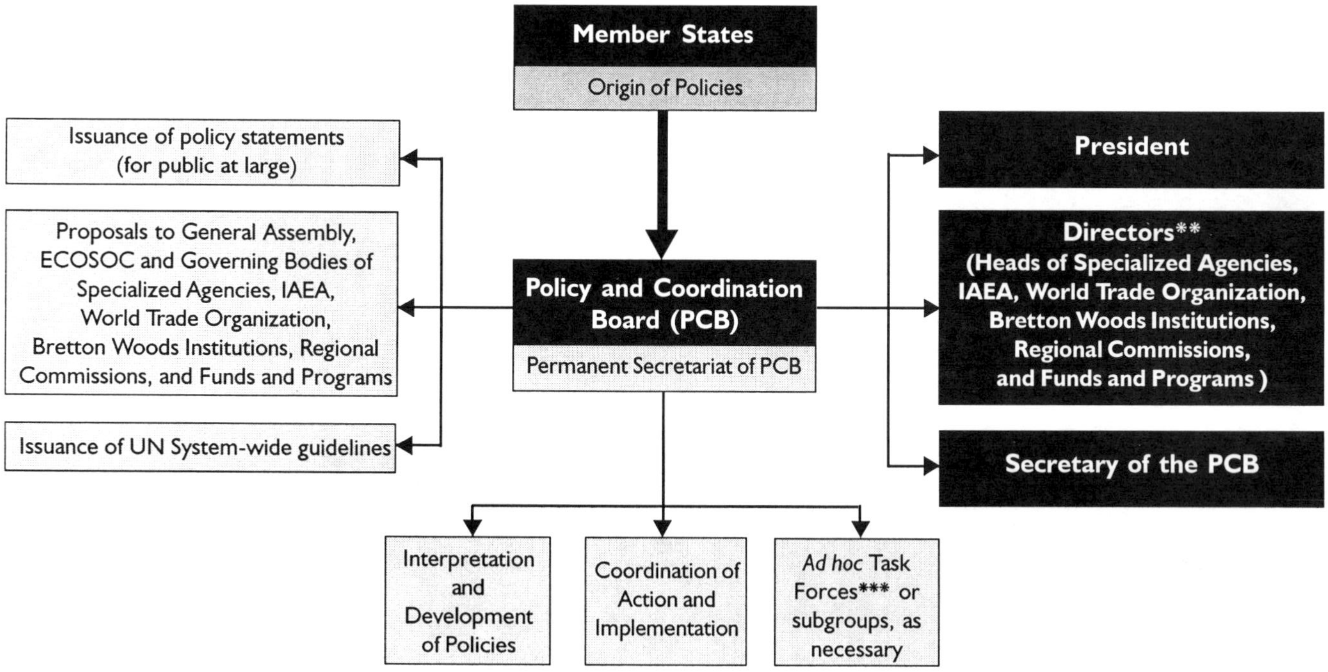

* Proposed replacement for the current Administrative Committee on Coordination (ACC)
** Regional Commissions to have one representative
*** One Task Force may be established to deal with *civil society* and the private sector.

130

An ACC of Substance

As stated earlier, the ACC has to be first and foremost relevant, and in becoming so, it has to change the way it works, starting first with the subjects it considers and the way it considers them. It is time to make coordination a means to an end, rather than an end in itself. It is time for the ACC to become a forum for informed and focused dialogue, involving all its members and ensuring the necessary contributions from outside, if necessary. It is time for ACC meetings to lead to written decisions that clearly enunciate results-oriented policies that can be translated into actions, with positive impact at the national and international levels.

The ACC must become a continuous ACC and not a two-day event, twice a year. It can do this without overtaxing the time of the Secretary-General and of the heads of Specialized Agencies if it is transformed into a PCB, as proposed. It must be ensured that subjects chosen are topical subjects of wide concern that truly reflect system-wide matters. The critically important needs of development and national capacity building must receive more sustained and constructive attention. Poverty eradication should always be high on any ACC agenda, until some impact has been made in this regard. This does not mean that less attention should be given to other pressing matters, such as humanitarian work resulting from the many political crises of the day. This is a subject, though, that may be allocated to a group within the ACC that is usually directly concerned with all aspects of the subject. This is an opportunity to allow the Secretary-General to ask the head of another agency to deputize for him and, if necessary, to test the machinery of the PCB by establishing an *ad hoc* working group to coordinate the United Nations contribution.

If the priorities are well set out within the PCB, the United Nations System will, over time, work more coherently and more effectively in addressing the challenges facing the international community. It is, therefore, important to give more thought to the agenda for the ACC meetings. It is mainly for this reason that we do not think that the generalists of the ACC (OC) can do justice to this. The world is changing continuously and fast and the agenda of the ACC should reflect this. Moreover, the agenda should not be encumbered with administrative and financial items that the new permanent secretariat can deal with in consultation with other parts of the ACC machinery. Administrative and financial matters with system-wide implications are certainly important for the System, but should not take precedence over matters like urgent humanitarian tragedies and longer-term problems like the eradication of poverty, which affect even more people. Exceptions should be kept to a minimum.

Such an ACC of substance would not only be of interest to the governing bodies of the Specialized Agencies of the System, but would also be of interest to the public at large. More importantly, it would point in the right direction by dealing with matters that affect the daily lives of millions of people rather than with matters of limited concern to the Specialized Agencies, as mandated in the founding resolution.[3] The new ACC (that is,

---

[3] ECOSOC resolution 13 (III) of 1946.

PCB) should not only deal with the most relevant subjects of the time but should also ensure that its work is known and appreciated outside the United Nations itself, namely in the world at large. Once the question of the subject matter is considered, it is important to concentrate on the best machinery that the ACC can have to accomplish its mission.

From an ACC to a PCB

There should be no doubt in anyone's mind that the present ACC has failed to fulfill its mission, in spite of about 50 years of reform and development. We think that this still can be done without the need to change the Charter of the United Nations or even the founding resolution of the ACC itself. This effort we believe would be worthwhile, since it would have ramifications beyond the ACC itself, and since we believe that the transformed ACC should play a pivotal role in the reform of the United Nations proper, as well as in the reform of the United Nations System. Diagram 6 of the PCB is striking in its simplicity. As can be seen, the emphasis is on reporting to the intergovernmental organs. All the present ACC machinery would be absorbed into the permanent secretariat of PCB as seen in Diagram 7. We think that it is also striking in its cost. This is confirmed in Annex IV. No one would be disappointed with a PCB doing what the ACC was supposed to do, but doing it better and at more or less the same cost. A lower cost would be an added bonus.

Irrespective of the subject matter and irrespective of how strongly one feels about whether the ACC plays a central role or not in the reform of the United Nations, one cannot escape the consequences of the cumbersome machinery of the ACC. Relevance comes first, but once it becomes relevant it will need the right machinery to do its work effectively.

Before referring to the machinery of the ACC, it is important for anyone who wants to understand the mission of the ACC to understand the name. This is not the first time that this matter is being brought up. The ACC, it is felt, is not a committee, it does not administer much, and finally it is not clear what it coordinates. Does it coordinate policy or the work of the United Nations and the Specialized Agencies?

We think that transparency can only come from clarity of purpose. A more appropriate name might help. We do not wish to imply that the change of name would right what is wrong with the ACC. Far from it. The new name, it is felt, would be the first concrete signal that the ACC means business, and from then on its business would be to make policy (or to be exact, to change legislative mandates into policy) and to coordinate this policy.

It is with this in mind that we propose a Policy and Coordination Board (PCB) of the United Nations, with all the heads of Specialized Agencies as Directors and the Secretary-General as the President. The President would report to and would receive mandates from the United Nations General Assembly, while the Directors would do the same with respect to their governing bodies. The PCB would work like any Board of Directors in the private sector, and, in the end, would be accountable to its shareholders, in this case the Member States, and, finally, the people of these Member States.

Diagram 7. The Mechanism of Policy and Coordination Board (PCB)

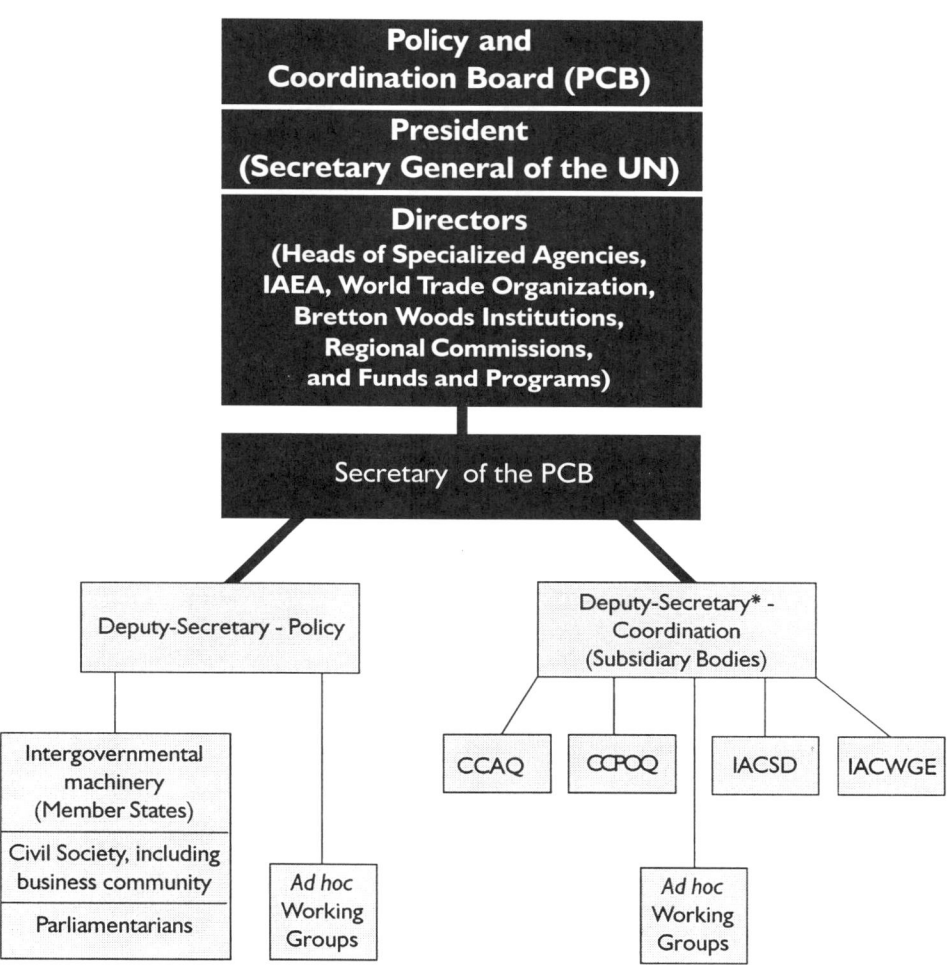

* Alternatively, to be divided between a Deputy-Secretary for the Consultative Committee on Administrative Questions (CCAQ), and a Deputy-Secretary for the Consultative Committee on Programme and Operational Questions (CCPOQ), the Inter-Agency Committee on Sustainable Development (IACSD), and the Inter-Agency Committee on Women and Gender Equality (IACWGE).

As already indicated, the PCB would develop policy statements with the help of a modest permanent secretariat, which could serve as a think tank. The permanent secretariat would be in regular touch with the secretariats of the whole system by monitoring and coordinating the implementation of agreed policy. Coordination in this context would become meaningful, and would be easy for anyone to understand. The PCB through its secretariat would also direct its work to the level of the people. Such actions could also be monitored and coordinated at the country level through the already existing network of Resident Coordinators. The present ACC already has some experience in this regard and has made important progress in using this network to assist some countries in the preparation of their national development plans and programs of technical cooperation, with inputs from the entire System, including the Bretton Woods Institutions.

Through its permanent secretariat, the PCB would be in 'continuous session', exploiting fully the advances in information technology, and the United Nations proper and the Specialized Agencies would be in constant consultation, without the need for the executive heads to meet twice a year. Such 'summit meetings' could certainly then take place once a year, if not even less frequently.

Such a transformation, as seen later, would also facilitate a closer relationship to the ECOSOC, to assist it in its role of coordination, and closer cooperation with other legislative bodies, as necessary.

It is felt that this would steer the ACC in the right direction. The present membership of the ACC, we think, could easily be modified for the transition to the PCB. It is also felt that this development would be welcomed by the governing bodies of the Specialized Agencies and would surely support it in a concrete way once its role has become clearer.

As indicated earlier, the Office for Inter-Agency Affairs could be strengthened to become the permanent secretariat of the PCB, to be headed by a senior staff member from the United Nations System (preferably by rotation for a period of up to three years). This office would report directly to the President of the ACC, and it would be authorized to establish *ad hoc* working groups, as and when necessary. We think that this would make it easier for heads of Specialized Agencies to second staff to it.

This, in fact, could be implemented immediately since, even in its present form, we think, the ACC would benefit from such a move. Moreover, this would redirect the recent initiative to establish the Office of Inter-Agency Affairs so that it would be seen as a move in the right direction, particularly if it reports directly to the Secretary-General, as President of the PCB, and is moved to a more appropriate place. In addition, we think that it would find its rightful place, if it replaces fully the OC and the other subsidiary machinery, as the various committees, subcommittees and panels complete their tasks (if such tasks would still be considered necessary). In future, all ACC tasks should be undertaken by *ad hoc* working groups, under the direct supervision of the new office, the future permanent secretariat of the PCB.

We believe that the ACC needs a transformation on the above lines, to enable it to be in a better position to play a role in bonding the United Nations System for the benefit of all the peoples of this planet.

The Brain of the PCB

Throughout this book it was never the intention to give the details of every proposal or recommendation made. In fact, it was always considered proper that it was the responsibility and the prerogative of Member States to work out the details once they agree with the proposed course of action. Ours is only an attempt to make proposals and recommendations for consideration and final decision by Member States, or the United Nations and the Specialized Agencies in the case of the ACC. It is, therefore, for the ACC itself to work out the details and the time frame for the implementation of the proposals made. We only suggest one alternative for implementation, but of course there may be others too.

Whether or not the above transformation of the ACC into the PCB is accepted, it is crucial to start the revival of the ACC by setting in motion the creation of the permanent secretariat, to assist guiding the ACC into the next millennium. It may be on the basis of the proposals in this chapter or on the basis of some other proposals, which would recognize the proper role of the new ACC in its quest for relevance.

The permanent secretariat, which could be established in New York or Geneva, should have two immediate objectives. The first is to phase out the work of the present machinery of the ACC, maintaining only those tasks which are still considered useful and which would fit within the new structure. The second is to set up the permanent secretariat with two deputies,[4] one to direct what is left of the machinery of the ACC, and the second to serve as the brain of the PCB. It is important that the permanent secretariat should be headed by a senior person who would have the complete confidence of the Secretary-General, whether he is situated in New York or Geneva.

As far as the first objective is concerned, it is important to phase out all activities of the ACC committees and subcommittees, if possible, within a period of 3 to 6 months, and to establish what is considered necessary within the new permanent secretariat, under one of the two deputies. It may be decided to have three deputies, in which case the machinery can be divided between the two. The four major committees of the ACC would have to be consolidated, under one or two deputies, as proposed. The creation of *ad hoc* working groups with clear objectives and time limits, and only when necessary, would restrict any expansion of the new PCB machinery to a minimum. Consideration should be given to the redeployment of the permanent staff of the ACC machinery to the new permanent secretariat.

The other deputy should be the main source for preparing a precise and action-oriented agenda for the PCB. This deputy should rely on the rest of the Secretariat for collecting raw material for the policy statements of the PCB. Such statements should always be the result of carefully selected topics that have been through rigorous strategic analysis. This should become the norm rather than the exception. It would also be the responsibility of this deputy to involve the other parts of the equation, namely the

---

[4] Depending on the size of the remaining machinery, it would also be possible to add another deputy. One could be in charge of the CCAQ, and the other could be in charge of what is left of CCPOQ, IACSD and IACWGE.

Member States, *civil society*, and other elements such as the business community and parliamentarians, if they can make a contribution. It would also be the responsibility of this deputy to exploit modern technology to keep meetings to a minimum and to create a continuous PCB to complement the continuous General Assembly of the United Nations.

It is believed that only a transformation along these lines as reflected in Diagram 7, can break the vicious cycle of over 50 years of tinkering with a machinery that never really worked, if the ACC is to have the crucial role outlined above. The details, as stated above, should be worked out by the Member States themselves and the United Nations and the Specialized Agencies, as appropriate. There should be no further delay, if it is expected that the new millennium will also be a millennium of hope for the peoples that have so far been left out of the progress enjoyed by some.

A CLEAR RELATIONSHIP BETWEEN THE ACC, THE ECOSOC AND THE GENERAL ASSEMBLY NEEDS TO BE ESTABLISHED

The PCB would facilitate this, since it would have to behave like the Board of Directors of a private company, which would be accountable to the Annual General Meeting and to the shareholders, who can dismiss it once it falls out of line. In this context, the Annual General Meeting would be the General Assembly of the United Nations and the Governing Bodies of the institutions of the United Nations System. The clear line of authority between the General Assembly, the Governing Bodies and the ECOSOC in this context, would need to be developed further.

The permanent secretariat of the PCB must give this matter urgent attention. It should set up an *ad hoc* working group on reporting, which should, within a year, first review the current reporting obligations, including those requested in the Agency agreements and consider recommending keeping only those reports which are absolutely necessary and compatible with the objectives and priorities of the PCB. Second, this working group would also develop the new reporting procedures of the PCB itself, paying particular attention to reports possibly being made directly or through the ECOSOC to other major organs of the United Nations. Third, it would be required to review all current decisions and resolutions that require reports from the United Nations and the System, some of which have become lengthy and cumbersome exercises.[5] The working group should recommend keeping only those reports with information that would not be readily available in the new and transparent *Better United Nations* and United Nations System.

In the spirit of the *Better United Nations*, the working group should include representatives of the Member States and *civil society*, as necessary. The group should also take into consideration the new roles proposed to the major organs of the United Nations and should endeavor to facilitate the transition of the ACC into the PCB and the present United Nations into the *Better United Nations*. This *Better United Nations* is expected to be more logical and streamlined, keeping in mind not only the new features

---

[5] All decisions and resolutions that require reporting particularly to ECOSOC from the United Nations and the System should be included in the review.

of the major organs like the General Assembly, the Security Council, the ECOSOC and the Trusteeship Council, but also the reduction of the committees of the General Assembly to only two. One committee, as seen later, would deal with political and security matters, in close cooperation with the Security Council, and the other with administrative and financial matters. All economic and social matters would be dealt with by the ECOSOC. The United Nations Secretariat would also be structured to service this new streamlining. Finally, the working group would have to establish clear lines of reporting, taking into consideration the new structure and architecture.

CHAPTER 9

A BETTER UNITED NATIONS
FOR THE FUTURE

SUMMARY

An outline of a fully transformed United Nations is presented in Annex III. As can be seen, this is a complete transformation of the United Nations that would require drastic changes in the Charter and in the Organization itself. Realistically, this cannot be achieved in the foreseeable future. It is expected, if one takes the present progress in the ongoing reform exercise as an indication, that such a transformation would be a lengthy process that would require the strongest political will. It would certainly require implementation in various stages.

The proposals for A *Better United Nations for the New Millennium* are presented in this chapter. This *Better United Nations* is a more realistic alternative to the fully transformed United Nations as proposed in Annex III. This alternative, although modest as compared with the ultimate United Nations described in Annex III, would also require a certain degree of political will. The critical difference is that it would require only modest changes, if any, to the Charter of the United Nations. What is of extreme importance, however, is the fact that acceptance of this blueprint will give a definite signal that the necessary political will exists for a meaningful reform of the United Nations. It will also show that, at this stage, there is no need to resort to a complete transformation of the United Nations and/or the Charter, as no one can guarantee that such a complete transformation will make the United Nations System work any better. The *Better United Nations* that we propose will have the necessary qualities that are essential for a millennium with a better chance for peace and less poverty. These qualities include relevance and efficiency, in that order, and, therefore, the United Nations proper and the United Nations System would cost much less and would do much more. However, if the *Better United Nations* fails to come about for lack of political will or for some other reason(s), then the fully transformed United Nations, on the lines presented in Annex III, would appear to be the only remaining alternative.

This chapter presents the *Better United Nations* of the future – an outline of the blueprint. This Organization would interact with the United Nations System at large, consisting more or less of the present Specialized Agencies, with the basic difference that only the Specialized Agencies which pass the rigorous test of relevancy, and then efficiency, would survive and form part of the *Better United Nations System* of the future.

The blueprint includes a United Nations that goes beyond the reform of the Secretary-General – taking the Second Generation United Nations into the new millennium! A holistic United Nations would include the Specialized Agencies, the Bretton Woods Institutions, the WTO and other global, regional and subregional institutions, whether intergovernmental or otherwise.

The *Better United Nations* would have a General Assembly energized by a summit-level session (as necessary), supplemented by a reinvigorated General Committee, two Substantive Committees (instead of the present six) and an Administrative Committee on Coordination (ACC) transformed into a Policy and Coordination Board (PCB) with a new mission and streamlined structure. This General Assembly would always be in session and would meet at either permanent representative or ministerial level. One of the first objectives of this better General Assembly would be to develop a system of representation of *civil society* and national parliaments in the Assembly itself. This United Nations would not only include the Specialized Agencies and entities in the present United Nations System but would also include other global, regional and subregional organizations, whether intergovernmental or otherwise. The process would require some time but there would be no reason not to include the work of these non-United Nations organizations immediately in the *Better United Nations*.

The Security Council would better represent the present geopolitical realities. It would eventually have to declare the veto anachronistic and would have to work more closely with the General Assembly, in the real spirit of the Charter, and with particular reference to Chapter III, Article 8.

An ECOSOC, as proposed in *A Second Generation United Nations*, would oversee development cooperation, which would be decentralized to the Specialized Agencies and Regional Commissions, under the coordination umbrella of the World Bank, as long as the World Bank were to receive legislative mandates from the General Assembly in addition to those from its Governing Board.

It would have a Trusteeship Council, as proposed by the Secretary-General and in *A Second Generation United Nations*, to hold in trust the heritage of present and future generations.

There would be a Secretariat, with a head chosen by established machinery that guarded against political pressures and which valued personal integrity, qualifications and proven leadership. It would be staffed by highly qualified officials governed by rules and regulations, which would be system-wide and protected by a unified system of administration of justice, if necessary under the supervision of the International Court of Justice. This would be designed to ensure that no staff member would lose his or her job purely as a consequence of the changes that would be necessary in the process of the transition to the *Better United Nations*.

THE BETTER UNITED NATIONS AS A MORE REALISTIC ALTERNATIVE TO A FULLY TRANSFORMED UNITED NATIONS

National Versus International Priorities

From experience of the pace of United Nations reform, it is not realistic to expect any significant progress any time soon. This is not a reason, however, to become indifferent. It is important to continue at least the momentum of the debate, even though very little significant reform has taken place. The reasons for this lethargy are varied and can be seen in the context of the relevance and efficiency criterion developed earlier.

One aspect of this dilemma, namely, why very little really changes in spite of near-unanimous agreement that the United Nations has to change, can be seen in the context of national versus international priorities.[1] Usually, national priorities predominate over international ones. A Member State, for example, may support a policy or program for the development of poor countries, as long as this policy or program does not adversely affect the Member State in question. In the past, Member States could support increased resources for the development of poor countries because it was usually put in the context of the possibilities of developing markets for the products of the Member States primarily contributing to such programs and policies. In other words, when national and international priorities coincided, things could be done, but this is now becoming more and more difficult. We see this again in the ongoing debate on globalization, which certainly coincides with the national priorities of the developed countries, although the developing countries, which feel left out, are becoming more and more skeptical of the drive towards globalization.

The United Nations, as well as some other organizations, were created to service and support a much different world from the existing one. It is, therefore, perceived by some that the *status quo* will continue to be in the interests of those countries that have gained most in the past, namely the developed countries. It continues to be in their interest to make the present institutions more efficient, rather than more relevant, which may mean changes that still favor primarily the developed countries.

---

[1] See de Marco and Bartolo, *op. cit*, Chapter 9.

A Rationale Based on Relevance over Efficiency

We often hear that a new and different United Nations is needed for a new and different world. We do not disagree, but this is easier said than done. It is, perhaps, easier to propose a new organization from scratch, like the one shown in Annex III. It is also rather tempting to propose solutions without examining the constraints prevalent at different times when efforts were made to reform the United Nations. At those times, as there was no political will, therefore, it was nearly impossible to change or modify the Charter of the United Nations.

It does not take one long to realize that there is no chance at all to replace the present United Nations proper with a completely new organization, like the one in Annex III, or another for that matter. Apart from the fact that we want to propose a realistic United Nations, which could be agreed upon with little or no change in the Charter, we believe that our rationale for the *Better United Nations* is a convincing one.

First, we believe that the *Better United Nations* could be a realistic alternative to a complete transformation as proposed in Annex III. Second, we do not accept that the United Nations has failed in all its endeavors. Therefore, it is rational to build on its successes. Third, the United Nations cannot be seen in isolation from the system of Specialized Agencies that had developed with, and in some cases even before, the United Nations proper, and which have been playing a useful role. The present set of reforms in most of these Specialized Agencies is bound to make them even more effective. Fourth, it is felt that the United Nations Charter in itself is generally sound, but that political developments and circumstances did not allow it to be implemented as hoped for and willed by the drafters. The major potential of the Charter of the United Nations is still latent, and needs to be turned into a reality.

These, we believe, are powerful reasons not to give up on the United Nations. We are convinced that the *Better United Nations* is within our grasp, if only we can make it relevant before we make it efficient. It is for this reason that we give so much importance to relevance over efficiency. The test of relevance is the test that determines what is included in the *Better United Nations* and the *Better United Nations System*.

Put in the context of the Charter, relevance should be easy to understand and to accept as the real test for a *Better United Nations*. In this regard only two references to the Charter suffice to prove, without any doubt, its power and our conviction of the enormous good that can be achieved by simply giving it a chance. The preamble of the Charter referring to 'we the peoples of the United Nations' is one clear and unmistakable implication that the United Nations was created for all and not for some of the people, which at the moment benefit most from the United Nations.[2] The other is Chapter III, Article 8 that states that '*The United Nations shall place no restrictions on the eligibility of men and women to participate in any capacity and under conditions of equality in its principal and subsidiary organs*'.[3]

---

[2] See pages 1 and 2 of the Charter of the United Nations for the full Preamble.
[3] *Ibid.*, p.7.

Can there be more eloquent statements in favor of the people? We do not think so. In all our references to relevance, the underlying theme has always been that the United Nations can only be relevant if it addresses all the peoples' problems and benefits them all.

Any proposals that required drastic changes in the Charter were not considered realistic in the current drive for reform. This, however, did not concern us greatly, since we believe that the Charter has not yet been fully implemented, and want to take the opportunity to unmask those who are using the Charter as an excuse to keep the Organization from rising to the challenges of the new millennium. It is for this reason that the *Better United Nations* would not require any major changes in the Charter. Thus, the opponents of this new and reformed United Nations would have to find other excuses to prevent meaningful reform. The acceptance of this *Better United Nations* would be significant, not only because it would give the signal that the time for a relevant United Nations has come, but also because it would demonstrate that a political will exists for a meaningful reform of the United Nations, whatever form this would take. Objections would no longer be raised to prevent the emergence of the Best United Nations for future generations, whether this is to be along the lines we propose, or along other lines.

THE BLUEPRINT FOR THE UNITED NATIONS PROPER

We propose a United Nations that goes beyond the reform proposed by the Secretary-General, by developing further the ideas of *A Second Generation United Nations,* as a basis for a more holistic organization for the new millennium. Diagram 8 redraws and refocuses the present United Nations into the *Better United Nations*, with the following highlights. It is not possible in a book of this kind and size, to deal with every aspect and subject of the United Nations. But it is felt that once the major organs and programs are reformed in the right direction, the rest will fall into place, whether it is in the important areas of human rights and disarmament or any other area, which the book does not deal with in any detail.

The General Assembly

We propose a General Assembly, as the supreme organ, meeting at the summit level as necessary but meeting normally at the level of permanent representatives and with more frequent meetings at the ministerial level. This assembly would meet all the year round with special sessions organized around selected topics. One of these early topics would be the reform of the Organization with particular reference to its new mission, to interpret the Charter as creating a United Nations of *all the peoples*, encompassing all other institutions, whether these be governmental, nongovernmental, global or regional, and its new structure, that is to say, a system of representation in the spirit of Chapter III, Article 8, with particular reference to *civil society* and national parliaments.

Diagram 8 : The Better United Nations

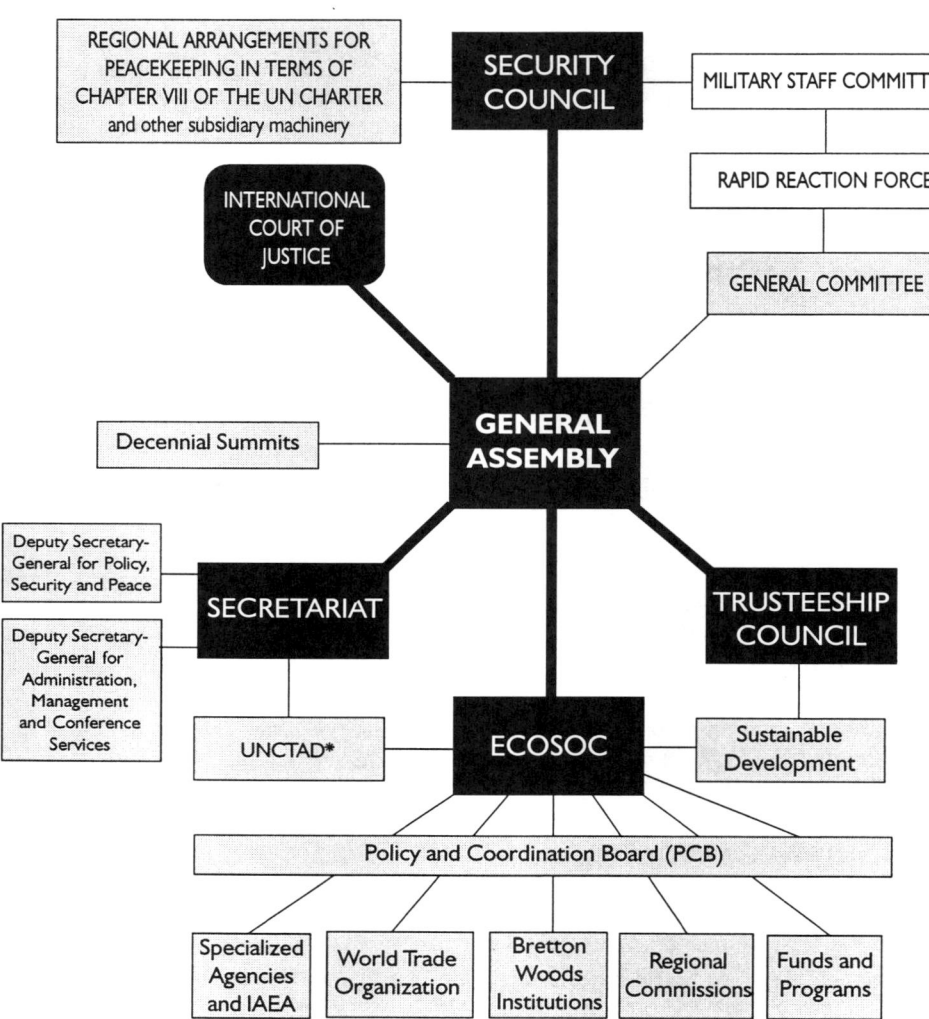

* UNCTAD: Also acts as Secretariat of ECOSOC.

It is, therefore, important to reconsider the matter of representation in the General Assembly to include also *civil society* (including the private sector, as appropriate) and parliaments. This should not come as a surprise to any one, since the delegations of some of the more advanced countries, including the United States, already do this. This would however need to be formalized, following the tripartite system of the International Labor Organization (ILO). While the ILO system includes the unions and the employers in addition to the governments, the proposed system at the General Assembly would include *civil society* and parliaments to ensure wider representation in the spirit of the Charter. This tripartite representation would then become standard at all levels of the United Nations.

We may anticipate that some governments may not feel comfortable sharing their decision-making responsibilities at the United Nations with either nongovernmental organizations or with members of parliament not forming part of the government. The important point in this wider representation is to give the opportunity of consultation with a greater number of people. The question of the role in the decision-making process of *civil society* and parliaments should at this stage be left to the individual delegations, who can best interpret the national consensus on this very delicate matter.

This General Assembly would be supported by a reinvigorated and strengthened General Committee and two substantive committees (one for political, peacekeeping and related matters and the other for administration and finance, all economic and social matters being entrusted to the ECOSOC). The two substantive committees would, as at present, have the same membership of the General Assembly with the same type of representation as referred to above. The committees would establish *ad hoc* working groups or commissions, as necessary, with flexible rules and procedures to facilitate their tasks. These *ad hoc* bodies would have very specific tasks assigned to them with strict time limits, to discourage the continuation of such bodies after their tasks have been completed.

The Political Committee may, for example, establish an *ad hoc* working group or commission to coordinate the humanitarian program in Kosovo. The United Nations is in the unique position to play a major role in this regard, to coordinate not only the United Nations contributions but also the program in its entirety. This *ad hoc* group could also include NATO, OSCE, the European Commission, the World Bank and other major contributors to the effort. Such machinery would prevent the establishment, as is currently usual, of coordination machinery in most, if not in all, of the above organizations – with the results still falling below expectations.

The Administration and Finance Committee could, for example, establish an *ad hoc* working group or commission to review the program and budget of the United Nations, before it is considered in the General Committee. This *ad hoc* working group could include, in addition to the representatives from the United Nations, experts from Member States both for program (now done by the Committee on Programme Coordination) and financial implications (now done by the Advisory Committee on Administrative and Budgetary Questions), as well as representatives from the Specialized Agencies of the System, other organizations, and anyone interested from the tripartite system referred to above. The modalities of organization should be left to the two committees themselves, with the participation of the General Committee.

Such an *ad hoc* or similar group could also meet with the political group on Kosovo, referred to above, to consider the financial implications of the humanitarian program, and to facilitate consideration and approval by the General Assembly. The Policy and Coordination Board (PCB) would also have the mandate and the expertise to participate in the *ad hoc* coordination groups of both committees to ensure a holistic and comprehensive program without duplication and waste. Coordination is neither the responsibility nor the prerogative solely of the United Nations System, nor is it solely that of the Member States. It is the responsibility and prerogative of both. This is the basic rationale behind our proposals.

The General Committee, with possibly different membership than at present, would be revitalized to control the agenda of the General Assembly and also to monitor and control the work of the two committees and the other organs that report to the General Assembly or receive mandates from it. The General Committee which, like the General Assembly itself, would meet continuously all-year round, and would also establish a special relationship with the Security Council, particularly in the area of operational activities for security purposes. In this context, the General Committee should be the focal point between the Security Council and the General Assembly in matters dealing with the mobilization of the Rapid Reaction Force, which would be an important feature in the *Better United Nations*. The new General Committee would also ensure that the proposed reduction in the number of committees would not result in any essential work being left out, which would hamper the smooth transition to the new and better General Assembly.

With the increase in importance of the General Committee the question of membership in this committee would require some consideration. The President of the General Assembly usually chairs the General Committee, and its membership includes the 21 Vice-Presidents of the General Assembly. The chairmen of the main committees are also members. Since the Vice-Presidents of the General Assembly are elected on the basis of an equitable geographical distribution, we would not want to see the membership changed drastically. Small committees are usually more practical and effective than much larger ones. Member States may want to decide on an open-ended membership or some kind of geographical representation like that of the ECOSOC. The tripartite type of participation proposed for the General Assembly would also apply in the case of the General Committee. In the light of the expanded role of the General Committee, it is proposed that the President of the ECOSOC and the President of the Security Council would also be members.

In the case of the ECOSOC this would be important, since it is proposed that the ECOSOC would replace the Second and Third Committees. As far as the Security Council is concerned, in addition to cooperation in the mobilization of the Rapid Reaction Force, it is expected that the proposed closer cooperation between the Security Council and the General Assembly could be facilitated by the General Committee.

Presidents of the General Assembly are usually well known personalities of international stature. Usually every President brings his or her own style to the Office, which continues to be generally ceremonial. We think that better use should be made of this high office and that it should not be left to the initiative and style of the individual. Both as a result of the increased role of the General Committee, which the President chairs, and the potential of the office, the President should not be left out of the consultations between the President of the Security Council and the Secretary-General. The concern that the President of the General Assembly could interfere with the work of the Secretary-General or that of the Security Council is not convincing. The President of the General Assembly should, therefore, be included in the regular consultations between the President of the Security Council and the Secretary-General and his office should be exploited to represent the views and wishes of the General Assembly, manifested in the resolutions and decisions taken by the Member States.

Finally, a direct link should be established between the General Assembly and the Policy and Coordination Board (PCB) to assist it in coordinating the work of the entire United Nations System and to focus this work in the context of the legislative mandates issued by the General Assembly itself and other major organs, such as the ECOSOC. The PCB should also serve as a link between the General Assembly and the ECOSOC in all matters related to the agreements between the Specialized Agencies and the United Nations.

The Security Council

Chapter 1 gives the reasons why, in our opinion, the discussions on the reform of the Security Council are at a stalemate. We think that in spite of all the efforts that went into the work on the reform of the Security Council, some of the entrenched positions on such an important and crucial subject for the future of the United Nations have been too quickly accepted. All agree that it is only fair for Member States to expect a Security Council that is more representative of the present world. There is, however, no agreement how this can be done.

We propose a Security Council that also has to take into consideration the spirit and letter of the United Nations Charter, particularly Chapter III, Article 8, referred to above. This can best be done if the Council is more representative of the present world and if it does not create various categories of Member States, namely some with the veto power and some without it. The Security Council would also be equipped, with the cooperation of the General Committee of the General Assembly, with a Rapid Reaction Force to give it the capability to intervene in a situation quickly to prevent its deterioration into a crisis presenting greater difficulties for the action of the United Nations.

Although we agree that it is the Member States themselves which need to reform the Security Council, it is becoming clearer than ever that the Permanent Members will never agree to relinquish their veto power and to share the responsibility and the authority of the Council more equitably. We, therefore, think that the proposal of the Secretary-General in this respect, to leave this matter entirely to the Member States, without any guidelines, is an alternative that would never result in any meaningful reform of the Council. Another alternative, which we would prefer, is to propose some guidelines on how to proceed with the possibility of breaking the stalemate.

We believe that the only way to move forward on this matter is to agree that the General Assembly, during its early session on reform, referred to above, should consider this matter and establish guidelines and a timetable, for a phased reform of the Council, with the proviso that, failing this, the General Assembly, by the year 2005, or another appropriate date to be agreed upon by all the Member States, would be free to take a vote on the matter, with a required two-thirds majority but without the need of positive votes from the five permanent members of the Security Council.

Although we harbor no illusions that the veto is implied in the Charter, we think that all the imaginative proposals to solve this matter have not yet been exhausted. The Millennium General Assembly should give the utmost attention to this and could consider the following points in establishing the guidelines referred to above. A system, for example, of *weighted voting* should be considered. This could gradually overcome the veto system by acknowledging, as in other institutions, that sometimes different responsibilities have to be given to countries considering their influence and position in the world. It should not be too difficult to develop such a system, which would be more equitable than the veto and yet would guarantee that no country, however powerful, would be allowed to stop a move by the United Nations that is considered by the majority to be in the interest of the world at large. The Security Council is too important an organ to depend solely on the wishes and decisions of a few.

The guidelines should also propose a study to investigate, first, whether the use of the veto in the Security Council could be considered a procedural matter and, therefore, could be dealt with in accordance with paragraph 2, Article 27, and, second, whether the *dispute* on the veto could be decided in accordance with paragraph 3, Article 27.[4]

The expansion of the Security Council has also been controversial. But we think that this matter will be settled eventually, once the question of the veto is solved. Various formulae for equitable distribution of participation exist in the United Nations System, and we are sure that a suitable one can be found for the Security Council. The original formula for the Economic and Social Council may offer some food for thought.[5]

In the meantime, we propose maintaining the momentum of Security Council reform, bearing in mind that while the questions of the veto and expansion of categories of membership are very valid, basic questions and other important issues, such as the transparency and openness of the Council should continue to be given the most urgent consideration. We think that this aspect benefits the greatest number of mankind.

Finally, we think that a *Better Security Council* would certainly have to have closer working relations with the new General Assembly. The new General Committee could undertake the monitoring of this new relationship of consultation between the Security Council and the General Assembly.

---

[4] Article 27.2 of the Charter of the United Nations states that procedural matters may be decided by an affirmative vote of nine members. Article 27.3 states that members party to a dispute shall abstain from voting.
[5] The amendment to Article 61 of the United Nations Charter, on 31 August 1965 enlarged the membership of ECOSOC from eighteen to twenty-seven. This was further increased to the present fifty-four.

The Economic and Social Council (ECOSOC)

We propose an ECOSOC which replaces the Second and Third Committees of the General Assembly, and which deals with all economic, social and related matters except human rights, which should be dealt with by the new Trusteeship Council, as proposed in *A Second Generation United Nations.* [6]

The *better* ECOSOC, as seen in Diagram 9, would oversee development cooperation, decentralized to the Specialized Agencies and the Regional Commissions under the coordination umbrella of the World Bank, as long as it receives mandates from the United Nations General Assembly, in addition to those from its Governing Board.

It should also be allowed to do its work as mandated by the Charter of the United Nations, considering that it was preempted from performing its tasks as spelled out by the United Nations Charter, with the establishment of the Bretton Woods Institutions.[7] It should also play its coordination role in close cooperation with the new and transformed ACC (PCB).

We think that no diplomatic language should hide the fact that the ECOSOC was not given the chance and the authority as mandated by the Charter to create the 'conditions of stability and well-being which are necessary for peaceful and friendly relations among nations'. Although not an easy matter, the question of whether the ECOSOC could ever realistically play an effective role in fostering an environment for development in the areas of international trade and finance needs to be addressed directly.

It certainly has not done so in the last fifty years or so. Again, as pointed out in Chapter 1, efforts at the revitalization of the ECOSOC have missed the point by emphasizing efficiency, while completely ignoring its role and position in the world of international trade and finance. In other words, as in other parts of the United Nations, there were no efforts to make it relevant before making it efficient. The ECOSOC was simply kept on the periphery of economic and financial institutions that have an impact in these fields. Few would argue that the leadership in the field in which the ECOSOC was to have had an impact has generally been in the hands of the most developed countries (G-7 or 8), the Bretton Woods Institutions, and, to some extent, the WTO.

The ECOSOC was never given a chance to play a critical role in the area of global macroeconomic policy, because other institutions were already playing such a role and Member States were satisfied with relegating the ECOSOC to a role in which it would cooperate with those institutions by contributing the input of the United Nations in accordance with the agreements between those institutions and the United Nations. As seen in Chapter 2 and elsewhere, these agreements never addressed the questions of the ECOSOC's role according to the Charter, but dealt primarily with the exchange of information and other related matters of secondary importance. The recent efforts, in the context of the revitalization of the ECOSOC, for closer cooperation with these institutions, did not change the situation significantly. Admittedly, putting the ECOSOC into the role envisaged by the Charter is not easy. The difference in the styles of

---

[6] See de Marco and Bartolo, *op. cit.,* p. 79.

[7] *Ibid.,* Chapter 7, p. 85.

Diagram 9. The Better United Nations Economic and Social Institutions

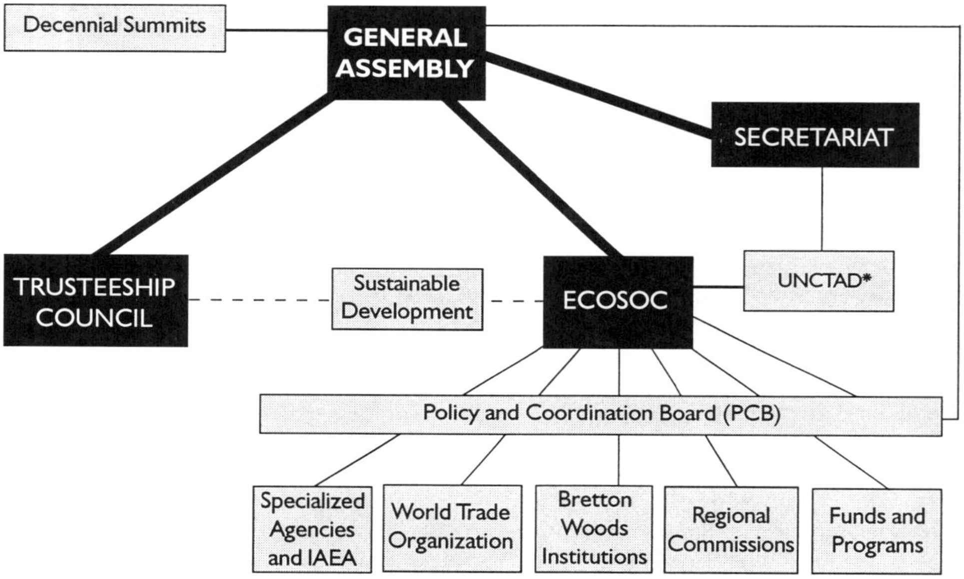

```
┌─────────────────────┐        ┌──────────────┐
│ Decennial Summits   │────────│   GENERAL    │──────────────────────────┐
└─────────────────────┘        │   ASSEMBLY   │                          │
                               └──────────────┘                          │
                                  /        \                             │
                                 /          \      ┌──────────────┐      │
                                /            \     │ SECRETARIAT  │      │
                               /              \    └──────────────┘      │
                              /                \          │              │
                             /                  \         │              │
┌──────────────┐    ┌──────────────┐    ┌──────────┐  ┌─────────┐       │
│ TRUSTEESHIP  │----│ Sustainable  │----│  ECOSOC  │──│ UNCTAD* │       │
│  COUNCIL     │    │ Development  │    └──────────┘  └─────────┘       │
└──────────────┘    └──────────────┘       /│││\                        │
                                          / │││ \                       │
                    ┌─────────────────────────────────────────────────────┐
                    │        Policy and Coordination Board (PCB)           │
                    └─────────────────────────────────────────────────────┘
                       /        |         |          |           \
          ┌──────────┐ ┌──────────┐ ┌──────────┐ ┌──────────┐ ┌──────────┐
          │Specialized│ │World Trade│ │ Bretton  │ │ Regional │ │Funds and │
          │ Agencies  │ │Organization│ │  Woods   │ │Commissions│ │ Programs │
          │ and IAEA  │ │          │ │Institutions│ │          │ │          │
          └──────────┘ └──────────┘ └──────────┘ └──────────┘ └──────────┘
```

* UNCTAD: Also acts as Secretariat of ECOSOC.

governance of the United Nations, on one hand, and the Bretton Woods Institutions and the WTO, on the other hand, is possibly the most difficult obstacle, but not the only one. We think that the disparity between the authority and influence of the ECOSOC and the authority and influence of the Bretton Woods Institutions in the area of financial flows, and policy regulating such flows, should be addressed. Nothing short of this will do.

A reformed ECOSOC must come closer to the institutions which have the major influence in fostering an enabling environment for development, namely, the International Monetary Fund (IMF) and the World Bank in the area of financial flows and investment, and the World Trade Organization (WTO) in the area of international trade. Only then do we feel that the ECOSOC would be in a position to function as envisaged in the Charter of the United Nations. No one is naïve enough to believe that this can be done unless the Bretton Woods Institutions and the WTO become full-fledged members of the United Nations System, not only sharing information with the United Nations but also bound to the mandates of the United Nations General Assembly. This new relationship would be facilitated by the Policy and Coordination Board (PCB), which would be equipped to bring out the best in the System.

Administratively, this new relationship would require a revision of the agreements referred to above, except of course in the case of the WTO, which would require a new agreement, considering that the WTO has signed no agreements at all with the United Nations. These agreements would have to come closer to the agreements signed by the Specialized Agencies like the ILO and the WHO. This would still allow the Bretton Woods Institutions to be under the direct management of their Governing Boards, but would require conformity with the mandates of the General Assembly. In return, we think that all development assistance and related activities should be transferred to the World Bank, which would continue to use the expertise of the Specialized Agencies and the Regional Commissions. This would free the United Nations from all such activities and from a number of Funds and Programs, with the exception of the specialized ones like UNICEF, UNHCR and WFP.

A reformed ECOSOC, as conceived in the Charter of the United Nations, could play a significant role in the *Better United Nations* of the future.

The Trusteeship Council

We propose a Trusteeship Council, reformed to hold in trust the heritage of present and future generations. This proposal would be in line with the comprehensive proposals of the Secretary-General,[8] and as proposed earlier in *A Second Generation United Nations*.[9] The Trusteeship Council would also take over the overall responsibility for human rights from the ECOSOC.

The proposals on the Trusteeship Council are detailed in *A Second Generation United Nations* and rely to a large extent on the comprehensive ideas introduced formally by Malta at the United Nations General Assembly (see General Assembly resolution 50/55

---

[8] A/51/950, 14 July 1997.
[9] de Marco and Bartolo, *op. cit*, Chapter 6 and Annex II.

of 17 December 1995). Therefore, we need only repeat the salient points of these proposals in order to place the new Trusteeship Council in the context of the *Better United Nations*.

If there is one thing that becomes clear throughout this book, we are sure it is that we did not hesitate to call for the abolition of parts of the United Nations that we thought were outdated or that have outgrown their usefulness. We think, however, that the Trusteeship Council will continue to be relevant and, therefore, will find its rightful place in the *Better United Nations*, by changing its focus from decolonization to the protection of the *common heritage* and the *common concerns* of mankind.

This would include the protection of the environment, extraterritorial spaces and zones, the resources of the sea and of the seabed, the climate, human rights, the rights of future generations, and the rights of peoples in situations where there has been a complete breakdown of the state or of the institutions guaranteeing the rule of law. We think that this could be done with only minor amendments, or even without any amendments, to the Charter of the United Nations.[10]

This idea of the new Trusteeship Council has received quite wide-ranging support. The only reasons given against it seem to have been largely economic, specifically that it would cost too much to do the work of already existing institutions. We think critics have misunderstood the proposal of the new Trusteeship Council, because the reasons mentioned above are not valid. The Trusteeship Council would only play a coordinating role, and, therefore, would not get involved in the work already being undertaken by existing institutions, for example, on the environment. It would certainly monitor this work and identify areas of duplication, attempting correction, if need be. In addition, the cost of the Trusteeship Council has always been one of the lowest in the Organization, due to the small number of staff involved in its work. It is not expected that this would change with its new role.

What we think is really needed at this stage is to give due recognition to the proposals for the transition to the new Trusteeship Council, by upgrading their consideration to the level that is being accorded to the Security Council and other important areas of the United Nations. This could be done by setting up a working group under the President of the General Assembly rather than leaving it buried within the reform exercise of the environment program. We think that the Millennium General Assembly needs to be apprised of this matter at the highest level. We are convinced that, once the Member States consider the importance of the proposals, they will also be convinced of their relevance and their contribution to *A Better United Nations for the New Millennium*.

The Secretariat

We propose that the Secretariat be headed by a Secretary-General chosen by established machinery, which minimizes political pressures and gives most importance to personal integrity, qualifications, and proven leadership.

---

[10] For a comprehensive analysis of the reasons why the changes proposed may not require basic changes in the Charter, refer to *ibid.*, pp. 71-74.

It should be staffed by highly qualified officials governed by rules and regulations which are system-wide and protected by a unified system of administration of justice, and, if necessary, under the supervision of the International Court of Justice. Since the staff would be expected to play a major role in the transition to the *Better United Nations*, they need to be assured that no one would lose their job purely as a consequence of the changes envisaged.

The Secretariat would be organized to support the new legislative structure proposed above. The Secretary-General would be assisted by two deputies, namely the Deputy Secretary-General of Political, Security and Related Matters and the Deputy Secretary-General of Administration and Finance. The structure of the Secretariat would be that of two major departments, to ensure transparency and accountability. The economic and social areas would be concentrated outside New York, with UNCTAD playing a central role in research and support for the ECOSOC. This structure would also emphasize decentralization, underscored by the fact that only the Regional Commissions and the other European headquarters would be headed by Under Secretaries-General (same rank as the Deputies).[11] All other units at headquarters would be within the two major departments, and generally never headed by anyone above the grade of an Assistant Secretary-General.

The streamlined Secretariat should undertake only those tasks which cannot be undertaken anywhere else in the system, and should start by divesting itself of all operational activities, especially when these involve technical cooperation or humanitarian activities.

United Nations Funds and Programs and Other Entities

The only major organ not included in the analysis of this book is the International Court of Justice (ICJ), apart from proposing a possible role for it in the area of administration of justice for the staff of the United Nations. No organization, however relevant, can function without effective dispute settlement machinery. The ICJ would, therefore, have a very important and necessary role in the *Better United Nations*. At the moment, less than one-third of the Member States accept its jurisdiction. It is, therefore, essential that all Member States accept the jurisdiction of the ICJ, since it would have to play a crucial role in the *Better United Nations* of the future, considering that this United Nations has to be more rule based and with wider representation.

Apart from the Funds and Programs, whose relevance is unquestionable, such as UNICEF, UNHCR and WFP, all other bodies and organs need to be reviewed in the context of the *Better United Nations* proposed above. For example, in the context of the new ideas on development cooperation, it would certainly be necessary to review UNDP, OPS and UNFPA to determine their place, if any, in the new and *Better United Nations*.

---

[11] This ranking of high officials would also bring some logic to the System. It is only reasonable to expect that the Secretary-General of the United Nations outranks the heads of Agencies. But no one else in the Secretariat should outrank or equal the rank of the Directors General of the Specialized Agencies, such as the ILO, the WHO, etc.

It is not possible in a book of this nature to review and analyze every single part of the United Nations. This does not mean, however, that any part of the United Nations that is not referred to should form part of the *Better United Nations*. We feel that our proposals would refocus the United Nations and orient it in the right direction. Once this is done, it will be easier for the rest of the system to follow suit. In the end, there is no doubt that it is the prerogative of the Members States to decide on reform. Therefore, it is not considered practical to go further than this. Any other reform will depend on the Member States accepting the main elements proposed above.

Neither does this mean that Funds and Programs whose relevance is unquestioned have no need to streamline their operations. We have maintained throughout this book that the process of reform in the United Nations has two stages. The first stage is to make the United Nations relevant and the second stage is to make it more efficient.

Cooperation with Other Global, Regional and Subregional Organizations

The introduction of more comprehensive representation within the General Assembly, and at every level of United Nations work, as pointed out earlier, should also be seen in the context of other global, regional and subregional organizations, which should certainly have closer relationship with the United Nations. Coordination and the avoidance of duplication should not only be sought within the United Nations but should be taken into consideration in all other institutions, whether intergovernmental or otherwise.

For example, in the humanitarian field, whether in Kosovo, East Timor or elsewhere, the United Nations should be responsible for coordinating all the work, starting of course from the planning and budgeting phases to the implementation and follow-up phases. Only this will ensure the best results at the lowest cost. This does not mean that the United Nations should do everything itself. It cannot. It would certainly have to include all the present organizations that are involved in this work. The only difference is that every organization would do only what it does best, with the others knowing what to do and when. This, we feel, is the best system to exploit the capabilities of all the organizations, with as little waste as possible and no duplication of resources and efforts.

A BETTER SYSTEM OF FINANCE AND CONTRIBUTIONS

No organization is expected to function properly unless it has the means to do so. The *Better United Nations* requires a better system of funding. This better system of funding needs to start with a fair distribution of the contributions and an imaginative plan to supplement such contributions when necessary. There may be good reasons to start the search for a solution to this problem by proposing to reduce the share of the largest contributor. We would still favor the proposal made in *A Second Generation United Nations* to find a solution where the largest contributor, the United States, would have its share reduced from, say, 25 to 20 percent of the budget of the United Nations.[12] It would not be difficult to make this up by slightly increasing the contributions of the Member States that are ready to take up more responsibilities at the United Nations. Member States should be expected to pay their assessed contributions, and those who do not should have their nationals barred from recruitment to United Nations posts, and from receiving United Nations contracts.

Other ideas for supplementary funds need to be considered, and these should certainly not be limited to the traditional ones. One such idea, that seems to gain ground every time the United Nations receives money from the private sector, is to tap the large multinational companies, by convincing them to donate reasonable sums of money in return for the maintenance by the United Nations and its programs of a peaceful environment to operate in. Another novel idea is to convince governments to donate all revenues derived from tax and levies on commercial transactions involving the United Nations. This should also include all transactions by business firms involved in procurement and contracts for and from the United Nations.

Costly items in the budgets of the United Nations and the system at large, such as communications and travel, should be seriously reviewed system-wide with the objective of reducing the costs. We think, in this respect, that there is scope to seriously consider the feasibility of a United Nations owned telecommunications company and travel agency. If this is not feasible, there is certainly scope for some formula of profit sharing with the companies that receive the business of the United Nations in these sectors.

We should not ignore the additional resources that can be saved from the better use of what is already available to the United Nations. It is for this reason that the *Better United Nations* would include strategic planning and result-based budgeting. As indicated in Annex IV, the *Better United Nations* would cost much less than the present United Nations on account of its more streamlined structure, since once the United Nations becomes more relevant, it would be much easier to make it more effective. These costs would be brought down even further by introducing strategic planning and result-based budgeting, first at the United Nations proper and then system-wide, with the ultimate objective of convincing other global, regional and subregional institutions to do the same.

Such a system of planning and budgeting has already been introduced in at least one of the Specialized Agencies and a number of other national and international organizations. Although this is a relatively new development, its advantages are already clear. This technique allows the Member States to establish policy and the head of the agency or organization to manage the planning, programming and monitoring of the work with transparency and clarity of purpose. This is done by providing the required transparency and opportunity for decision-making at all stages of the cycle, on the basis of a set of predefined objectives and expected results, identification of related resource requirements, and the measurement of achievement by performance indicators. The focus on results, on output rather than input, which is the hallmark of the *Better United Nations*, helps to test the relevance of the agency or institution and to improve its effectiveness and efficiency, once its relevance is established.

---

[12] de Marco and Bartolo, *op. cit,* p. 118.

The *Better United Nations*, therefore, should not only strive for relevance and efficiency as an end but as means to tackle the enormous problems facing mankind and also to influence the performance and quality of all the other institutions, which in one way or another, cooperate and work towards the same objectives of peace, security, and prosperity for all.

CHAPTER 10

A BETTER
UNITED NATIONS SYSTEM

SUMMARY

A *Better United Nations System for the New Millennium* is a consolidated United Nations with one set of rules, and which, above all, is not duplicated by other international and regional institutions, whether intergovernmental or not. Also, and just as important, it would have a staff governed by a common set of rules and regulations including a common United Nations Administration of Justice, as a basic requirement for an effective and unified personnel system, with the possibility of resorting to the International Court of Justice (ICJ), if necessary.

In addition to the elements of the blueprint referred to above, other aspects and characteristics of the *Better United Nations System* are analyzed and scrutinized. These include the desirability of using the ILO tripartite system in other parts of the United Nations when such consultation is considered necessary. The role of NGOs, or the preferred term *'civil society'*, is considered and ways of formalizing this role is discussed. The model of the role of *civil society* in United Nations humanitarian activities is analyzed to determine how, without duplicating this feature; this input can also be used by other parts of the United Nations, when considered necessary.

On the same lines, the input and contribution of other governmental and nongovernmental institutions, such as the European Commission and the Organization of African Unity (OAU), are discussed, to propose their permanent input to United Nations activities in all areas of their work. This is considered to be essential in *A Better United Nations for the New Millennium.*

FROM A BETTER UNITED NATIONS
TO A BETTER UNITED NATIONS SYSTEM

One Set of Rules – No Exceptions

The United Nations proper, reformed as proposed in the previous chapter, would be the foundation of a United Nations System with one set of rules, with no exceptions, and which, above all, would not duplicate any work being done by any international or regional institutions, whether these are intergovernmental or not.

This is easier said than done. To ensure that the United Nations System functions in a coherent, holistic, and organic manner, it is essential that a mechanism is put in place that helps to develop a common and shared understanding of the proper mission, goals, and objectives of the entire system and of each of its component parts. The strategic planning process, result-based budgeting, predefined objectives and expected results, and, above all, objective, verifiable, and preagreed performance indicators, we believe, can and should play a vital role in ensuring the development of a truly common, single set of codified rules to govern the policies, programs, and activities of a *Better United Nations System*. The role of the PCB in the interpretation and development of policies, and in coordinating their implementation, as explained in Chapter 8, will be crucial for the success of this approach.

At the same time, it would be helpful if an early effort is made to coordinate the policy formulation and program development activities of the present United Nations System with major entities in the intergovernmental sphere that also deal with the same set of issues at the national, regional or global levels. Indisputably, the G-7 is the most influential group in all areas of international affairs, whether economic or political, with the summit of this group usually setting the norms and practices for others to follow. Other global, regional, and subregional organizations like the European Union, the OAU, the Asia-Pacific Economic Cooperation (APEC), and their counterparts in other regions, also have influence that sometimes exceeds that of the United Nations System itself. Since these organizations have tasks and objectives not too dissimilar from those of the United Nations, it would be reasonable, therefore, that their capabilities and resources be coordinated to be more productive and effective.

As a first step, the need for such coordination should be acknowledged and channels of communication established linking the United Nations System with such groups and organizations. The existence of the Internet and the World Wide Web has made such consultations and information sharing an easy and cost-effective possibility. It is only a matter of applying astute and farsighted leadership and vision in order to translate this concept into reality.

The *Better United Nations System* must have a staff governed by a common set of rules and regulations, with no exceptions, including a common United Nations Administration of Justice as a basic requirement for an effective and unified United Nations personnel system. Staff should be secure in their conviction of fairness and equity, and when necessary such machinery would provide the possibility of resorting to the International Court of Justice (ICJ). However, the enlargement of the network, by inclusion of other non-United Nations intergovernmental organizations, may entail a rethinking of the conditions of service of the personnel in the United Nations proper as well as in the component parts of the System. This will include rethinking the modalities for hiring, training, promoting, motivating, disciplining and terminating employment of the staff at all levels. In short, human resources management would have to be overhauled, perhaps along the lines of many modern transnational corporate entities. A greater use of competitive examinations would have to be made for hiring professional staff. This should not be limited, as it is at the United Nations proper, to the more junior levels.

The ability to draw fresh talent from the private sector and national governments would have to be enhanced at all levels of professional staff, including the director (D1 and D2) levels. A competitive salary structure and conditions of employment, greater professionalism, and depoliticization of recruitment are issues that require systemic and system-wide solutions. In the first place, the Bretton Woods Institutions must agree to a system-wide arrangement. Otherwise, this would encourage other organizations (as in the case of the WTO) to break away from the common system. If the common system conditions are not adequate, these should be improved. The *Better United Nations System* should never deny fair conditions to its staff. In the long run, the extra costs would certainly result in higher productivity.

Without these measures, a mere reduction in the size of the system-wide bureaucracy may only demoralize those who remain. In that situation, the cost of United Nations System might decrease, but productivity and effectiveness would decrease even more. The PCB would, therefore, have to review the scope and mandate of the International Civil Service Commission in this regard, and make recommendations for an improved body that would have the trust and confidence of all the organizations and their staff. At the same time, the Office of Internal Oversight Services (OIOS), at the United Nations headquarters could play a role in overseeing the human resource functions system-wide. In view of the creation of the OIOS, the role and functions, or even the existence, of the JIU needs to be considered afresh and the two entities may be amalgamated.

TO KEEP THE BEST OF THE UNITED NATIONS PROPER AND THE BEST OF THE UNITED NATIONS SYSTEM

The ILO and the Tripartite System

The application of the yardstick of relevance developed earlier would help in ascertaining the relevant parts of the United Nations and the System that should survive. The previous chapter dealt with the United Nations proper. Here, we concentrate on the United Nations System, that is, on the Specialized Agencies. While discarding inefficient machinery and expired projects and programs, elements that have proved useful and effective should be applied system-wide. In this regard, we strongly support the system-wide introduction of a tripartite system that would include, apart from representatives of Member States, representatives of *civil society* and parliament. As explained earlier, we prefer a broad definition of *civil society* that includes the business or market sector as well.

The tripartite system of the ILO, which brings together representatives of governments, employers, and workers in its executive bodies, has worked very well from the beginning in the General Conference of the ILO, namely, the International Labour Conference, which is its plenary organ. Every state has two representatives of government and one representative from each side of the labor market – the employers and the workers. This tripartite mode of representation exists in all the subsidiary organs of the ILO by virtue of special rules on nomination and voting. For example, of the 56 members of the governing body, 28 are government members, 14 employer members, and 14 worker members. States of chief industrial importance permanently hold ten of the government seats. Representatives of other Member States are elected at the Conference every three years, taking into account geographical distribution. The employers and workers elect their respective representatives.

This successful experiment with formalized tripartite representation, with over 87 annual sessions of the International Labour Conference, should be sufficient to convince one of the need to adopt the tripartite approach, with suitable modifications, for the General Assembly and the ECOSOC, to begin with. Of course, many of the other parts of the United Nations network, especially the Specialized Agencies, Funds and Programs, could also employ this tripartite model for their governing and plenary organs, adjusting the representation as necessary, depending on the nature of the work.

Civil Society and Humanitarian Activities

It is especially in the areas of humanitarian assistance, human rights, women and children's concerns and, of course, environmental issues, that *civil society* organizations have been playing a very significant role over an extended period of time. This participation is especially focussed and productive, for example, in the Office of the United Nations High Commissioner for Refugees (UNHCR) which, from its inception, has worked closely with *civil society*. A landmark in this cooperation was the PARinAC (Partners in Action) Global Conference in Oslo in 1994. The plan of action adopted in that conference has become the framework for the UNHCR's partnership activities with NGOs. Amongst other things, this framework seeks to:

(a) increase NGO participation in dialogues with national authorities concerning refugee policies and programs;
(b) encourage early involvement of national NGOs in the UNHCR's programs, including support and training to build local capacity; and
(c) encourage closer coordination between the UNHCR and NGOs and among NGOs themselves.

In 1998, the UNHCR entered into project agreements with 506 NGOs (400 national and 106 international) to implement operational activities involving USD265 million or approximately 25 percent of the UNHCR's 1998 budget. In addition, NGOs participate as observers in a Standing Committee of the Executive Committee of the UNHCR. In October 1998, the Executive Committee extended NGO observer participation through the year 2000. The UNHCR acknowledges that NGO involvement frequently makes the difference between failure and success. Besides 'traditional' cooperation in emergency deployment or in technical areas, such as the provision of water or shelter, the UNHCR and NGOs have pooled their complementary expertise in the fields of protection, advocacy, social services, and other sectors.

Red Cross and Red Crescent Societies

In the area of humanitarian assistance, the role of the International Federation of Red Cross and Red Crescent Societies (formerly called the League of Red Cross Societies) continues to be very important, and, therefore, merited examination, to see whether it had valuable lessons for other parts of the United Nations System.

The International Federation of Red Cross and Red Crescent Societies is an international humanitarian organization with a unique worldwide network. The Federation exists to improve the situation of the world's most vulnerable people. It provides assistance without discrimination as to nationality, race, religious beliefs, class, or political opinions. The Federation, founded in 1919, has a presence in almost every country in the world today through its national Red Cross and Red Crescent Societies. This global spread is supported by a Federation Secretariat in Geneva, Switzerland, and its 'delegations' strategically located to assist and advise Red Cross and Red Crescent activities in various regions of the world. This network enables an effective and rapid response to a crisis, which should be envied and reproduced by the United Nations Security Council. The Federation provides humanitarian relief to people affected by disasters or other emergencies as well as development assistance to empower vulnerable people to become self-sufficient.

The Governing Body of the Federation is its General Assembly, comprising all member national societies. This supreme organ of the Federation meets every two years. The smaller, elected Executive Council acts between meetings of the Assembly. The Federation Secretariat is responsible for coordination and cooperation in directing and mobilizing international relief assistance. It helps in planning and implementing disaster preparedness and long-term development programs, along with a multitude of other humanitarian activities including community based health care. It acts as the official representative of its member societies in the international field.

Apart from the Federation and the National Societies, the third element of the International Red Cross and Red Crescent 'Movement' is the International Committee of the Red Cross (ICRC), which is an impartial, neutral, and independent organization whose exclusively humanitarian mission is to protect the lives and dignity of victims of war and internal violence, and to provide them with assistance. It directs and coordinates the international relief activities conducted by the 'Movement' in situations of conflict. It also endeavors to prevent suffering by promoting and strengthening humanitarian law and universal humanitarian principles. Established in 1863, the ICRC is at the origin of the International Red Cross and Red Crescent Movement. All the three elements of the 'Movement' are guided by the same seven fundamental principles: humanity, impartiality, neutrality, independence, voluntary service, unity, and universality. The relevance of the ICRC is that it facilitates coordination and cooperation and fosters the best use of available resources, which are usually very scarce indeed.

In its field operations, the Federation depends on its Emergency Response Units (ERUs) which are standard units of trained personnel along with all their technical equipment. The ERUs are ready to be deployed at 48 hours notice and capable of working for up to three weeks before being integrated into a Federation 'delegation'. The ERUs are built up and trained by national Red Cross and Red Crescent societies and are deployed at the request of the Federation Secretariat into Federation programs. There are various types of specialized ERUs dealing with, for example, production and distribution of drinking water, providing sanitation facilities to large populations, providing basic health care facilities, providing first-level medical referral services, providing telecommunications facilities within a disaster area, and providing logistical support.

Between March 1996 and August 1999, 21 ERUs were deployed in Albania, Congo, Honduras, Kenya, Macedonia, Nicaragua, Nigeria, Peru, Poland, Rwanda, Tanzania, Turkey, and Uganda, to render assistance during earthquakes, hurricanes, the Balkan crisis, floods, and for the return of refugees. In many of these situations, the Federation works in close cooperation and coordination with the United Nations Office for the Coordination of Humanitarian Affairs (UNOCHA), the UNHCR, UNICEF, WHO, and others. When the resources and skills of the United Nations System are mobilized in this context, the system usually performs up to expectations. Should not this performance under the leadership of an organization outside the United Nations be considered significant enough to encourage duplicating it in other areas of United Nations endeavors?

When the initiative comes from outside the United Nations System, particularly in the humanitarian area, the results always appear to be better, and the United Nations input to it also more effective. There are many initiatives that the NGOs have taken on as a group. For example, the 'Sphere Project', launched in July 1997, seeks to develop a set of standards in core areas of humanitarian assistance in order to improve the quality of assistance provided to people affected by disasters, and to improve the accountability of the Specialized Agencies. In October 1998, the Sphere Project Management Committee, with the participation of over 700 individuals from over 228 organizations in over 60 countries, completed the preliminary edition of the *Sphere Humanitarian Charter and Minimum Standards in Disaster Response*. In 1999, the humanitarian agencies were testing its application and evaluating its usefulness as a working tool, with a view to improving it. As a major inter-agency collaborative process, the Sphere Project involves front line NGOs, donor governments and United Nations Specialized Agencies. Nongovernmental networks, namely, the *Steering Committee for Humanitarian Response* (SCHR) and *Inter Action* lead this effort, with VOICE (a consortium of European Voluntary Organizations In Cooperation in Emergencies), the ICVA (International

Council of Voluntary Agencies), and the ICRC hold observer status on the Project Management Committee. United Nations agencies including the UNHCR, the UNOCHA, the UNICEF, the WFP, and the WHO have also supported and directly participated in the project.

The SCHR, which comprises seven international networks, including the International Red Cross Movement, concerns itself with policy and strategic questions relating to humanitarian aid and, since the early 1970s, has been an avenue for dialogue with the United Nations System with regard to emergency response. With the establishment of the UNOCHA it was hoped that an effective coordinating mechanism in the United Nations would be created to respond to natural and complex disasters. While UNOCHA has played a very useful role, it still needs to become far more active and also more sensitive to the concerns of the *civil society* to be able to provide the looked-for complementarity and synergy in humanitarian responses worldwide. The recommendations in this respect made in *A Second Generation United Nations* are still valid.[1]

The basic point that we wish to emphasize is that the United Nations System has a lot to learn from the way *civil society* functions. The efforts made by the *civil society* organizations mentioned above, to respond effectively and in a flexible, transparent, and accountable manner to world needs and to come to grips with short-, medium- and long-term problems, have useful lessons for the various components of the United Nations System. This is not to imply that the United Nations System is alone in having something to learn from the *civil society* organizations. In fact, *civil society* organizations, like the rest of the community to which they belong, come in all shapes, sizes and colors, as, by their very nature, they are the products of a human response to specific challenges. As a result, their focus, at times, is very specialized and narrow. This often creates difficulties in their efforts to mobilize sufficient resources or to have a major impact at the macro level. There is no dearth of *civil society* organizations, that are not as effective as others and that, sometimes, mars the good name of the rest.

Our focus should remain, however, on learning systematically from the *civil society* organizations that have performed admirably over the years, decades and, sometimes, for well over a century. The need to learn is greater today than ever before, as the interdependence of nations is producing new stresses and strains on the fabric of intergovernmental organizations — whether these are under the influence of the United Nations System or outside it. For this reason alone, the *civil society* organizations deserve the place we recommend for them in the *Better United Nations*.

As stated earlier, it is not expected that the United Nations System is going to look very different at the start of the new millennium than it does now, as is shown in Diagram 1 (Current United Nations System) in Chapter 1. It would, however, certainly be more relevant, as a result of the series of reforms discussed earlier. It would also be more

---

[1] de Marco and Bartolo, *op. cit.*, pp. 112-113. It was proposed that the DHA (the predecessor of the OCHA) would not be involved in operations in the field but would concentrate its efforts towards ensuring a consolidated approach to emergencies by bringing all the necessary inputs together quickly and efficiently, without overlapping and duplication. Failing this, it was proposed to give this role to a more suitable organization in the System.

efficient and effective, as result of the closer cooperation with the *civil society* organizations, and, therefore, better prepared for the challenges that lie ahead.

THE BLUEPRINT – FOR A BETTER UNITED NATIONS SYSTEM

While examining a blueprint, one should look not so much at its actual contours but more at the rationale, principles, and vision behind its various elements and their inter-linkages. The *Better United Nations System* would be governed by one set of rules and procedures, whether this was at the level of governance or at the level of staff management. This would mean that all cooperation agreements between the Specialized Agencies and the United Nations, the General Assembly and other organs would have to be similar and standard. The Bretton Woods Institutions would be fully a part of this system, with a major role to play in directing and coordinating development assistance, in cooperation with other parts of the System and, even more importantly, with the major bilateral donors.

The WTO should seriously consider joining the United Nations System at the opportune time, but preferably sooner rather than later, before it moves even further away from it. In *A Second Generation United Nations,*[2] the WTO was left to function independently for two reasons. The first was that, as a newly created organization with a set of rules approved by consensus following a lengthy round of global negotiations on the modalities of world trade, it was considered reasonable to allow it to settle down first, before asking it to take any major decision on its relationship to other organizations and institutions. The second reason was that it was considered impractical to propose that the WTO join the United Nations System, before the United Nations had first put its own house in order. On the eve of the next global round of trade negotiations, it is now considered opportune that the WTO seriously consider joining the United Nations System, to take the lead in its area of competence, namely international trade, and to establish its niche in a *Better United Nations System* before it moves further away from it. The work in UNCTAD would be with emphasis on development and, therefore, would cooperate closely with the WTO.

In the aftermath of the Second World War, the leaders of the victorious powers, in particular, envisioned and realized a United Nations which sought to preserve for ever certain ground rules and assumptions. Much has changed since then. For example, the total number of countries in the world today is much larger than anyone could have imagined in the final years of the first half of this century. The political and economic strengths of many of the world powers of the 1940s have undergone major upheavals. In a certain sense, the playing field of the international arena has become more level, particularly in the political sphere.

In the other spheres, especially the economic and social, the disparities have increased, not only across international borders but also within countries and in certain countries even within neighborhoods. In these new and ever evolving circumstances, it is

---

[2] de Marco and Bartolo, *op. cit.,* p. 95.

too much to assume that a State-centered United Nations Charter and a State-centered organizational structure is all that the world can and should have. As suggested earlier, there is still considerable scope for constructive interpretation of the Charter of the United Nations to enable, in practice, a necessary and greater democratization of the intergovernmental system. If *'we the peoples'* has to be translated into a meaningful vision, which is relevant to present times, then *civil society*, including the business community, together with parliaments will have to play a much bigger role in *A Better United Nations for the New Millennium*.

The dependence of the present system on the interaction of representatives of governments alone is not adequate to meet the challenges of our era, in which the democratic credentials of a very large number of countries in the developing world are still not firmly established. In fact, for short-term considerations, even the most advanced and democratic countries have supported governments and regimes whose track record was blemished by outright violation of international norms especially in the field of human rights.

In a world where the western concepts of human dignity and human rights seem to have been accepted by more and more peoples with totally different cultural, social, and political traditions, in Asia, Africa, Latin America, and the Arab World, there is an absolute need to support and nurture such aspirations at the international level in the United Nations System. We reiterate that this can be done by enhancing the status of *civil society* organizations and of parliamentarians, including representatives of the political parties sitting on the opposition benches, through creative mechanisms that enable their voice to be heard in international forums and organizations. In some situations, this may take on a feminist flavor, when women's issues are taken up. In other situations, it may respond to special concerns, such as child labor or child soldiers. Without ensuring a principled, transparent, ethical, and open debate and discussion, it will not be possible to resolve such issues to the satisfaction of all, and, in particular, to the satisfaction of those affected.

It, therefore, stands to reason that a hallmark of a *Better United Nations System* will be most of the present Specialized Agencies, the major ones of which have passed the test of relevance in their areas of specialization. No doubt, greater coordination of the positions taken by the national delegations, along with the inputs from *civil society* and parliamentarians will help in further improving their focus for reducing overlap and duplication in the work of the United Nations System.

In a *Better United Nations*, the United Nations proper would be much more rational and focused, as it would have given up a large number of economic and social activities as well as operational activities, be they of a humanitarian or developmental nature. Only then would the Secretary-General be able to devote the time and energy required for the more urgent political and security matters and to the PCB, which would need his direct intervention, in order to carry out its mandated tasks. The PCB must have a long-term strategic perspective to guide its day-to-day work. It should operate in a transparent manner with its accountability mechanisms to the Member States strengthened by its direct relationship with the ECOSOC and the General Assembly.

It is, therefore, clear to us that the *Better United Nations System* would include only those elements of the present system that have passed the test of relevance. Thereafter, for the purpose of efficiency and effectiveness, their organizational links would have to be adjusted, modified, and refashioned so that a rational division of labor exists. The United Nations System, in addition to including the Bretton Woods Institutions and the WTO, would seek to absorb major elements of the existing intergovernmental bodies and entities, which are at present outside its ambit.

A BETTER UNITED NATIONS SYSTEM
A HOLISTIC APROACH

A *Better United Nations System* would, in turn, ensure that all existing institutions, whether international or regional, would not duplicate the work being done within the System.

We have focused on a holistic approach, as that is one way of harmonizing the approaches of different Member States, different types and levels of *civil society* organizations, and of parliamentarians in responding to the global challenges. Some 50 years ago, the overwhelming concern was in preventing the recurrence of a 'World War', while today global, regional, or national security is hardly threatened by military adventurism, with very rare exceptions. Increasingly, in today's world, the complex issues concerning nations, big and small, are climate change, environmental degradation, loss of biodiversity, continuing rapid growth of populations, water scarcity, economic instability, terrorism, and the like. The international community is expected to respond to intrastate conflicts and national fragmentation in a globalizing and highly interdependent world – such are the paradoxes and contradictions created by the legalistic and theoretical underpinnings of the existing institutions at the international level. There is a need to depart from too rigid a theoretical basis, and be guided by ethical concerns which respond to the needs and aspirations of the most needy, so that the interdependence of all living and nonliving things on our planet is managed in a global and holistic perspective to plan for a complete transformation of the material, moral, and spiritual dimensions of human existence, with a view to achieving the greatest happiness for all in the long run.

A *Better United Nations System* is foreseen as a small step in this direction. It is a quest on a journey during which we will be satisfied if we are making progress in the right direction, for who knows when we shall arrive at the final destination. As in the case of a *Better United Nations* proper we do not hold any illusions that a *Better United Nations System* would be accepted by all concerned. The objectives and priorities of individual countries and, above all, the concept of what the United Nations System should do, are so different and varied, that to reach a consensus on this matter is well nigh impossible. We have kept this stark reality in mind when making our recommendations and proposals. This is just an honest and pragmatic approach to the question of the reform of the United Nations proper or the United Nations System. There is no doubt that the matter is now in the hands of Member States. There is no doubt that the Millennium General Assembly and the preparations for this will discuss the matter fully. But let there be no doubt that changes will come. Let us take part in this quiet and gradual revolution with vision and perseverance, and let us not give the more violent elements reason to gain the upper hand.

CONCLUSION

THE BLUEPRINT AND THE VISION

SUMMARY

International institutions are usually the result and the product of the world at a certain time. Times change and so should the institutions. This book is an attempt to reflect on how the important institutions, which are the subject of this study, should reflect the changes in the world and its affairs. It is common knowledge that, while events in the world have their own dynamics, institutions usually suffer from a lack of similar dynamics, and tend to propagate with little or no relevance to what is happening around them. It is for this reason that the institutions occasionally need to be administered a dose of reality, and be brought back to relevance. Those that fail to shape up should also fail to survive. Diagrams supplement the blueprint, and the vision attempts to project it into the future.

ANY ORGANIZATION CAN ONLY BE AS RELEVANT AND AS EFFECTIVE AS THE MEMBER STATES WANT IT TO BE

The United Nations is a product of its Founding Members and it functions as the most influential of them intend it to function, considering the conditions prevailing at the time. The problem is that when these conditions change, institutions do not change as rapidly, or not at all.

The problem of change for an organization as complex as the United Nations becomes more challenging because the membership has increased and the Founding Members are no longer in the majority. The objectives for the Organization in the opinion of the present majority may not coincide with the objectives of some of those Founding Members. This factor has been observed in the reform debate since its beginning. One

169

has only to look at the stalemate, primarily in the work undertaken by the *ad hoc* group on the Security Council, and also in the work undertaken by other *ad hoc* groups.

We kept this sobering thought in mind while making some realistic assumptions and following some practical guidelines, adopting as pragmatic an approach as possible.

One question that is not asked often enough in the debate on United Nations reform is whether the original drafters of the United Nations Charter would have approved of the Organization as it actually developed. We think that the promise, high ideals, and yearning for universal participation in the proceedings and decisions of the Organization, as enshrined in the Charter, were not reflected in the United Nations that was established, and are still not reflected in the United Nations of today. Something strange happened on the way to the Conference in San Francisco. We see another gap here, between the ideals and promise put forward by the eminent personalities who drafted proposals of the Charter at Dumbarton Oaks and the blueprint put together by the technocrats and bureaucrats who journeyed to San Francisco.[1]

National and Global Priorities and Targets do not Always Coincide – This may be One of the Major Problems with United Nations Relevance and Effectiveness

It should be the major task of international organizations to narrow the gap between national and global objectives. That is why we think that such a task could be more realistically accomplished with the intervention of regional organizations, to which more work should be decentralized. The rationale for this is that the organizations in the regions normally have priorities and targets which are closer to those of the countries in those regions.

If one puts the yardstick of relevance developed in Chapter 3 in this context, one may see rather dramatically the various gaps and paradoxes that slow and sometimes block completely the road to reform. For example, is it in the interest of the most powerful Member States to make the United Nations more universal, not in numbers only, but also in influence, as implied by the Charter of the United Nations, and as quoted in the first and foremost condition of the yardstick of relevance? The answer is clearly no. It has been obvious that no Member State is ready to relinquish its present control and influence in the Organization by democratizing it in the spirit of the Charter, for example, by surrendering the rights and privileges of the veto in the Security Council. If anything, we see a movement in the opposite direction, in the actions of other countries wishing to join

---

[1] It must be pointed out that the Charter passed through three formal stages before being approved in San Francisco on 24 June 1945. The first stage was the intellectual stage at Dumbarton Oaks, at a meeting of diplomatic experts from the four great powers of that time, namely the United States, the United Kingdom, the Soviet Union, and China, which took place from 21 August to 7 October 1944. These eminent personalities could be referred to as the Founding Fathers of the Charter, and therefore of the United Nations. The second stage was the Yalta Conference, where at the political summit level, the question of voting (i.e., the veto) and the question of membership (i.e., seats for the Soviet Republics), left over from Dumbarton Oaks, were resolved. The third stage was the final approval of the Charter in the San Francisco Conference, by diplomatic representatives of the 26 Founding Members of the United Nations.

the ranks of the five permanent Members of the Security Council, arguing that this would reflect better the present political and economic situation in the world. The question of the right to veto in the Security Council is one instance where the national and global priorities and objectives do not coincide, or even come close to doing so.

Concerning the second condition of the yardstick of relevance on poverty, we see the phenomenon, mentioned earlier as another important gap, that statements in this case do not coincide with deeds. Especially at the highest levels, it is common to hear statements and pledges to eradicate poverty but they are not followed up with real or significant action. All the projects and programs to eradicate poverty have fallen greatly below expectations. The figures referred to in the Introduction are undeniable evidence of this.

In the area of economic and social affairs, as stated in the third condition of the yardstick of relevance, national and global priorities certainly do not coincide, and they never will, unless the marginalization of most of the developing countries, in efforts towards globalization, is stopped.

Similarly, in the political area, the fourth condition of the yardstick of relevance, the chasm between national and global priorities and objectives is probably the most striking. One need only reflect on the conflicts of the recent past to draw this conclusion. The analysis of the other conditions of the yardstick of relevance also points to the same conclusion.

As stated more than once earlier, proof of the good intentions of the major players to support meaningful reform of the United Nations and the System, will come only with the proof that they are ready to bridge the gap between national and global priorities and objectives.

Some Necessary Reflections

The United Nations was never intended to solve all the problems of the world. It simply cannot. So it is very important to keep realistic expectations of what the United Nations can do. On the other hand, the United Nations should not take upon itself impossible tasks, and should resist becoming a dumping ground for perennial problems.

It is also important to understand that, in an organization with a system of democratic governance, every single Member State has to be given the opportunity to express its views. The decision-making process becomes more complex for these reasons.

We, therefore, gave the most prominence to the United Nations General Assembly, where every Member State is equal, since every country has one vote.

In the context of reform, the consensus process may not work, so the only alternative is to take the decision to the highest organ, the General Assembly, and to the highest level of participation, the summit level, without forgetting the necessary participation proposed earlier, namely *civil society* and parliaments. As seen from experience, the positions of the various groups, which we see most often causing the stalemate in the debate on reform of the United Nations, are seen to be less rigid at the summit level. Therefore, there are more chances of reaching agreement on them at that highest level. It is for this reason that we think that, if there is a chance of an agreement or consensus, it has to be at that level.

Diagram 10. Transformation from the Current to the Better United Nations

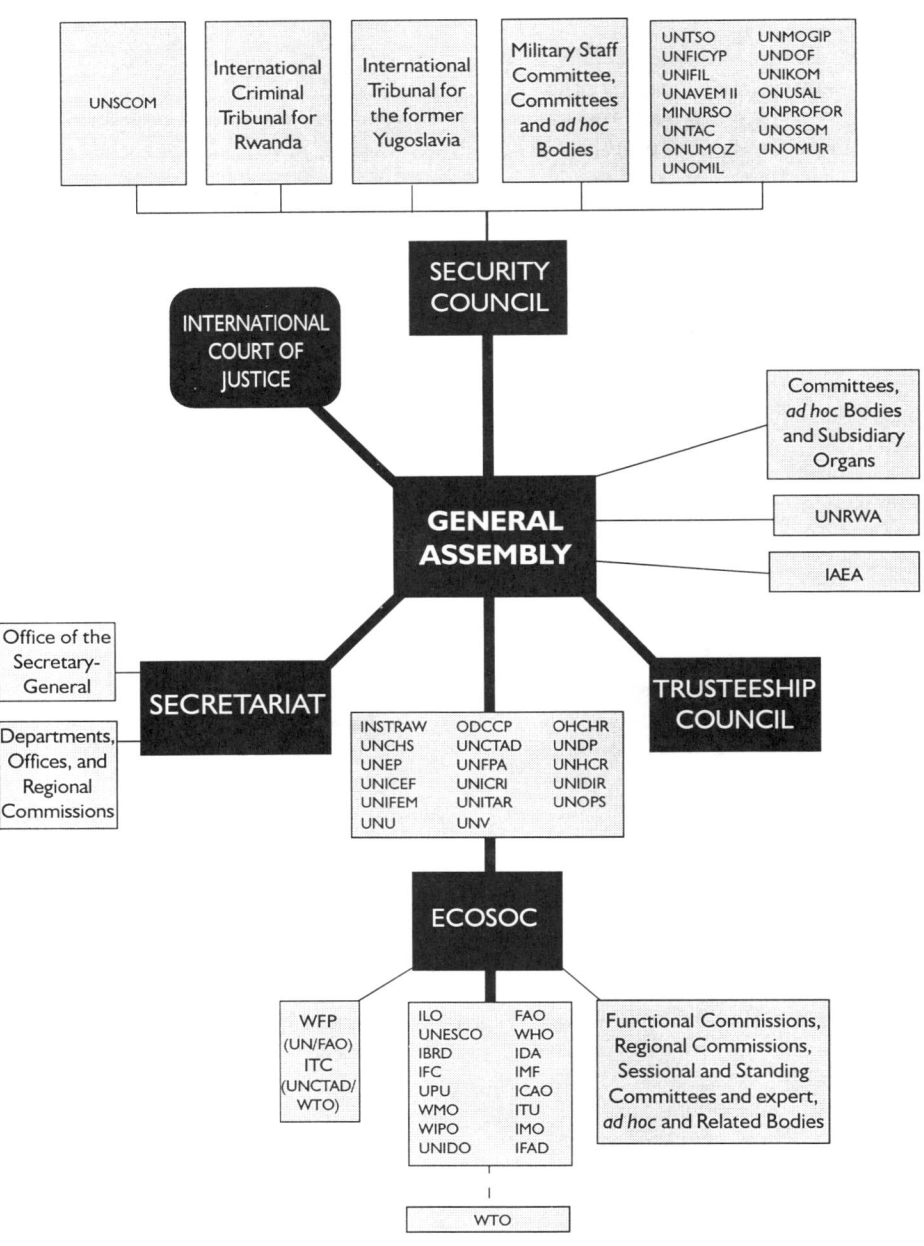

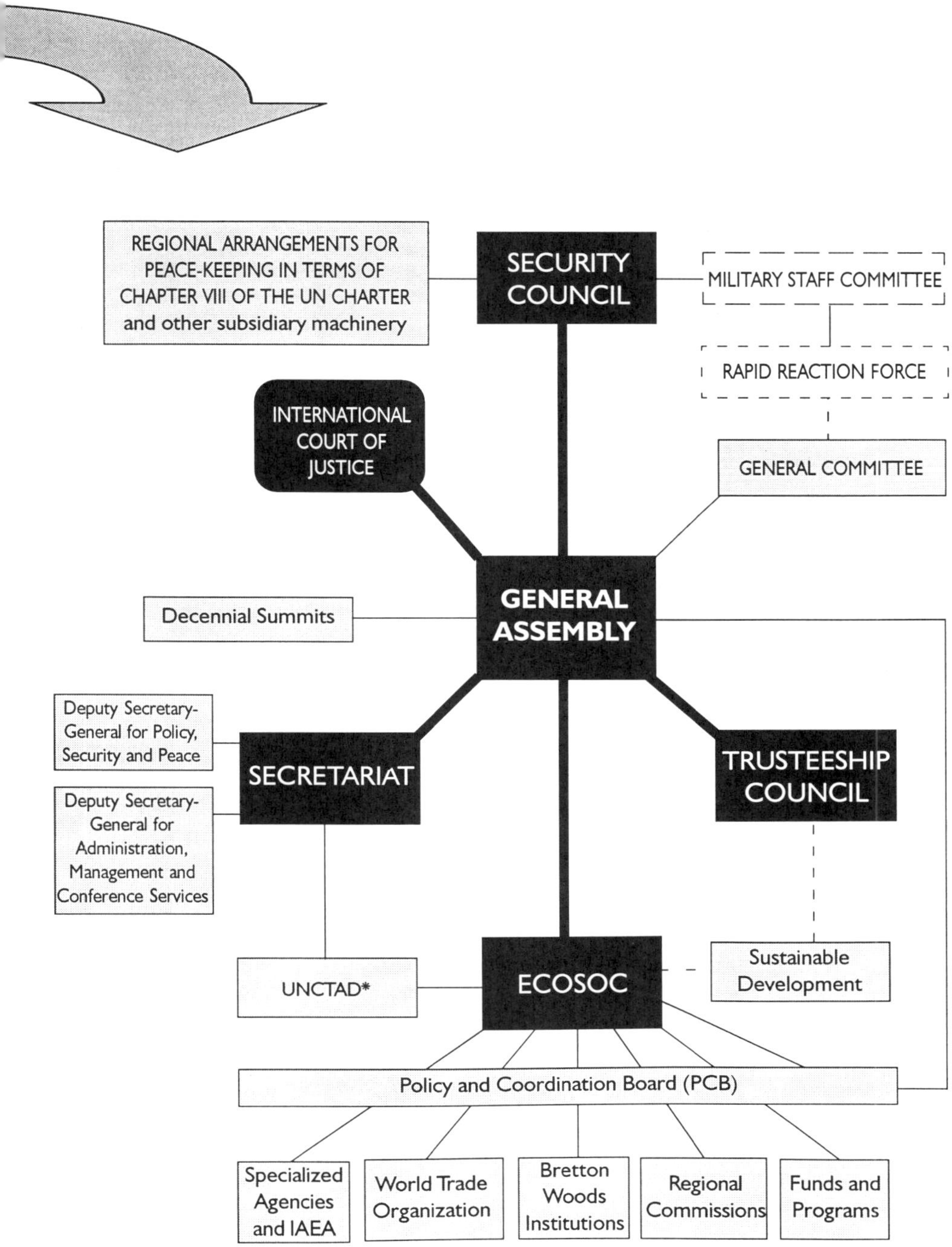

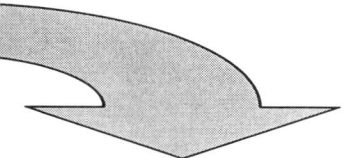

REGIONAL ARRANGEMENTS FOR PEACE-KEEPING IN TERMS OF CHAPTER VIII OF THE UN CHARTER and other subsidiary machinery	**SECURITY COUNCIL**

MILITARY STAFF COMMITTEE

RAPID REACTION FORCE

GENERAL COMMITTEE

INTERNATIONAL COURT OF JUSTICE

GENERAL ASSEMBLY

Decennial Summits

Deputy Secretary-General for Policy, Security and Peace

SECRETARIAT

Deputy Secretary-General for Administration, Management and Conference Services

TRUSTEESHIP COUNCIL

UNCTAD*

ECOSOC

Sustainable Development

Policy and Coordination Board (PCB)

Specialized Agencies and IAEA	World Trade Organization	Bretton Woods Institutions	Regional Commissions	Funds and Programs

* UNCTAD: Also acts as Secretariat of ECOSOC.

Diagram 11. Transformation from the ACC to the PCB

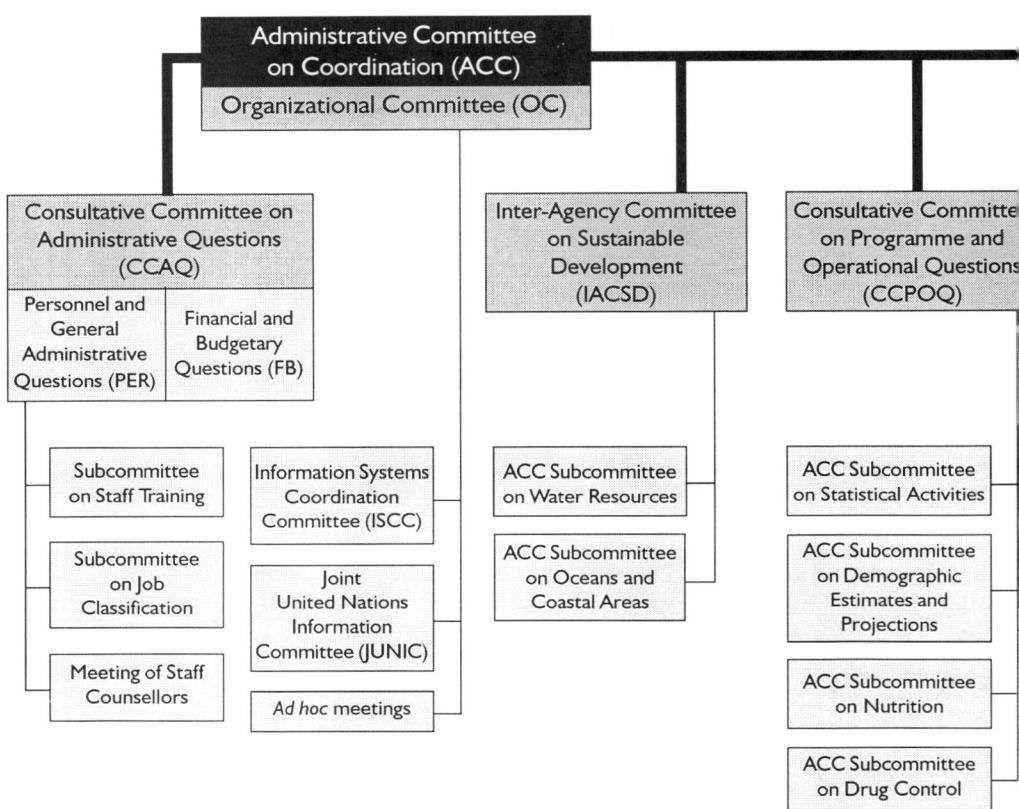

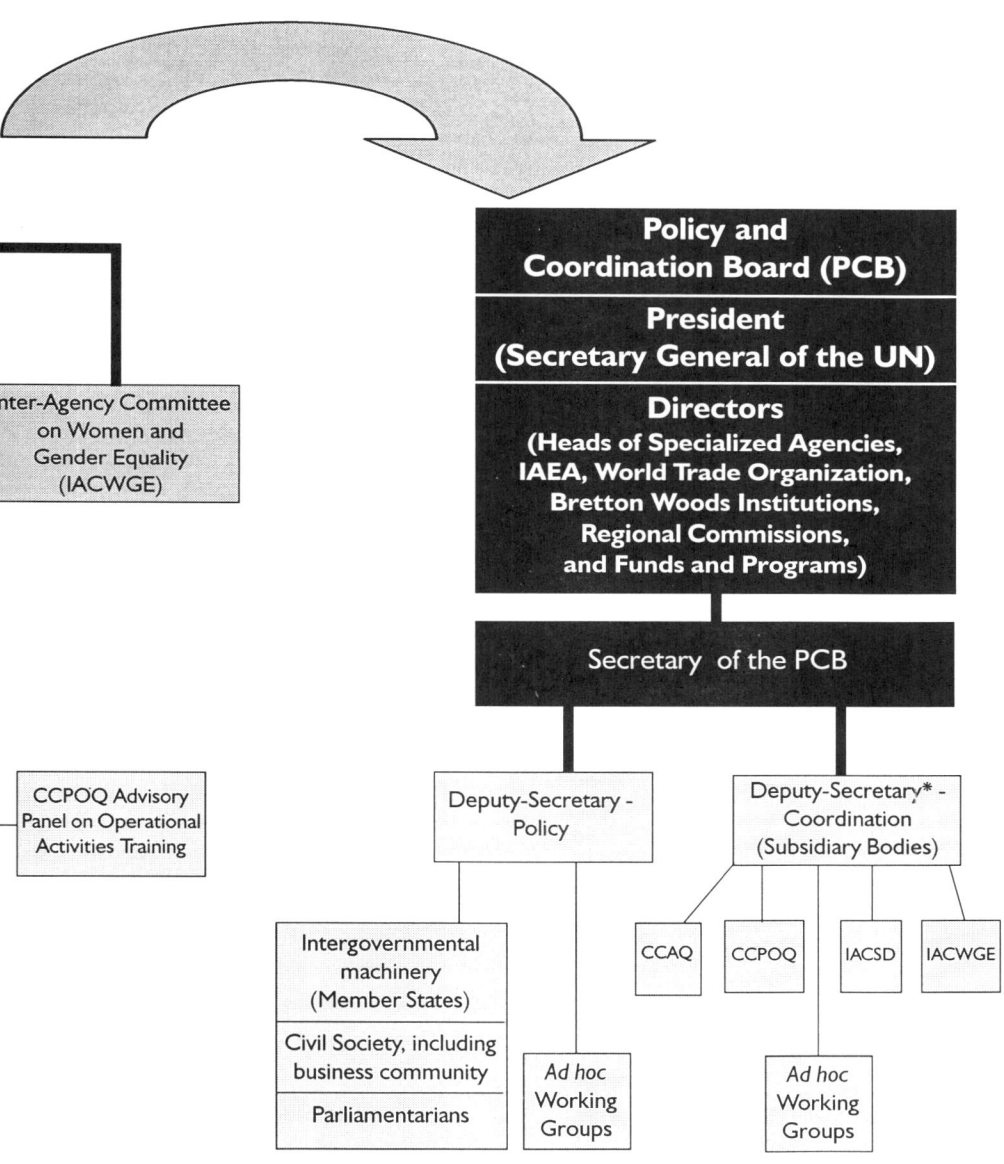

* Alternatively, to be divided between a Deputy-Secretary for the Consultative Committee on Administrative Questions (CCAQ), and a Deputy-Secretary for the Consultative Committee on Programme and Operational Questions (CCPOQ), the Inter-Agency Committee on Sustainable Development (IACSD), and the Inter-Agency Committee on Women and Gender Equality (IACWGE).

THE BLUEPRINT

Chapter 9 gives the blueprint of the *Better United Nations*, which we think passes the tests of relevance and goes a long way in the area of streamlining, which is reflected in the cost savings pointed out in Annex IV. The *Better United Nations System*, as seen from Chapter 10, did not require so striking a change to pass the tests of relevance owing to the areas of specialization. Some agencies did, however, need drastic streamlining and realignment. A completely new and transformed Policy and Coordination Board (PCB) would ensure the necessary coordination in the system and necessary cooperation with the Member States and the organizations outside the System. The two diagrams in this chapter present the *Better United Nations* and the *Better United Nations System* and the transformation of the ACC into the PCB pictorially. The blueprint would include the following highlights, which can be seen graphically in Diagram 10, which compares the current United Nations with the proposed *Better United Nations*.

The result would be a United Nations that is much closer to the vision and hopes of the original drafters of the Charter rather than to the actual Charter itself. It would be a United Nations which still falls short of a utopian United Nations but is still more representative of the wishes and hopes of the majority, and, therefore, more relevant to their needs and priorities.

A United Nations with a reformed General Assembly is proposed, supreme in governance and overseeing a United Nations that is relevant and streamlined to the core, recognizing the full autonomy and expertise of the System, including the Bretton Woods Institutions and the WTO, and supplemented by other outside global, regional and subregional institutions, functioning also as part of the System.

A new Security Council is proposed, eventually with no veto and with wider representation, supported by an ECOSOC as originally conceived in the Charter and a Trusteeship Council updated and refocused to respond to the concerns and priorities of present and future realities. Dispute settlement machinery is proposed, under the supervision of the International Court of Justice (ICJ), whose authority needs to be recognized and accepted *ipso facto* with membership in the United Nations.

A Policy and Coordination Board (PCB) is proposed, bonding the United Nations and the system and taking the lead in policy and coordination, by involving the tripartite partners and other institutions outside the United Nations in giving impetus to the work of the United Nations and the System. The transformation of the ACC into the PCB is shown in Diagram 11.

A less costly United Nations System is foreseen that would introduce strategic planning and results-oriented budgeting, first to the organizations of the System and later to all other organizations outside the System but cooperating with the United Nations.

A United Nations System is proposed that concentrates its method of work around groups working on issues, rather than around geographical groups, and supported by contributions from various quarters, as long as these contributions are the most competitive in quality and cost.

THE VISION

We are not naïve enough to think that our proposals have a chance of being accepted by all, without any reservations or modifications. In fact, we are aware of the fact that some of our proposals go against the traditional positions of both the South and the North, and, therefore, neither side will be fully satisfied. In spite of this we think that it is opportune to make an objective study for the best alternative United Nations, presented without political constraints and seen from a perspective wider than that of any one country or group of countries.

It is not the intention to criticize anyone in this book. Neither is it a reflection on individuals, whenever posts or parts of the United Nations are identified for abolition. This is not a call for a quick and violent revolution, because we know that such a strategy will not work. This is a rational call for things to change – on terms agreed to by the most influential countries, the only ones who can foster change.

This is an effort to develop institutions that can facilitate this change. These institutions, led by the United Nations, supported by an ACC transformed into a PCB, have to show that change is necessary, not only for the benefit of the poor, but also for the developed and advanced countries: these countries, by improving the life of those presently poor, are going to ensure their own continued progress by developing a world that can exploit the advances in science and technology for wider benefits to be enjoyed by more people. To do this, the people themselves will have to take the initiative to make the United Nations, and other international institutions, work for them. It will also be easier, in this context, to harness the power of the private corporations, particularly those at the cutting edge of technology, whether in communications, pharmaceuticals or some other area, to find solutions to problems of poverty. Here, we are referring not to charity but to ingenious and innovative endeavors that are rewarding to the corporations as well. Therefore, this scenario is advantageous to all.

Few doubt the advantages of globalization. The concern here is that the advantages are not distributed fairly, and that the system of free trade and commerce needs an institution to transfer some of these gains to the less competitive countries, until these countries can compete in a fairer market, where the playing field has been leveled and the strengths of the players made more, and not less, equal. As pointed out again and again, the present structure of trade and financial flows needs to change. It would be a folly not to heed this warning.

For us, it is not the time frame for reform or change that is most important, but the very need to realize the fact that this change is necessary and, just as important, that there is an agreement to start the process of renewal. As we have said already, one cannot change a situation overnight that has developed over centuries. This will take time. What has to take priority is the understanding of the problem and the decision to correct it.

It is the Member States, with the help of the *Better United Nations*, in the context of the tripartite arrangement proposed, that would have to work out the details and the time frame. We think that the *Better United Nations*, as proposed, can be instrumental in this regard. It is now for the governments to take the decisive steps, in the full knowledge that those governments whether elected by the people or not should represent the people.

Governments are also brought down by the people, whether in a democratic process or otherwise.

It is, for these reasons that we propose a United Nations, which, recognizing the urgent need for reform, should steer itself in the right direction, as soon as possible. But no deadlines are set for its complete overhaul, either as proposed in the *Better United Nations* or in the more drastic transformation proposed in Annex III. Setting unrealistic deadlines would hamper and probably even prevent any progress. The crucial part of the vision is to recognize the problem and to set in motion the steps necessary for a solution. If it is to take another fifty years, let it be so.

The alternatives to this vision would not augur well for peace, security, and economic well-being in the new millennium.

We do not underestimate the objections that some of the proposals of the *Better United Nations* would encounter. We do not overlook the nearly impossible task of trying to bridge the chasm between the views of the developed and the developing countries, not only on substantive subjects, but also on matters concerning reform. But we have not shied away from making an honest and comprehensive contribution to the debate on United Nations reform. We believe that our contribution is free of political constraints and is objective and fair to all concerned. We do this, fully conscious of the fact that in the end it is the Member States, and only the Members States, that have the authority to deliberate effectively on an issue as important as the reform of the United Nations, and certainly only the Member States can decide the outcome. This responsibility rests very clearly on the Member States. Let it be recorded that no stone was left unturned to assume this responsibility, with the intention that the United Nations of the new millennium would not only be better, but would also be fairer. It would be a *Better United Nations* because it would facilitate changes in the world to benefit more people. It is for this reason that the *Better United Nations* would also be a fairer United Nations.

ANNEX I

COMPARATIVE ADVANTAGE – ITS USE AND MISUSE IN THE DEBATE ON THE REFORM OF THE UNITED NATIONS

COMPARATIVE ADVANTAGE AND UNITED NATIONS REFORM

The term *comparative advantage* is significant in the context of the debate on reform of the United Nations for two reasons. The first is the importance of the term for free trade in the present international economic relations and the role that international organizations play, particularly at this stage of the debate on globalization. The second is the constant misuse of the term in the debate on reform. For these two reasons, it is important to take some time to understand the real meaning of the term *comparative advantage*.

ABSOLUTE VS COMPARATIVE ADVANTAGE

Before David Ricardo, who introduced the concept of *comparative advantage* in the 19th century, economic theory as it related to trade was much simpler. This probably made people happier because they understood and accepted Adam Smith's *absolute advantage*, which appeared to them straightforward enough. The gains from trade in Adam Smith's time, a century before Ricardo, resulted from specialization. This meant that in a simple example of two countries and two products, each country specialized in the product in which it had an *absolute advantage*, namely, in the product that it was better at producing than the other country.

If, for example, the first country was better at producing clothes, while the second country was better at producing beer, when the two countries produced the item they were better at, the end result was that total production was greater. By trading, both countries benefited from the gains.

In this example, one has to assume that both countries had an *absolute advantage* in one of the two products, clothes or beer. Otherwise, the example would not apply. In other words there could only have been gains from trade when there was specialization. What a happy and simple world!

With Ricardo, namely with *comparative advantage*, things would be different and somewhat more complicated. In the case of *comparative advantage* there would always be gains from trade. To take the same example, even if one country was not as good as the other in producing either of the two products, it would still have had a *comparative advantage* in one of the products. It would have had a *comparative advantage* in the product where the margin of inferiority was smaller. Alternatively, the country that was better in producing both products would still have a *comparative advantage* in only one product, namely, in the product where its margin of superiority was greater.

The reader has to take our word for this. The alternative would be to consult a basic economics text and to go through the logic, the graphs and accompanying figures that convincingly show the mystery, or for some the miracle, of trade and gains from it, resulting from the theory or doctrine of *comparative advantage*. In real life, however, as stated in the main text (see particularly the Introduction), things are not that simple, and not everyone shares in the gains from trade.

DAVID RICARDO, ZINEDINE ZIDANE AND JACQUES CHIRAC

David Ricardo is known as an 19th century economist, mentioned above for his theory of *comparative advantage*. Zinedine Zidane is the hero of the 1998 football (soccer) World Cup, when France beat Brazil with a score of 3-0, two of the goals being scored by Zidane. He is certainly the best in France and arguably also in Europe and the World. Jacques Chirac is the President of France and the ardent supporter of the World Cup champions, France.

No one would argue that Zidane is best at playing football. Those who saw him play would also agree that he is very athletic and a good sprinter. It would, therefore, be fair to conclude that Zidane is better than President Chirac at both football and sprinting. So he has an *absolute advantage* in both. But it would be a grave mistake in the light of what we learned above, however, to say that he has a *comparative advantage* in both football and sprinting. Zidane is better at football than at sprinting, so if he would be asked to choose his best activity he would have to choose football. According to the logic of the theory of *comparative advantage*, it would be correct to say then that President Chirac has a *comparative advantage* over Zidane at sprinting. Incredible though it may sound it is perfectly correct to come to that conclusion because President Chirac is less inferior (his margin of inferiority is smaller) to Zidane at sprinting than at football. On the other hand Zidane has a *comparative advantage* over President Chirac at football because he is superior (his margin of superiority is greater) in football than in sprinting.

The conclusion is very clear. If the national coach of France has to fill, according to *comparative advantage*, two vacant spots for the millennium games, one in football and one in sprinting and the two candidates are Zidane and President Chirac, he would have no alternative but to select Zidane for football and President Chirac for sprinting. On the other hand, if the selector applies the *absolute advantage* criteria Zidane would get both spots. In actual fact the coach would use neither of these two criteria and would, in this example, simply use his common sense and fill the two spots with Zidane.

The term *comparative advantage* has a specific meaning and significance and should only be used in the right context. Any different use, such as the way it is normally used in the debate on United Nations reform, is bound to be wrong.

THE USE OF COMPARATIVE ADVANTAGE

Most of the supporters of free trade use Ricardo's theory of *comparative advantage* as the justification for the present system of international trade. However, as in other parts of economic theory, the assumptions, that one has to make, take the situation further away from real life. The debate on terms of trade referred to in the Introduction is only one such example. Analysis of empirical evidence did not support the theory that all countries gain from free trade. The present debate on globalization and the marginalization of the poorer countries revisits some of the argumentation of the previous debate on the terms of trade.

THE MISUSE OF COMPARATIVE ADVANTAGE

When the term is used, as it is often done, in the debate on United Nations reform to show, for example, the superiority or advantage of one agency or entity over another, it is always used wrongly. It is also used wrongly when a country, or anyone for that matter, calls for a specific agency or entity of the United Nations to concentrate its work in an area where it has a *comparative advantage*.

In both examples given above, an agency or an entity may have a *comparative advantage* in an area and yet another agency or entity can be better in that area. It is certain that the intention is not to abolish the better agency or entity and keep the other, which is not as good.

It should not be implied that only Member States make this mistake. A look at the literature on United Nations reform would show that this practice is also prevalent within the United Nations, where sometimes managers try to convince Member States that they have a *comparative advantage* over other managers.

FINAL WORD

It appears that, since the term *comparative advantage* sounds nice, and some may feel good about using it because it sounds scholarly, it will continue to be misused in some quarters, particularly by the media. We do not think that this should cause undue concern. The term in this book is used correctly. We hope that from now on others too will use it correctly.

ANNEX II

EXPERT COMMENTS
FROM SOME EMINENT PEOPLE

We wish to thank all those who provided help, comments, and encouragement during our work on this book. Their input helped us significantly to sharpen the focus of the thoughts and ideas that have been put forth in this book. First and foremost, we wish to convey our gratitude to the former President of South Africa, Mr. Nelson Mandela, for providing the clarity and perspective embodied in the foreword, which served as our constant guide. We are also indebted to the President of Malta, Professor Guido de Marco, for sharing his deep insight and concern about the need and nature of reforms required to create a *Better United Nations* for the new millennium and for contributing the preface for the book.

We were particularly encouraged by the enthusiastic support that we received from many in the international diplomatic community, most of whom have themselves done a considerable amount of thinking and writing about reforming the United Nations System. In particular, we wish to thank Mr. Francis Blanchard, former Director General of the International Labour Organization, Dame Margaret J. Anstee, former Under Secretary-General of the United Nations, Mr. Flavio Cotti, former Federal Counselor, Switzerland, and many of our colleagues in Geneva and elsewhere.

The support and ideas of the late President of Tanzania, Mr. Julius K. Nyerere, who was Chairman of the South Centre, have helped us in rethinking our draft at various points. We, therefore, are grateful for his ideas, good will, and encouragement.

In general, there was agreement that reform measures designed to make the United Nations System more relevant, integrated, and effective are needed today more than ever before. It was also generally agreed that, so far, there has been no dearth of excellent reform proposals, but these have remained largely on paper. The chief reason for their nonimplementation continues to be lack of political will. In addition, the resistance of the

United Nations bureaucracy and the absence of logical consistency in the agreed proposals arrived at after political compromises in the General Assembly, should never be allowed to thwart attempts to implement reforms.

We agree with many of those who commented that strong leadership at the top plays a crucial role in transforming an organization. Without it, any changes in the organigram or coordination structures alone will not bring about the desired results. At least one of them suggested a fundamental change in the method of selecting and appointing the Secretary-General and heads of Specialized Agencies, in that the best possible person be selected on the basis of an objective, independent assessment and not by political horse trading as happens in most cases. It was also suggested that there be a single term of office (no reelection) for all such top personnel, to ensure their independence and insulation from political pressure. We must hasten to add that this comment is not meant to be a criticism of the high quality and dedication of the personalities that are part of the present leadership of the United Nations and most of the Specialized Agencies. It is only the method of selection that is under scrutiny.

Many of the eminent persons have stressed that developing a shared vision in the whole United Nations System-wide bureaucracy is a key element for meaningful coordination. In other words, the 'missions' of all the United Nations Specialized Agencies and the United Nations proper should be 'aligned'. One of them has suggested that a single budget for the whole United Nations System would eliminate most of the coordination problems at once.

Many of them share our concern for defining 'security' in a broad, integrated context, so as to embrace sustainable economic and social development, just governance based on the rule of law and democratic principles, efforts at reduction of inequalities and disparities, and practical steps and measures to ensure equal treatment of all races, religions, sexes, and peoples. Only this approach, it was agreed, could provide a life of dignity and respect for everyone on this earth.

Many comments were made on the financial implications of the reform exercise. Some felt that an attempt should have been made to go into greater depth to determine the savings that would result from the proposed reforms. Others felt that financial savings should not be a primary concern, as the overall resources devoted to the United Nations System are rather small. In fact, they feel that more resources should be made available to the United Nations System, in a way that precludes undue influence being exerted by major donors. What is more important is that the available resources are utilized on relevant policies and programs, and in a manner which avoids duplication and waste.

One eminent person commented that the President of the PCB should not become a judge of his own actions. However, there was wide agreement that reform of the United Nations System could begin with reform of the ACC, although some wondered why give so much emphasis to a machinery that is hardly known outside of the United Nations.

One eminent person commented that the agreements between the United Nations and the Specialized Agencies were very verbose, and that this verbosity contributed to their ineffectiveness. Short, crisp and to the point agreements would improve cooperation significantly. Another commented that it was perhaps premature for the authors to reveal their long-term vision (presented in Annex III) at this stage. One eminent person commented that the book dealt too much with the past, including the League of Nations and that this was unnecessary, since the focus should be entirely on proposals for the future.

Another eminent person commented that it was too optimistic to even suggest the incorporation of other global, regional and subregional intergovernmental organizations into the United Nations System. At best, developing a working relationship with such non-United Nations organizations is all that could be considered in the foreseeable future.

Many of them supported the greater use of information technology in improving transparency, coordination, dialogue and information sharing. The need for constant exchange of views and dialogue, when an assembly, or committee, or working group was not in session, through a *quasi* 'chat room' on the Internet was considered by some to be a suggestion on the right lines.

Concerning development cooperation, one of the commentators referred to the continuing bickering over sharing of UNDP funds amongst the United Nations Specialized Agencies. This unproductive exercise was the result of lack of clarity concerning the relative importance of the programs and activities of the different Specialized Agencies and unclear guidelines for the planning, programming, monitoring and evaluation of technical cooperation activities.

Most agreed that it was time to review the representation element in the work of the United Nations. There was close to unanimous agreement on the involvement of the *civil society*, less so with regard to parliaments. The way to do this was also controversial.

Many of the suggestions have been taken into consideration. All their criticism has been given due attention, while we discussed and debated the various ideas and issues that have been elaborated in this book. While many of their comments have colored our final output, we ourselves remain solely responsible for the final product, particularly in so far as the shortcomings and errors are concerned. There were many other suggestions with which we were unable to agree. But even such important points of intellectual differences could only improve our final product. The differences of opinion continue to be essential elements for spurring further novel, creative thinking and for finding solutions in all areas of human endeavor.

ANNEX III

TRANSFORMING THE UNITED NATIONS SOME IDEAS

A GLOBAL ASSEMBLY
WITH TRIPARTITE MEMBERSHIP

A fundamental transformation of the United Nations calls for a radical approach that may require changes in the Charter of the United Nations. Without such changes the United Nations might find its role and importance rapidly diminishing in providing leadership for peace and security in the world. Such changes are also considered essential for increasing its relevance for effectively dealing with the other multifarious challenges before the global community.

The General Assembly is the only major organ of the United Nations where all Member States are permanent members, and, therefore, the only organ that can really empower all the peoples of the world, by allaying the suspicion that the United Nations is run by the five permanent members of the Security Council. It is crucial that the most important decisions should be taken at the level of the General Assembly. It is, therefore, this organ that needs to be strengthened above all others, to give the United Nations a new credibility and relevance. This is no Utopia. In Utopia there would be no need for a United Nations.

First and foremost, the title and structure of the General Assembly need to be changed. It would be more appropriate to rename it the Global Assembly. The reconstituted Global Assembly would have a very broad-based and diverse membership. This would enable its moral authority to extend beyond that provided by the conventional representation of national governments.

The proposed Global Assembly, even if it is to have a new constitution must still have to conform better to the spirit of the Charter, and must have a tripartite representation as follows:

(a) representatives of national governments, (some believe, provided they are legitimate legal representatives of their respective peoples);
(b) representatives of national parliamentary assemblies; and
(c) representatives of *civil society*.

The principle of a tripartite arrangement has been tried in the United Nations System (e.g., ILO). It is proposed to build on this principle.

It should be appreciated that the increasing democratization of governance at different levels of society, will inevitably result in democratization at the international level. There are already clear signs of this development in international organizations, as in the governance of WIPO. This basic change would underpin the relevance and effectiveness of the United Nations in the context of global governance.

REPLACING THE SIX MAIN COMMITTEES OF THE GENERAL ASSEMBLY BY COMMISSIONS

The present constitution of the six committees, their functioning, and the results achieved leave much to be desired. In general, these committees are too time-consuming and not result-oriented; often they are doing work that is largely being done elsewhere in the United Nations System or, not uncommonly, is of peripheral relevance to the core concerns of the global community.

It is recommended that a number of commissions replace the six main committees. Each commission would have a defined mandate, and a specified number of representatives, reflecting the tripartite character of the Global Assembly.

The name 'commission' is not intended to downgrade the work of the present main committees. The word is chosen to represent more flexibility, and in some ways informality, to allow the new machinery to get down to business without the conventional constraints of the present committee structure.

Each commission would, in general, have some 50 members who would be elected for a term of two years by the Global Assembly. There would be a specific quota for each geographical region. It must also be borne in mind that the membership of each commission would depend on the subject matter and the tripartite character referred to above. Some commissions, if not all, should also have representation from the secretariats of the United Nations System. Each commission would establish its own working methods and procedures and would include all United Nations activities in the respective areas. Flexibility, transparency and a concerted effort to move away from the conventional committee machinery would be the hallmarks of the commissions.

The recommendations arising out of the deliberations of the commissions would be considered by the Global Assembly, to ensure that no one who wanted to make an input was prevented from doing so.

These commissions would be the focal points in the United Nations of the specialized activities assigned to each. Their main characteristics would be that each commission would be responsible for aspects of work of the United Nations, of the Specialized Agencies and of the Funds and Programs, and would ensure the tripartite representation referred to earlier, and would be the hallmark of the Global Assembly itself. These commissions would also govern activities in other forums and institutions outside the United Nations, and would establish the minimum of subsidiary machinery.

The following commissions are proposed:

1. **Civil society Commission**
   This would give 'we the peoples' in the Preamble of the Charter a new meaning by entrusting responsibility to this commission to ensure the participation and input of *civil society*.

2. **Peacekeeping and Disarmament Commission**
   This commission would include all security-related and disarmament matters and would have a special relationship to a reformed Security Council. In the event of the Security Council's failure to reform, it would replace it.

3. **Economic and Social Commission (or Development Commission)**
   This commission would replace and supersede all intergovernmental entities involved in these areas, including the Second and Third Committees of the General Assembly, and also the ECOSOC, if it continues to fail to play the role given to it by the Charter.

4. **Environment Commission**
   If the Second Generation United Nations Trusteeship Council (also supported by the Secretary-General) is not allowed to become a reality, this commission would absorb all environment-related intergovernmental entities, including the current Commission on Sustainable Development.

5. **International Law Commission**
   This would be responsible for making recommendations for progressive development and codification of international law, which would form the basis of decisions in this regard by the Global Assembly. This would replace the present International Law Commission, would absorb all intergovernmental legal entities and would establish links with the International Court of Justice, as long as all Member States accept its jurisdiction.

6. **Human Rights Commission**
   This commission would include the present Human Rights Commission and Human Rights Committee and streamlined subsidiary machinery with a strong relationship to the Civil Society Commission.

7. **Administration and Finance Commission**
   This would absorb and reorganize the work of the Fifth Committee, ACABQ and CPC work and, if necessary, of the General Committee of the General Assembly too.

8. **International Civil Service Commission**
   This would be reformed, to include strong staff representation.

9. **Consultation and Coordination Commission (Successor to ACC and CPC)**
   This commission would deal with consultation and coordination at both the intergovernmental and United Nations System levels. The executive heads of the Specialized Agencies and the heads of remaining United Nations programs would be joined by representatives of the Member States, as necessary. The Secretary-General and a representative of the Member States would co-chair the meetings of this commission.

Other existing commissions would be absorbed under one of the commissions above. If in some cases this is not desirable, for example in the cases of crime and drugs, it would be possible to add one or two other commissions at most, as long as these followed the guidelines referred to above.

This transformation would necessitate a complementary transformation in other parts of the United Nations System. Some of this transformation would include the following:

RESTRUCTURING THE UNITED NATIONS SECRETARIAT IN NEW YORK

In line with the mandate of each commission, the Secretariat of the United Nations in New York would be regrouped into functionally coherent clusters, corresponding to the established commissions. These clusters would be organized under one or two Deputy Secretaries-General, who would deputize for the Secretary-General, whenever necessary.

MERGER OF THE SPECIALIZED AGENCIES AND/OR PROGRAMS

To eliminate duplication and to improve coordination and collaboration, a number of Specialized Agencies and/or Programs would have to be merged.

For example, the merger of WIPO and UNESCO would bring education, culture, science and technology into one logical framework.

If not accomplished already as part of the strategy for a *Better United Nations*, all economic and social matters, including development matters, should not be part of the United Nations proper. Except for specialized programs like UNICEF, UNHCR and WFP, which are considered relevant, all other Programs and Funds should be phased out, with the work still considered necessary to be entrusted to the World Bank in the case of development activities (with the full participation of the Specialized Agencies and the Regional Commissions), and to UNCTAD in the case of research, and support activities to either the ECOSOC or the appropriate Economic and Social Commission (or Development Commission).

EXPANSION OF THE SECURITY COUNCIL

To reflect the new realities, the Security Council would be made more representative and would thereby move towards its eventual democratization. In the meantime, the emphasis should be on evolving a consensus as a basis for decision-making. If this does not materialize, the Peacekeeping and Disarmament Commission should take over its role.

BRETTON WOODS INSTITUTIONS

These institutions and WTO would come under the Global Assembly for legislative guidance.

REGIONAL COMMISSIONS

The transformation of the United Nations would depend on decentralization. The Regional Commissions would have to be renamed and would have to assume a major role in the new system. Depending on how such a complete transformation of the United Nations develops, the Regional Commissions might have to undertake other tasks, not restricted to economic and social matters. As proper regional arms of the United Nations they might have to deal with all matters that are dealt with by the United Nations.

SUPPORT BY THE SPECIALIZED AGENCIES
TO THE BUDGET OF THE GLOBAL ASSEMBLY

A certain minimum amount and/or percentage of the budget would be contributed by each Specialized Agency and organization, an essential element of the new relationship created by agreement between the Specialized Agencies and organizations and the Global Assembly of the United Nations.

IMPLEMENTATION OF STRATEGIC PLANNING AND BUDGETING SYSTEM-WIDE

The secure financial flows will enable the preparation and implementation of a medium- (or long-) term strategic planning and budget system for the United Nations and all the Specialized Agencies and organizations cooperating with it. Eventually, this would be extended to all other organizations (global, regional and subregional), whether governmental or otherwise, as long as these were involved in the work of the United Nations.

REVIEW OF OTHER ORGANS

All the other organs and entities, such as the ECOSOC and the Trusteeship Council, at one level, and the ACC and ACABQ at another, would be reviewed, and their role would be evaluated in the context of the transformed Global Assembly and its established commissions, to ensure that the duplication in the present system, as between the ECOSOC and the Second and Third Committees, would be avoided.

REVIEW OF OTHER ORGANIZATIONS

All other organizations, whether global, regional, subregional, intergovernmental or nongovernmental, would be reviewed to ensure their relevance in the context of the fully reformed United Nations; *civil society* would be very well represented, and would, therefore, not need its own organizations and associations to make their input. This would also apply to other intergovernmental organizations, whether global, regional or subregional, since parliaments, like the *civil society*, would be fully represented in the transformed United Nations. Economic and political institutions that, in the view of the Member States, need to exist in parallel to the United Nations, would certainly need to cooperate closely with the United Nations, so that a new spiral of organizations and institutions would not be encouraged, and overlapping and duplication would be avoided.

A DRASTICALLY REVISED CHARTER OR A NEW CONSTITUTION?

This fully transformed United Nations would certainly require drastic changes in the present Charter. Some say that it would require a completely new Constitution. Probably both statements are correct. In either case, we are sure of one fact that the dreams and hopes of the drafters of the original proposals of the present Charter for all the peoples of the world, as reflected in the many quotations from the Charter all through this book, will have to be included again. Also, in either case, the universal participation and the supremacy of the Global Assembly in governance must continue to be paramount. No one has ever suggested that there was anything wrong with these noble aspirations. What was clearly wrong was the manner in which these aspirations were thwarted by the manipulation of the final wording. Also, further manipulation was done during the implementation of the Articles of the Charter to accommodate the views and wishes, first of the victors of the World War II, and, second, of the countries which, by their economic and political supremacy, controlled the decision-making processes concerning major events at the international level during the last fifty years or so. This transformed United Nations, like the *Better United Nations*, would be for everyone.

COST BENEFIT OF THE BETTER UNITED NATIONS SOME TENTATIVE FIGURES

THE COST OF PEACE AND DEVELOPMENT SHOULD NEVER BE CONSIDERED EXCESSIVE

When something works, like the attempt to land a man on the moon or rescuing of a child trapped under the ruins produced by an earthquake, usually the cost is not questioned. It is only when something does not work, or does not work up to expectations, that cost is scrutinized.

It is certain that if the United Nations worked more effectively in keeping peace and in promoting development no one would seriously question its cost. After all, the public perception about the budget of the United Nations is that it is not that excessive, particularly, if one compares it to the military spending of some countries, including some developing countries.

SOME TENTATIVE COST FIGURES

It is very difficult and challenging to find out what the United Nations spends today on its different missions. This is not the place, nor is it our purpose to criticize the budget of the United Nations as lacking transparency. But during the research for this book it was rather difficult to obtain figures for our analysis. An apparent straight forward question, like how much did the United Nations System spend in 1998, in all its peace missions, from all sources of funding, met with all sorts of difficulty. Apparently this question was far from a straightforward one.

Since we could not obtain such figures we attempted to figure it out ourselves. According to the ACC, the United Nations Secretariat and its Specialized Agencies had a regular budget of some USD3.2 billion per year, for each one of the years in the period 1996 to 1999.[1] Of these totals, USD1.3 billion would be the annual budget of the United Nations Secretariat. To that figure, the amount of expenditures covered by voluntary contributions has to be added. These expenditures amounted to USD5.5 billion in 1996 and USD6.2 billion in 1997.[2] Of these totals, USD0.2 billion would be the annual voluntary contributions to the United Nations Secretariat. System-wide figures for 1998 and 1999 are not yet available. These figures neither include the cost of peacekeeping operations nor Bretton Woods Institutions, and seem to grossly underestimate extra-budgetary resources available to the Secretariat.

According to the United Nations Secretariat, its regular budget is USD2.6 billion for each one of the 1996-1997 and 1998-1999 biennia (i.e., USD1.3 billion per year), [3] and its extra-budgetary resources are USD4.5 billion and USD4.4 billion for each one of the two biennia, respectively (i.e. USD2.2 billion per year). [4]

Finally, according to the ECOSOC, the estimated expenditure of the United Nations System, all sources of funds was USD14.9 billion in 1994-1995 (i.e. USD7.4 billion per year).[5] These figures did not include the cost of the United Nations Secretariat. Similar surveys for 1996-1997 and 1998-1999 are not available.

From all the above, we could conclude that the annual cost of the United Nations System is in excess of USD11 billion per year, made up of USD3.5 billion spent by the Secretariat and USD7.5 billion spent by the rest of the System. These figures would not include peacekeeping operations or the annual program costs of the World Bank and the International Monetary Fund.

SOME POSSIBLE SAVINGS

No one is suggesting that because the United Nations budget seems not to be very transparent, its programs are not necessary or useful. It could be argued, however, that the more transparent and accountable an organization, the more likely it would be that its resources are used more efficiently and are more effective in achieving the desired impact. Among other reforms proposed in the book, the following could yield significant savings.

A Better Committee Structure of the General Assembly, including a reduction of the main committees of the General Assembly from six to two, and the strengthening of the

---

[1] A/53/647, Table 1.
[2] A/34/647, Table 7.
[3] A/52/6 Rev. 1, Table 3.
[4] A/52/6 Rev. 1, Table 9.
[5] E/1995/64, Table 1.

role of the General Committee could reduce the cost considerably.

A *Better Secretariat* structure organized under two Deputies Secretary-General. The new Secretariat would only have two major departments instead of the current seven. Some offices would continue doing legal, administrative, budget, financial, public information, and other matters. This *Better Secretariat* would divest itself of all operational activities, particularly in the areas of development and humanitarian affairs. The savings here, could also be substantial.

A *Better United Nations Development Assistance*, giving overall responsibility to the World Bank, would make some of the present organizations redundant, resulting in more savings and in consolidation of the remaining dispersed United Nations programs.

The transformation of the Administrative Committee on Coordination (ACC) into the Policy and Coordination Board (PCB), and the resulting reduction of the number of meetings and the subsidiary machinery could reduce significantly the overall budget of the ACC, when one considers the substantial costs to the Specialized Agencies.

The benefits that could be expected from the implementation of the above reforms would be very large, both in terms of the impact of the *Better United Nations*, as a result of it being more relevant, and in terms of the cost savings due to the resulting streamlining and more efficient machinery. We do not wish to prejudge decisions that have to be taken by Member States on the new and reformed United Nations, but it is not unreasonable to expect that annual savings from the *Better United Nations* proposed would be in the range of billions of United States Dollars rather than in the millions.

WHAT HAPPENS TO THE SAVINGS RESULTING FROM REDUCTIONS IN COSTS?

The Member States would have to decide what happens to the savings resulting from these reductions in costs, on the basis of the global priorities and role of the more relevant and efficient United Nations and United Nations System. However, this less expensive and more effective United Nations should be the most effective confidence building measure for Member States. No Member State would be justified anymore not to pay its mandated obligations.

LIST OF ABBREVIATIONS

ACABQ	Advisory Committee on Administrative and Budgetary Questions
ACC	Administrative Committee on Coordination
ALECSO	Arab League Educational, Cultural and Scientific Organization
APEC	Asia-Pacific Economic Cooperation
ASEAN	Association of South East Asian Nations
CCAQ	Consultative Committee on Administrative Questions
CCPOQ	Consultative Committee on Program and Operational Questions
CCSQ	Consultative Committee on Substantive Questions
CEFACT	Center for Facilitation of Administration, Commerce and Trade
CIS	Commonwealth of Independent States
CPC	Committee on Programme Coordination
CSCE	Conference on Security and Cooperation in Europe
DHA	Department of Humanitarian Affairs
EBRD	European Bank for Reconstruction and Development
ECAFE	Economic Commission for Asia and the Far East
ECE	Economic Commission for Europe
ECLAC	Economic Commission for Latin America
ECOSOC	Economic and Social Council
ERUs	Emergency Response Units
EU	European Union
FAO	Food and Agriculture Organization
FB	Financial and Budgetary Questions
GA	General Assembly
GATT	General Agreement on Tariffs and Trade
GDP	Gross Domestic Product
GNP	Gross National Product
HDI	Human Development Index
IACSD	Inter-Agency Committee on Sustainable Development
IAEA	International Atomic Energy Agency
IATF	Inter-Agency Task Force
IACWGE	Inter-Agency Committee on Women and Gender Equality
IBRD	International Bank for Reconstruction and Development (World Bank)
ICAO	International Civil Aviation Organization

ICJ	International Court of Justice
ICRC	International Committee of the Red Cross
ICVA	International Council of Voluntary Agencies
IDA	International Development Association
IFAD	International Fund for Agricultural Development
IFC	International Finance Corporation
ILO	International Labour Organization
IMF	International Monetary Fund
IMO	International Maritime Organization
INSTRAW	International Research and Training Institute for the Advancement of Wom
IRO	International Road Transport Organization
ISCC	Information Systems Coordination Committee
ISESCO	Islamic Educational, Scientific and Cultural Organization
ITC	International Trade Centre
ITU	International Telecommunications Union
JCGP	Joint Consultative Group on Policy
JIU	Joint Inspection Unit
JUNIC	Joint United Nations Information Committee
LDC	Least Developed Country
MINURSO	United Nations Mission for the Referendum in Western Sahara
NATO	North Atlantic Treaty Organization
NGO	NonGovernmental Organization
NIEO	New International Economic Order
OAS	Organization of American States
OAU	Organization of African Unity
OC	Organizational Committee
ODA	Overseas Development Assistance
ODCCP	Office for Drug Control And Crime Prevention
OECD	Organization for Economic Cooperation and Development
OHCHR	Office of the United Nations High Commissioner for Human Rights
OIOS	Office of Internal Oversight Services
ONUMOZ	United Nations Operation in Mozambique
ONUSAL	United Nations Observer Mission in El Salvador
OPE	Office of Project Execution
OPS	Office of Project Services
OSCE	Organization for Security and Cooperation in Europe
PARinAC	Partners in Action
PCB	Policy and Coordination Board
PER	Personnel and General Administrative Questions
SAPs	Structural Adjustment Programs
SCHR	Steering Committee for Humanitarian Response
SG	Secretary-General
UN/OPS	United Nations Office of Project Services
UNAIDS	Joint UN Program on HIV/AIDS

UNAVEM II	United Nations Angola Verification Mission II
UNCHS	United Nations Centre for Human Settlements (Habitat)
UNCTAD	United Nations Conference on Trade and Development
UNDAF	United Nations Development Assistance Framework
UNDCP	United Nations International Drug Control Programme
UNDG	United Nations Development Group
UNDOF	United Nations Disengagement Observer Force (Syrian Golan Heights)
UNDP	United Nations Development Programme
UNEP	United Nations Environment Programme
UNESCO	United Nations Educational, Scientific and Cultural Organization
UNFICYP	United Nations Peace Keeping Force in Cyprus
UNFPA	United Nations Population Fund
UNHCR	United Nations High Commissioner for Refugees
UNICEF	United Nations Children's Fund
UNCHS	United Nations Center for Human Settlements
UNICRI	United Nations Interregional Crime and Justice Research Institute
UNIDIR	United Nations Institute for Disarmament Research
UNIDO	United Nations Industrial Development Organization
UNIFEM	United Nations Development Fund for Women
UNIFIL	United Nations Interim Force in Lebanon
UNIKOM	United Nations Iraq Kuwait Observation Mission
UNITAR	United Nations Institute for Training and Research
UNMOGIP	United Nations Military Observer Group in India and Pakistan
UNOCHA	United Nations Office for the Coordination of Humanitarian Affairs
UNOG	United Nations Office in Geneva
UNOMIL	United Nations Observer Mission in Liberia
UNOMUR	United Nations Observer Mission Uganda Rwanda
UNOPS	United Nations Office for Project Services
UNOSOM	United Nations Operation in Somalia
UNPROFOR	United Nations Protection Force (former Yugoslavia)
UNRWA	United Nations Relief and Works Agency for Palestine Refugees in the Near East
UNSCOM	United Nations Special Commission (Iraq)
UNTAC	United Nations Transitional Authority in Cambodia
UNTSO	United Nations Truce Supervision Organization (Jerusalem)
UNU	United Nations University
UNV	United Nations Volunteers
UPU	Universal Postal Union
USSR	Union of Soviet Socialist Republics
WFP	World Food Programme
WHO	World Health Organization
WIPO	World Intellectual Property Organization
WMO	World Meteorological Organization
WTO	World Trade Organization

BIBLIOGRAPHY

Aga Khan, Sadruddin. *Improving the Disaster Management Capabilities of the United Nations.* (New York: UNA-USA, 1988).

Alagappan, Alagappa. *Personnel Administration in the United Nations: Some Aspects of Article 101 of the Charter.* (Ann Arbor, MI, USA: University Microfilms, 1968).

Alger, Chadwick F. Lyons M. Gene, Trent E. John (eds). *The United Nations System: The Policies of Member States.* (Tokyo, New York: United Nations University Press, 1995).

Alger, Chadwick F. 'Thinking About the Future of the UN System'. *Global Governance,* Vol.2/No. 3 (Sep.-Dec. 1996).

Alger, Chadwick F. *The Future of the United Nations System: Potential for the Twenty-First Century.* (New York: United Nations University Press, 1998).

Allbright, M. 'America and the League of Nations: Lessons for Today'. Address to the Woodrow Wilson International Centre for Scholars, 4th March 1994.

Ameri, Houshang. *Politics of Staffing the United Nations Secretariat.* (New York: Peter Lang, 1996).

American Academy of Political and Social Science. 'The United Nations and the Future'. Patterson, Ernest Minor (ed.). *Annals of the American Academy of Political and Social Science,* v. 228. (Philadelphia, 1943).

American Academy of Political and Social Science. 'Making the United Nations Work'. Patterson, Ernest Minor (ed.). *Annals of the American Academy of Political and Social Science,* v. 246. (Philadelphia, 1946).

American Academy of Political and Social Science. 'World Government'. Patterson, Ernest Minor (ed.). *Annals of the American Academy of Political and Social Science,* v. 264. (Philadelphia, 1949).

Annan, Kofi. 'Renewing the United Nations: A Programme for Reform'. (New York: UN DPISG/SM/6284 or GA/9282, 16 July 97 and attachments). <http://www.un.org/reform/track2/> 1997.

Annan, Kofi. *Renewal Amid Transition*: Annual Report on the Work of the Orgnization, 1997, by the Secretary-General of the United Nations. (New York: UN DPI/1927 of Sales No.: E.97.1.23 – Sep 1997).

Arnold, Tim. *Reforming the UN: Its Economic Role.* (London: Chatham House/RIIA, 1995).

Ashby, Lowell D. *The United Nations Economic Institutions and the Need for Restructuring.* (Washington, D.C, USA: The Center for U.N. Reform Education, 1991).

Baehr, Peter R. and Leon Gordenker. *The United Nations: Reality and Ideal.* (New York: Praeger, 1984).

Baehr, Peter R. and Leon Gordenker. *The United Nations in the 1990s.* (2nd edn, Basingstoke, England: MacMillian, 1994).

Bailey, Sydney D. *The General Assembly of the United Nations: A Study of Procedure and Practice.* (New York: Praeger, 1960).

Bailey, Sydney D. *The Troika and the Future of the U.N.* (New York: Carnegie Endowment for International Peace, 1962).

Bailey, Sydney D. *The Secretariat of the United Nations.* (New York: Praeger, 1964).

Balogh, T. *The Economics of Poverty.* (London: Weidenfeld & Nicolson, 1965).

Barnaby, Frank (ed.). *Building a More Democratic United Nations: Proceedings of Camdun-1.* (Frank Cass & Co., 1991).

Baratta, Joseph Preston (ed.). *Strengthening the United Nations: Bibliography on United Nations Reform and World Federalism.* (London: Greenwood Press, 1987).

Barratta, Joseph Preston. *United Nations System.* (New Brunswick, NJ, USA: Transaction Publishers, c1995).

Barros, James (ed.). *The United Nations: Past, Present, and Future.* (New York: Free Press, 1972).

Barry, Tom and Leaver Erik. *The Next Fifty Years: The United Nations and the United States.* (Inter-Hemispheric Resource Center, 1996).

Bartolo, Michael. *Limitations of United Nations Technical Assistance.* (ENDA-DAKAR, 1976).

Bartolo, Michael and Guido de Marco. *A Second Generation United Nations: For Peace in Freedom in the 21st Century.* (London and New York: Kegan Paul International, 1997).

Beckel, Graham. *Workshops for the World*: *The Specialized Agencies of the United Nations.* (New York: Abelard-Schuman, 1945).

Becker, Benjamin Max. *Is the United Nations Dead?* (Philadelphia, USA : Whitmore Publishing Co., 1969).

Bedjaoui, Mohammed. *The New World Order and the Security Council: Testing the Legality of its Acts.*(Dordrecht, Netherlands; Boston, MA, USA: M. Nijhoff Publishers, 1994).

Beigbeder, Yves. *Management Problems in United Nations Organizations: Reform or Decline?* (London: F. Pinter, 1987).

Beigbeder, Yves. *Threats to the International Civil Service.* (London: F. Pinter, 1988).

Beigbeder, Yves. *Reforming the Economic and Social Sectors of the United Nations: An Incomplete Process.* (Opladen, Germany: Leske Budrich, 1995).

Beigbeder, Yves. *The Internal Management of United Nations Organizations: The Long Quest for Reform.* (New York: St. Martin's Press, 1996, and Babingstoke: MacMillian Press, 1997).

Bellamy, Christopher. *Knights in White Armour: The New Art of War and Peace.* (London: Hutchinson-Random House, 1996).

Bennett, Alvin LeRoy. *International Organizations: Principles and Issues.* (6th edn, Englewood Cliffs, NJ, USA: Prentice Hall, 1995).

Bennys, Phyllis. *Calling the Shots: How Washington Dominates Today's UN.* (New York: Olive Branch Press, 1996).

Bernhard, John T. *United Nations Reform: An Analysis.* (Los Angeles, USA: University of California, 1950).

Bertrand, Maurice. *Some Reflections on Reform of the United Nations.* (Joint Inspection Unit, JIU/REP/85/9: United Nations, Geneva, 1985).

Bertrand, Maurice. *The U.N. in Profile: How its Resources are Distributed.* (New York: UNA-USA, 1986).

Bertrand, Maurice. *Planning, Programming, Budgeting, and Evaluation in the United Nations.* (New York: UNA-USA, 1987).

Bertrand, Maurice. *The Role of the United Nations in the Economic and Social Fields.* (New York: UNA-USA, 1987).

Bertrand, Maurice. *The Third Generation World Organization.* (Dodrecht, Netherlands; Boston, MA, USA: M. Nijhoff Publishers, 1989).

Bibliography

Bertrand, Maurice. *L'ONU*. (Paris: La Découverte, 1994).

Bertrand, Maurice and Warner Daniel (eds). *A New Charter for a Worldwide Organisation?* (Nijhoff Law Specials, Vol. 22, The Hague: Kluwer Law International, 1997).

Bertrand, Maurice. *The United Nations: Past, Present and Future* (Nijhoff Law Specials, Vol 25, January 1997, The Hague: Kluwer Law International, 1997).

Blodgett, Steven Alvah. *The Evolving Relationship Between the United Nations and International Non-Governmental Organizations: An Assessment of the Need for Institutional Reform.* (Ann Arbor, MI, USA: University Microfilms International, 1984).

Bloomfield, Lincoln P. *The United Nations and US Foreign Policy: A New Look at the National Interest.* (Boston, MA, USA: Little, Brown and Co., 1967).

Blum, Yehuda Z. *Eroding the United Nations Charter.* (Martinus Nijhoff, March 1993).

Borgese, Elisabeth Mann. *Ocean Governance and the United Nations.* (Dalhousie University, 1995).

Boudreau, Thomas Eugene. *The Secretary-General and Satellite Diplomacy: An Analysis of the Present and Potential Role of the United Nations Secretary-General in the Maintenance of International Peace and Security.* (New York: Council on Religion and International Affairs, 1984).

Boudreau, Thomas Eugene. *Sheathing the Sword: The U.N. Secretary-General and the Prevention of International Conflict.* (New York; Westport, CT, USA: Greenwood Press, 1991).

Bourantonis, Dimitris and Jarrod Weiner (eds). *The United Nations in the New World Order: The World Organization at Fifty.* (New York: St. Martin's Press, 1995).

Bourantonis, Dimitris and Marios L. Evriviades (eds). *A United Nations for the Twenty-First Century: Peace, Security, and Development.* (The Hague: Kluwer Law International, 1996).

Boutros-Ghali, Boutros. 'Empowering the United Nation'. *Foreign Affairs*, 71 (Winter 1992-93).

Brecher, Jeremy, John Brown Childs and Jill Cutler (eds*). Global Visions: Beyond the New World Order.* (Boston, MA, USA: South End Press, 1993).

Bustelo, Mara R. and Philip Alston. *Whose New World Order: What Role for the United Nations?* (Annandale, Australia: Federation Press, 1991).

Campaign for U.N. Reform (United States). *Elements of U.N. Reform.*(Wayne, NJ, USA: Campaign for U.N. Reform, 1977).

Campaign for U.N. Reform (United States). *The 14-point Program to Reform and Restructure the U.N. System.* (Washington, D.C., USA: Campaign for U.N. Reform, 1992).

Canadian Committee for the Fiftieth Anniversary of the United Nations. *Canadian Conference on UN Reform Proceedings of the First Canadian Conference on UN Reform, Montreal, Quebec, 23-25 March 1995.* (Canadian Committee for the Fiftieth Anniversary of the United Nations, 1995)

Carlsson, Ingvar. 'The U.N. at 50: A Time to Reform'. *Foreign Policy*, Number 100 (Fall 1995), pp. 3-18.

Carnegie Commission on Preventing Deadly Conflict: Final Report (New York: Carnegie Corporation, 1997).

Carr, William George. *One World in the Making; the United Nations.* (Boston, USA: Ginn,1947)

Chiang, Pei-Heng. *Non-Governmental Organizations at the United Nations: Identity, Role, and Function.* (Praeger Pub. Text, 1982).

Childers, Erskine B. and B. Urquhart. *A World in Need of Leadership.* (Dag Hammarsköld Foundation, 1990).

Childers, Erskine B. and B. Urquhart. *Reorganisation of the United Nations.*(February, 1991; unpublished).

Childers, Erskine B. 'Never Again'. Lecture to the Society for International Development, Amsterdam, 9th May 1991.

Childers, Erskine B. and B. Urquhart, *Towards a More Effective United nations.* (Dag Hammarsköld Foundation, 1991).

Childers, Erskine B. 'Restoring the Role of the United Nations in Economic and Social Leadership'. *Malta Review of Foreign Affairs*, Special Issue (1993).

Childers, Erskine B. *In a Time Beyond Warnings: Strengthening the United Nations System.* (London: Catholic Institute for International Relations; Pax Christi, Christian Peace Education Centre, 1993).

Childers, Erskine B. (ed.). *Challenges to the United Nations: Building a Safer World.* (London: CIIR, Catholic Institute for International Relations, 1994).

Childers, Erskine B. and B. Urquhart. *Renewing the United Nations System.* (Uppsala, Sweden: Dag Hammarskjöld Foundation, 1994).

Childers, Erskine B. 'The United Nations and Global Institutions: Discourse and Reality'. *Global Governance*, Vol. 3/No.3 (Sep-Dec 1997).

Claude, Inis L. Jr. *Swords into Plowshares: The Problems and Progress of International Organization.* (4th edn, New York: Random House, 1971).

Cleveland, Harlan. *Birth of a New World: An Open Moment for Internaitonal Leadership.* (San Francisco, CA, USA: Jossey-Bass Publishers, 1993).

Coate, Roger A. (ed.). *U.S.Policy and the Future of the United Nations.* (New York: Twentieth Century Fund Press, 1994).

Codding, George A. Jr. 'The Relationship of the League and the UN with Independent Agencies: A Comparison'. *Annals of International Studies*, (1970), p. 82.

Cohen, Benjamin. *The United Nations: Constitutional Development, Growth and Possibilities.* (Cambridge, MA, USA: Harward University Press, 1961).

Commission on Global Governance. *Our Global Neighbourhood: The Report of the Commission on Global Governance.* (Oxford, England; New York: Oxford University Press, 1995).

Commission on Global Governance. *A Call to Action – Summary of Our Global Neighbourhood.* (Geneva, 1995).

Commission to Study the Organization of Peace. *Charter Review Conference.* (New York: Commission to Study the Organization of Peace, 9th report,1955).

Commission to Study the Organization of Peace. *Strengthening the United Nations.* (New York: Harper, 1957).

Commission to Study the Organization of Peace. *Developing the United Nations: A Response to the Challenge of a Revolutionary Era.* (New York: Commission to Study the Organization of Peace, 13th report, 1961).

Commission to Study the Organization of Peace. *New Dimensions for the United Nations: The Problems of the Next Decade.* (New York: Commission to Study the Organization of Peace, 17th report, 1966).

Commission to Study the Organization of Peace. *The United Nations: The Next Twenty-five Years.* (New York: Commission to Study the Organization of Peace, 20th report, 1969).

Commission to Study the Organization of Peace, and Stanley Foundation. *Restructuring the United Nations System for Economic and Social Co-operation and Development: Twenty-Seventh Report.* (Muscatine, IA, USA: Stanley Foundation, 1980).

Commonwealth Secretariat. *Common Index and Glossary to the Brandt, Palme and Brundtland Reports of the Independent Commissions on International Development*

Bibliography

Issues, Disarmament and Security, and Environment and Development. (London: Commonwealth Secretariat, 1990).

Conceptual Framework Project on UN Reform. *A Procedural Agenda for the Discussion of United Nations Reform.* (Berkeley, CA, USA: Institute of International Studies, University of California at Berkeley, 1995).

Conetta, Karl and Charles Knight. *Vital Force: a Proposal for the Overhaul of the UN Peace Operations System and for the Creation of a UN Legion.* (Cambridge, MA, USA: Commonwealth Institute, 1995).

Conforti, Benedetto. *Law and Practice of the United Nations.* (The Hague: Kluwer Law International, 1996).

Cooker, Chris de (ed.). *International Administration: Law and Management Practices in International Organizations.* (Dordrecht, Netherlands; Boston, MA, USA: M. Nijhoff, 1990).

Council on Foreign Affairs (New York). *Independent Task Force. American National Interest and the United Nations: Statement and Report of an Independent Task Force.* (New York, USA: The Council, 1996).

Cox, Robert W. and Harold K. Jackobson. *The Anatomy of Influence: Decision-Making in International Organizations.* (New Haven, CT, USA: Yale University Press, 1973).

Culpeper, Roy. *The United Nations and the World Economy* (Ottawa: UNAC, 1997).

Dagory, Jacques. 'Les Rapports Entre les Institutions Spécialisées et l'ONU', *RGDIP* 1969-2.

Dallen, Russell M. (Compiler). *A U.N. Revitalized: A Compilation of UNA-USA Recommendations on Strengthening the Role of the United Nations in Peacemaking, Peacekeeping and Conflict Prevention.* (New York: UNA-USA, 1992).

Damsgaard, Anders Carsten. *Staffing an International Civil Service: Principles and Practices: The United Nations Secretariat, 1981.* (Aarhus, Denmark: University of Aarhus, 1981).

De Gara, John P. *Administrative and Financial Reform of the United Nations: A Documentary Essay.* (Hanover, NH,USA: Academic Council on the United Nations System, 1989).

De Marco, Guido. Ministry of Foreign Affairs, Malta, *Presidency with a Purpose.*

De Marco, Guido and Michael Bartolo. *A Second Generation United Nations: For Peace in Freedom in the 21st Century.* (London and New York: Kegan Paul International, 1997).

Dell, Sydney. 'Relations Between the United Nations and the Bretton Woods Institutions'. *Development* , No. 4, SID, Rome (1989).

Dicke, Klaus. 'Reform of the UN', Wolfrum (ed.). *United Nations: Law, Policies and Practice, Vol. 2.* (Dordrecht-Boston-London: M. Nijhoff, 1995), p. 1013.

Diehl, Paul Francis (ed.). *The Politics of International Organizations: Patterns and Insights.* (Chicago, IL, USA: Dorsey Press, 1989).

Dijikzeul, Dennis. *The Management of Multilateral Organizations.* (The Hague: Kluwer Law International, 1997).

Durch, William J. and Barry M. Blechman. *Keeping the Peace: The United Nations in the Emerging World Order.* (Washington, D.C., USA: The Henry L. Stimson Center, 1992).

Economist, The. 15 Feb 97: Reworking the UN (17-18); United Nations: Towards Reform (38-39); Iraq and the UN: Oil But No Food. (39-40).

Economist, The. 19 Jul 97: Another Go at Reviving the UN. (40).

Economist, The. 22 Nov 97: The Best World Club We Have. (8,49-50).

Elmandjra, Mahdi. *The United Nations System: An Analysis.* (London: Faber and Faber, 1973).

Evans, Gareth. *Cooperating for Peace – The Global Agenda for the 1990s and Beyond.* (St-Leonards, Australia: Allen & Unwin, 1993).

Falk, Richard A. and Saul H. Mendlowitz (eds). *The United Nations.* (New York: World Law Fund, 1966).

Falk, Richard A. *The Promise of World Order: Essays in Normative International Relations.* (Brighton, UK: Wheatsheaf Books, 1987).

Falk, Richard A., Samuel S. Kim, and Saul H. Mendlowitz (eds). *The United Nations and a Just World Order.* (Boulder, CO, USA: Westview Press, 1991).

Fawcett, Eric and Hanna Newcombe (eds). *United Nations Reform: Looking Ahead After Fifty Years.* (Toronto; Heddington, Oxford; Niagara Falls, New York: Science for Peace, distributed by Dunburn Press, 1995).

Fedder, Edwin H. (ed.). *The United Nations: Problems and Prospects.* (St. Louis, MO, USA: Center for International Studies, University of Missouri, 1971).

Ferencz, Benjamin B. *New Legal Foundations for Global Survival: Security Through the Security Council.* (New York: Oceana Publications, 1994).

Finger, Seymour Maxwell and John Mugno. *The Politics of Staffing the UN Secretariat.* (New York: The Ralph Bunche Institute on the United Nations, 1974).

Finger, Seymour Maxwell and Joseph R. Harbert (eds). *U.S. Policy in International Institutions: Defining Reasonable Options in an Unreasonable World.* (Boulder, CO, USA: Westview Press, 1982).

Finkelstein, Lawrence S. (ed.). *Politics in the United Nations System.* (Durham, NC, USA: Duke University Press, 1988).

Finkelstein, Lawrence S. *The United States and International Organizations.* (Cambridge, MA, USA: The MIT Press,1969).

Fisas, Vicenc. *Blue Geopolitics: The United Nations Reform and the Future of the Blue Helmets.* (London; New Haven, CT, USA: Pluto Press, 1995).

Fomerand, Jacques. *Strengthening the United Nations Economic and Social Programs: A Documentary Essay.* (Hanover, NH, USA: Academic Council on the United Nations System, 1990).

Ford Foundation. *Financing an Effective United Nations. Independent Advisory Group on United Nations Financing:A Report of the Independent Advisory Group on U.N. Financing.* (New York : Ford Foundation, 1993).

Forum on the Future of the United Nations (1995, Vienna). *Reforming the United Nations: A View from the South.* (Geneva, Switzerland: South Centre, 1995).

Franck, Thomas M. *Nation Against Nation: What Happened to the U.N. Dream and What the U.S. Can Do About It.* (New York: Oxford University Press, 1985).

Franck, Thomas M., John P. Renninger and Vladislav B. Tikhomirov. *A Diplomat's Views on the United Nations System: An Attitude Survey.* (New York: United Nations Institute for Training and Research, 1982).

Franz, Mark A. and Robert Winters. *At the United Nations, Reform Has a Long Way to Go.* (Washington, D.C., USA: Heritage Foundation, 1988).

Fromuth, Peter J. *The U.N. at 40: The Problems and Opportunities.* (New York: UNA-USA, 1986).

Fromuth, Peter J. and Ruth Raymond. *U.N. Personnel Policy Issues.* (New York: UNA-USA, 1987).

Fromuth, Peter J. (ed.). *A Successor Vision: The United Nations of Tomorrow.* (New York: United Nations Association of the United States of America, 1988).

Bibliography

Galtung, J. *The United Nations Today: Problems and Some Proposals.* (Princeton, NJ, USA: Center for International Studies, 1986).

Gardner, Richard N. *The United States and the United Nations: Can We Do Better?* (New York: Columbia University Press, 1972).

Gardner, Richard N. *Sterling Dollar Diplomacy in Current Perspective.* (New York: Columbia University Press, 1980).

Gati, Tobi Trister. *The 'New' UN: Through Soviet and American Eyes.* (New York: UNA-USA, 1989).

Gati, Tobi Trister (ed.). *The US, the UN and the Management of Global Change.* (New York: New York University Press, 1983).

Gauci, Victor J. 'Malta and the Security Council'. *Malta Review of Foreign Affairs,* No.6, (January 1995).

Gemeinsame Verantwortung in den 90er Jahren: die Stockholmer Initiative zu globaler Sicherheit und Weltordnung: die Charta der Vereinten Nationen = Common responsibility in the1990ties: The Stockholm Initiative on Global Security and Governance: The Charter of the United Nations. (Saarbucken, Germany: Breitenbach, 1991) Note: Text in English and German.

Gibbons, S. R. *International Co-Operation: The League of Nations and UNO* (Harlow, England: Modern Times, 1992).

Goodrich, L., E. Hambro, et al. *Charter of the United Nations.* (New York: Columbia University Press, 1969).

Goodrich, Leland Mathew. *The United Nations in a Changing World.* (New York: Columbia University Press, 1974).

Gordenker, Leon. *The UN Secretary-General and the Maintenance of Peace.* (New York: Columbia University Press, 1967).

Gordenker, Leon. *Thinking About the United Nations System.* (Hanover, NH, USA: Academic Council on the United Nations System, 1990).

Gordenker, Leon. *The UN Tangle: Policy Formation, Reform, and Reorganization.* (Cambridge, Mass., USA: World Peace Foundation, WFP Report No. 12, 1996).

Gordon, Wendell. *The United Nations at the Crossroads of Reform.* (Armonk, New York, USA: M.E. Sharpe, 1994).

Goulding, Marrack. 'The Evolution of United Nations Peacekeeping'. *International Affairs,* No.3, Vol.69 (July 1993).

Government of Canada. *Towards a Rapid Reaction Capability for the United Nations.* (Ottawa: Canadian Government, Sep 1995).

Graham, Norman A. and Robert S. Jordan (eds). *The International Civil Service: Changing Role and Concepts.* (New York: Pergamon Press, 1980).

Gregg, Robert W. *About Face?: The United States and the United Nations.* (Boulder, CO, USA: L. Rienner, 1993).

Groom, A.J.R., Paul Taylor and Andrew Williams. *The Study of International Organization: British Experiences.* (Hanover, NH, USA: Academic Council for the United Nations System, 1990).

Guggenheim, Paul. 'Legal and Political Conflicts in the League of Nations. A Contribution to the Reform of the League' by Professors of the Graduate Institute of International Studies, Geneva, *The World Crisis* (London-New York-Toronto: Longmans, Green and Co., 1938).

Gutteridge, Joyce Ada Cooke. *The United Nations in a Changing World.* (Manchester, NY,USA: Oceana Publications, 1969).

Gwin, Catherine in Mahbub Ul Haq, Richard Jolly, Paul Streeten, Khadija Haq (eds). *The UN and the Bretton Woods Institutions; New Challenges for the 21ˢᵗ Century.* (New York: St. Martin's Press, 1950).

Haag, Ernest van den and John Phillips Conrad. *The U.N.: In or Out?/A Debate Between Ernest van den Haag and John P. Conrad.* (New York: Plenum Press, 1987).

Haas, Ernst B. *The Web of Interdependence: The United States and International Organization.* (Englewood Cliffs, NJ, USA: Prentice-Hall, 1970).

Haas, Ernst B. *Why We Still Need the United Nations: Collective Management of International Conflict.* 1945-1984. (Berkeley, CA, USA: Institute of International Studies, 1986).

Hall, Brian. 'Blue Helmets, Exporting Guns'. *New York Times Magazine*, 2 January,1994.

Halper, Stefan. *A Miasma of Corruption: The United Nations at 50.* (Washington, D.C., USA: Cato Institute, 1996).

Handler, Antonia Chayes, Abram Chayes and George Raach. 'Beyond Reform: Restructuring for More Effective Conflict Intervention'. *Global Governance,* Vol. 3 /No. 2 (May-Aug 1997).

Haq, Ul Mahbub, Richard Jolly, Paul Streeten, Khadija Haq (eds). *The UN and the Bretton Woods Institutions: New Challenges for the Twenty-First Century.* (New York: St. Martin's Press, 1950).

Harrison, Haynes Lukas. 'Great Power Relations and the United Nations'. *Oxford International Review*, Vol. VII/No. 2 (Spring 1996).

Harrod, Jeffrey and Nico Schrijver (eds). *The UN Under Attack.* (Aldershot, England; Brookfield, VT, USA: Gower, 1988).

Hata, Kazuhiko. *The Personnel Management System of the United Nations Secretariat: A Systems Approach.* (Ann Arbor, MI, USA: University Microfilms, 1975).

Hayter, Teresa. *Aid as Imperialism.* (New York: Penguin Books, 1971).

Hazzard, Shirley. *Defeat of an Ideal: A Study of the Self-Destruction of the United Nations.* (Boston, Mass., USA: Little, Brown and Co., 1973).

Heritage Foundation. *The United Nations: Its Problems and What to Do About Them.* (September 1986).

Higgins, Rosalyn. *The New United Nations: Appearance and Reality.* (Hull: University of Hull Press, 1993).

Hill, Martin. 'The ACC' in Luard, Evan (ed.). *The Evolution of International Organizations* (New York: Praeger, 1966), p. 127.

Hill, Martin. *Towards Greater Order, Coherence and Co-ordination in the United Nations System.* (New York: United Nations Institute for Training and Research, 1974).

Hill, Martin. *The United Nations System: Coordinating its Economic and Social Work.* (Cambridge, England; New York: Cambridge University Press, 1978).

Hoffmann, Walter. *United Nations Security Council Reform and Restructuring.* (Livingstone, NJ, USA: The Center for U.N. Reform Education, 1994).

Hoffmann, Walter and Scott Hoffman. *A New World Order: Can It Bring Security to the World's People?: Essays on Restructuring the United Nations.* (Washington, D.C., USA: World Federalist Association, 1991).

Holtje, James. *Divided it Stands: Can the United Nations Work?* (Atlanta, GA, USA: Turner Publishing Inc., 1995).

Hopkinson, Nicholas. *The United Nations in the New World Disorder.* (London: HMSO, 1993).

Bibliography

Hudson, Michael. 'Epitaph for Bretton Woods'. *Journal of International Affairs*. No.2, Vol.12, (1969).

Hufner, Klaus (ed.). *Agenda for Change: New Tasks for the United Nations*. (Opladen, Germany: Leske & Budrich, 1995).

Imber, Mark F. *Environment, Security and UN Reform*. (New York: St. Martin's Press, 1994).

Independent Advisory Group on U.N. Financing. *Financing an Effective United Nations: A Report of the Independent Advisory Group on U.N. Financing*. Shijuro Ogata (co-chairman) et al. (New York, NY, USA: Ford Foundation, c1993).

Independent Commission on Disarmament and Security Issues. *Common Security: A Blueprint for Survival*. (New York: Simon and Schuster, 1982).

Independent Commission on Disarmament and Security Issues. *A World at Peace: Common Security in the Twenty-First Century*. (Stockholm: Palme Commission on Disarmament and Security Issues, 1989).

Independent Commission on International Development Issues. *North-South: A Program For Survival: The Report of the Independent Commission on International Development Issues / Under the Chairmanship of Willy Brandt*. (Cambridge, MA, USA: MIT Press, 1980).

Independent Commission on International Development Issues. *Common Crisis North-South: Co-Operation for World Recovery: Memorandum of the Independent Commission on International Development Issues*. (London, Sydney: Pan Books, 1983).

Independent Working Group on the Future of the United Nations. *The United Nations In Its Second Half-Century: The Report of the Independent Working Group on the Future of the United Nations*. (New York: Ford Foundation, 1995).

International Conference on a More Democratic United Nations (1st: 1990: New York). *Building a More Democratic United Nations: Proceedings of CAMDUN-1*. (London; Portland, OR, USA: Frank Cass, 1991).

International Conference on a More Democratic United Nations (2nd: 1991: Vienna). *The United Nations and the New World Order: Keynote Addresses from the Second International Conference on a More Democratic United Nations*. (Vienna: International Progress Organization, 1992).

Italian Society for International Organization. *Prospects for the Reform of the United Nations System* International Symposium, Rome, 15-17 May 1992. (Padova: Cedam, 1993).

International Symposium on the Role and Future of the United Nations (1983: Geneva). *The Role and Future of the United Nation*. (World Federation of the United Nations Associations, 1985).

Jackson, R. *A Study of the Capacity of the United Nations Development System*. 2 Volumes. (Geneva, Switzerland : United Nations, November 1969).

Jacobson, Max. *The United Nations in the 1990s: A Second Chance?* (New York: Twentieth Century Fund, UNITAR, 1993).

James, R. *Staffing the United Nations Secretariat*. (Brighton, England: Institute for the Study of International Organisation, University of Sussex, 1970).

Japanese-German Center (Berlin). *Symposium 'The role of the United Nations in the 1990'*. (Berlin, 1990).

Jenks, Wifred C. 'Amendment of the Covenant'. *British Yearbook of International Law* (1937), Vol. 18.

Jenks, Wilfred C. 'Coordination: A New Problem of International Organization. A Preliminary Survey of the Law and Practice of Intergovernmental Relationships'. *RCADI*, 1950 - II.

Johansen, Robert. 'The Future of United Nations Peacekeeping and Enforcement: A
    Framework for Policymaking'. *Global Governance.* Vol. 2/No. 3, Sep-Dec (1996).
John, Charles Daly, J.William Fulbright, et al. *The Future of the United
    Nations:* a Round Table held on November 16, 1976. (Washington: American Enterprise
    Institute for Public Policy Research, c1977).
Jonah, James O.C. *Differing State Perspectives on the United Nations in the Post-Cold War
    World.* (Academic Council on the United Nations System, 1993-4).
Jordan, Robert S.(ed.). *Dag Hammarskjold Revisited: The UN Secretary-General as a
    Force in World Politics.* (Durham, NC, USA: Carolina Academic Press, 1983).
Jordan, Robert S.(ed.). *International Administration: Its Evolution and Contemporary
    Applications.* (New York: Oxford University Press, 1971).
Jutte, Rudiger and Annemarie Grosse-Jutte (eds). *The Future of International
    Organization.* (New York: St. Martin's Press, 1981).

Kanninen, Tapio. *Leadership and Reform: The Secretary-General and the UN Financial
    Crisis of the Late 1980s.* (The Hague; Boston, MA, USA: Kluwer Law International, 1995).
Karns, Margaret P. and Karen A. Mingst (eds). *The United States and Multilateral
    Institutions: Patterns of Changing Instrumentality and Influence.* (Boston, MA, USA:
    Unwin Human, 1990).
Kaufmann, Johan. *United Nations Decision Making.* (Alphen aan den Rijn, Netherlands;
    Rockwville, MD, USA: Sijthoff & Noordhoff, 1980).
Kaufmann, Johan. *The Evolving United Nations: Principles and Realities.* (Providence, RI, USA:
    Academic Council on the United Nations System, c1994)
Kaufmann, Johan, Dick A. Leurdijk and Nico Schrijver. *Changing Global Needs: Expanding
    Roles for the United Nations System: Report.* (Academic Council for the United Nations
    System, 1990).
Kaufmann, Johan, Dick A. Leurdijk and Nico Schrijver. *The World in Turmoil: Testing the
    UN's Capacity.* (Hanover, NH, USA: The Academic Council on the United Nations
    System, 1991).
Kaul, Inge, Grunberg Isabelle and Stern A. Marc (eds). *Global Public Goods, International
    Cooperation in the 21st Century.* Published for The United Nations Development
    Programme (UNDP). (Oxford University Press,1999).
Kay, David K.(ed.). *The Changing United Nations: Options for the United States.* (New
    York: Academy of Political Science, 1977).
Kay, David K. *The Functioning and Effectiveness of Selected United Nations System
    Programs.*(St. Paul, MN, USA: West Pub. Co., 1980).
Keenleyside, H. L. *International Aid: A Summary.* (New York: J. H. Heinemann Inc., 1966).
Keith, Krause, et al. *Canada, the United Nations and the Reform of International Institutions*
    Draft paper by Centre for International and Strategic Studies, York University, Toronto
    (1990).
Kennedy, Paul and Russett Bruce. 'Reforming the United Nations'. *Foreign Affairs*, Vol.
    74/No. 5 (Sep/Oct 1995), p. 56.
Kilbourne, Lewis Buckner. *Organizational and Political Conflict Within the United Nations
    Secretariat.* (Ann Arbor, MI, USA: University Microfilms, 1978).
Kincaid, Cliff. *Global Taxes for World Government.* (Lafayette, Louisiana, USA: Huntington
    House Publishers, 1997).
Kirdar, U. *The Structure of United Nations Economic Aid to Underdeveloped Countries.* (The
    Hague, 1966).

Bibliography

Kissinger, Henry. *Diplomacy*. (New York, London, Toronto, Sydney, Tokyo, Singapore: Simon and Schuster, 1994).

Knipping, Franz and Hans Von Mangoldt (eds). *The United Nations System and Its Predecessors: Predecessors of the United Nations*. (Oxford: Oxford Univ Press, 1997)

Kostakos, Georgios. *Reforming the United Nations, 1985-1989*. (Canterbury, England: 1989). Note: Thesis (Ph.D.) University of Kent at Canterbury, 1989.

Kunugi, Tatsuro, et al. *Towards a More Effective UN: Research Project on a More Effective United Nations And Japan's Options*. (Tokyo: PHP Research Institute, 1996).

Landsberg, Chris. 'Another Debate on Order?: Restructuring the United Nations Security Council'. Universiteit van Pretoria, Institute for Strategic Studies; (1995). ISSUP bulletin; 3/95.

Langhorne, Richard. *Reforming The United Nations: The International and Institutional Contexts of Reform*. (London: HMSO, 1995).

Langrod, George S. *The International Civil Service: Its Origins, Its Nature, Its Evolution*. (Leyden, Netherlands: A. W. Sythoff, 1963).

Larson, Arthur. *Appointment of the Secretary-General of the United Nations Without a Recommendation of the Security Council*. (Durham, NC, USA: School of Law, Duke University, 1961).

Laurenti, Jeffrey. *National Taxpayers, International Organizations: Sharing the Burden of Financing the United Nations*. (New York: UNA-USA, c1995).

Lawson, Stephanie (ed.). *The New Agenda for Global Security: Cooperation for Peace and Beyond*. (Canberra: Allen & Unwin in association with the Department of International Relations, Australian National University, 1995).

Lee, John M. *To Unite Our Strength: Enhancing the United Nations Peace and Security System*. (Lanham, MD, USA: University Press of America, 1992).

Legault, Albert Craig, N. Murphy, W. B. Ofuatey-Kodjoe. *The State of the United Nations*. (Academic Council on the United Nations System, 1992).

Lemoine, Jacques. *The International Civil Servant: The Endangered Species*. (The Hague, Netherlands; Boston, MA, USA: Kluwer Law International, 1995).

Leng, Russell John. *United States Response to the United Nations Financial Crisis*. (Ann Arbor, MI, USA: University Microfilms, 1967).

LeRoy, Bennett. *International Organizations: Principles and Issues*. (5th Edition, New Jersey: Prentice Hall Inc., 1991).

Liberal International. *Strengthening of the United Nations*. (London: Liberal International, 1993).

Lister, Frederick K. *Fairness and Accountability in UN Financial Decision-Making*. (New York: UNA-USA, 1986).

Lichenstein, Charles M. *The United Nations: Its Problems and What to Do About Them: 59 Recommendations Prepared in Response to General Assembly Resolution 40/237*. (Washington, D.C., USA: Heritage Foundation, 1986).

Lichenstein, Charles M. *United Nations Reform: Where's the Beef?* (Washington, D.C., USA: Heritage Foundation, 1987).

Liu, B. 'Quality of Life: Concept, Measure and Results'. *The American Journal of Economics and Sociology*, January 1975, Vol. 34, No. 1.

Luard, Evan. *The United Nations: How It Works and What It Does*. (New York: St. Martin's Press, 1994).

Luard, Evan (ed.). *The Evolution of International Organizations*. (New York: Praeger, 1966).

Malone, David. 'Security Council Decision-Making and the Future of UN Peace-Keeping'.
    Oxford International Review, Vol. VII/No. 2 (Spring 1996).
Martin, Andrew and J.B.S. Edwards. *The Changing Charter: A Study in the Reform of the
    United Nations.* (London: Sylvan Press in Association With the David Davies Memorial
    Institute of International Studies, 1955).
Mason, Edward Sagendorph. *The World Bank Since Bretton Woods: The Origins, Policies,
    Operations, and Impact of the International bank for Reconstruction and Development.*
    (Brookings Institution, 1973).
Matanle, Emma. *The UN Security Council: Prospects For Reform.* (London: The Royal
    Institute of International Affairs, 1995).
Maynes, Charles William and Richard S. William (eds). *United States Foreign Policy and
    the United Nations System.* (New York: W.W. Norton & Co., 1996).
Maynes, Charles William. *What's Wrong with the United Nations – And What's Right.*
    (Washington: Department of State, Bureau of Public Affairs, Office of Public
    Communication, 1978).
Mendlovitz, Saul H. and Weston Burns H. (eds). *Preferred Futures for the United
    Nations.* (Irvington, NY, USA: Transnational Publishers Inc., 1995).
McCarthy, Patrick A. 'Positionality, Tension, and Instability in the UN Security Council'.
    Global Governance, Vol. 3/No. 2 (May-Aug 1997).
McLaren, Robert I. *Civil Servants and Public Policy: A Comparative Study of Internaitonal
    Secretariats.* (Waterloo, Canada: Wilfrid Laurier University Press, 1980).
Meron, T. *The United Nations Secretariat: The Rules and Practice.* (Lexington, MA, USA:
    Lexington Books, 1977).
Michelak, Stanley Jacob. *The Senate and the United Nations: A Study of Changing
    Perceptions About the Utilities and Limitations of the United Nations as an Instrument of
    Peace and Security, and Its Role in American National Security Policy.* (Ann Arbor, MI,
    USA: University Microfilms, 1968).
Minford, P., J. Riley and E. Nowell. 'The Elixir of Growth: Trade, Non-traded Goods and
    Development'. (London: CEPR Discussion Paper. No.1165, May 1995).
Mingst, Karen A. and Margaret P. Karns. *The United Nations in the Post-Cold War Era.*
    (Boulder, CO, USA: Westview Press, 1995).
Ministry of Foreign Affairs, Sweden. *Financial Management in International Organizations.*
    Stockholm (1994).
Mirza, Ahmar Sharif. *Peacekeeping, Peacemaking, and World Order: A Study of the Post-
    Cold War United Nations System and Some Proposals For Operational Reforms.*
    (Kingston, Canada: Department of Political Science, Queen's University, 1993).
Moore, Raymond A. (ed.). *The United Nations Reconsidered.* (Columbia, USA: University of
    South Carolina Press, 1963).
Morrow, Robert. *Proposals for a More Equitable General Assembly Voting Structure.*
    (Livingston, NJ, USA: Center for U.N. Reform Education, 1989).
Müller, Joachim. *The Reform of the United Nations.* (New York: Oceana Publications,
    1992).
Müller, Joachim. *Reforming the United Nations; New Initiatives and Past Efforts.* (The Hague,
    Kluwer Law International, 1997).
Muller, Robert and Douglas Roche. *Safe Passage into the Twenty-First Century: The United
    Nations'Quest for Peace, Equality, Justice and Development.* (New York: Continuum,
    1995).
Muller, Robert. *The Birth of a Global Civilization: With Proposals For a New Political
    System For Planet Earth.* Anacortes. (WA: World Happiness & Cooperation, 1991).

Bibliography

Murray, Gilbert. *1866-1957. From the League to U.N.* (London, New York: Oxford Universiry Press, 1948).

Nerfin, Marc. 'The Future of the United Nations System'. *Development Dialogue*, No.1, 1985.
Newcombe, Hanna. *Design for a Better World.* (Lanham, MD, USA: University Press of America; 1983).
Nicholas, H. G. *The United Nations as a Political Institution.* (London: Oxford University Press, 1975).
Nicol, Davidson and Margaret Croke (eds). *The United Nations and Decision-Making: The Role of Women.* (New York: UNITAR, 1978).
Nicol, Davidson. *The United Nations Security Council: Towards Greater Effectiveness.* (New York: UNITAR, 1982).
Nordic U.N. Project. *Perspectives on Multilateral Assistance*, Report No. 10, (Stockholm, 1989).
Nordic U.N. Project. *Financing the Multilateral System*, Report No. 13, (Stockholm, 1990).
Nordic U.N. Project. *The Agencies at a Crossroads*, Report No. 15, (Stockholm, 1990).
Nordic U.N. Project. *Responding to Emergencies*, Report No. 16, (Stockholm, 1990).
Nordic U.N. Project. *The United Nations: Issues and Options*: Five studies on the Role of the UN in the Economic and Social Fields, (Distributed by Almqvist & Wiksell International, Stockholm, Sweden: 1991).
Nordic U.N. Project. *The United Nations in Development: Reform Issues in the Economic and Social Fields: A Nordic Perspective: Final Report.* (Distributed by Almqvist & Wiksell International, Stockholm, Sweden: 1991).
Noyes, John E. *The United Nations at 50: Proposals for Improving its Effectiveness* (Washington: American Bar Association, 1997).

O'Brien, Conor Cruise. *Conflicting Concepts of the United Nations.* (Cambridge: Leeds University Press, 1964).
Owen, David. *Balkan Odyssey* (New York: Harcourt Brace & Co., 1995).

Paolini, Albert J., Anthony P. Jarvis and Christi Reus-Smit (eds). *Between Sovereignty and Global Governance: The United Nations, the State and Civil Society.* (Basingstoke, London: MacMillian Press Ltd., 1998)
Payer, Cheryl. *The Debt Trap: The IMF and the Third World.* (Penguin Books, 1974).
Pearson, Lester B., E. A. Gross and Sir P. Dean. *A Critical Evaluation of the United Nations.* (Vancouver, Canada: University of British Columbia, 1961).
Peck, Connie. *The United Nations as a Dispute Settlement System: Improving Mechanisms for the Prevention and Resolution of Conflict.* (The Hague; Boston: Kluwer Law International, c1996).
Perry, Estelle Siegal. *Streamlining the United Nations System. Part A – Wanted: A UN Personnel System That Works.* (Livingston, NJ, USA: Center for U.N. Reform Education, 1993).
Petersmann, E.-U. 'How to Constitutionalize the United Nations? Lessons from the International Economic Law Revolution'. *Liber Americorum Günther Jaenicke-Zum.* Springer, (1998). p. 321.
Peterson, M. J. *The General Assembly in World Politics.* (Boston, MA, USA: Allen & Unwin, 1986).
PGA. 'Towards a Global Security System for the 21st Century: A Submission to the Secretary – General of the United Nations'. *PGA Newsletter,* June 1993, pp.6-7.

Pinder, John. *U.N.Reform: Proposals for Charter Amendment*. (2nd edn, London: Federal Union, 1953).

Pines, Burton Yale (ed.). *A World Without a U.N.: What Would Happen if the U.N. Shut Down?* (Washington, D.C., USA: The Heritage Foundation, 1984).

Pitt, D. and T. Weiss (eds). *The Nature of the United Nations Bureaucracies*. (London: Croom Helm, 1986).

Prebisch, Raul. *The Economic Development of Latin America and its Principal Problems*. (New York: United Nations. 1950).

Prebisch, Raul. *Theorectical and Practical Problems of Economic Growth*, (Mexico: United Nations,1950).

Prebisch, Raul. *Interpretación del Proceso de Desarrollo Latinoamericano En 1949*, Santiago: ECLA, 1951).

Prebisch, Raul. 'A Critique of Perpheral Capitalism'. *CEPAL Review* 1 (First Semester): 9-76 (1976).

Prebisch, Raul. *Towards a Global Strategy of Development*: (New York: United Nations, 1968).

Preston Baratta, Joseph. *Strengthening the United Nations*. (New York: Greenwood Press, 1987).

Protheroe, David R. *The United Nations and its Finances: A Test for Middle Powers*. (Ottawa: The North-South Institute, 1988).

Puchala, Donald J. and Roger A. Coate. *The State of the United Nations*, 1988. (Hanover, NH, USA: Academic Council on the United Nations System, 1988).

Puchala, Donald J. and Roger A. Coate. *The Challenge of Relevance: The United Nations in a Changing World Environment*. (Hanover, NH, USA: Academic Council on the United Nations System, 1989).

Puchala, Donald. 'Outsiders, Insiders and UN Reform'. *Washington Quarterly*, Vol. 17/No. 4 (Autumn 1994), p. 161.

Qureshi, Moeen, Richard von Weizsacker, et al. *The United Nations in its Second Half-Century: A Report of the Independent Working Group on the Future of United Nations* (New York: Ford Foundation, 1995).

Rajan, Mannaraswamighala Sreeranga. *The Expanding Jurisdiction of the United Nations*. (Bombay, India: N.M. Tripathi; Dobbs Ferry, NY, USA: Oceana Publication, 1982).

Ramcharan, B.G. *Keeping Faith with the United Nations*. (Dordrecht; Boston: M. Nijhoff/Kluwer Academic Publishers, 1987).

Ranshoffen-Wertheimer, Egon F. *The International Secretariat*, (Washington, D.C., USA: Carnegie Endowment, 1943).

Ray, Jean. *Commentaire du Pacte de la Sociètè des Nation Selon la politique et la Jurisprudence des Organes de la Sociètè*. Paris, Sirey, (1930), pp. 652-60.

Renninger, John P. *ECOSOC: Options for Reform*. (New York: United Nations Institute for Training and Research, 1981).

Renninger, John P., et al. *Assessing the United Nations Scale of Assessments: Is It Fair? Is It Equitable?* (New York: United Nations Institute for Training and Research, 1982).

Renninger, John P. *Can the Common System be Maintained: The Role of the International Civil Service Commission*. (New York: United Nations Institute for Training and Research, 1986).

Renninger, John P. 'Improving the UN System'. *Journal of Development Planning*, No. 17, (1987), p.85.

Bibliography

Renninger, John P. (ed.). *The Future Role of the United Nations in an Interdependent World.* (Dordrecht, Netherlands; Boston, MA, USA; London: M. Nijhoff, 1989).

Reymond, Henri and Sydney Mailick. *International Personnel Policies and Practices.* (New York: Praeger, 1985).

Rife, Roseanne. *The Current Financial Crisis and Prospects for More Dependable U.N. Revenue.* (Livingston, NJ, USA: Center for U.N. Reform Education, 1987).

Riggs, Robert E. and Jack C. Plano. *The United Nations: International Organization and World Politics.* (2nd edn, Belmont, CA, USA: Wadsworth Pub. Co., 1994).

Riggs, Robert Edwon. *Politics in the United Nations: A Study of United States Influence in the General Assembly.* (Urbana, IL, USA: University of Illinois Press, 1958).

Righter, Rosemary. *Utopia Lost: The United Nations and World Order* (New York: Twnetieth Century Fund Press, 1995).

Rivlin, Benjamin and Leon Gordenker (eds). *The Challenging Role of the UN Secretary-General: Making the Most Impossible Job in the World Possible.* (Westport, CT, USA: Praeger, 1993).

Roberts, Adam and Benedict Kingsbury. *Presiding Over the Divided World: Changing UN Roles, 1945-1993.* (Boulder, CO, USA: Lynne Rienner Pub., 1994).

Roberts, Adam and Benedict Kingsbury (eds). *United Nations, Divided World: The UN's Roles in International Relations.* (2nd edn, Oxford: Clarendon Press,1995).

Rochester, Martin J. *Waiting for the Millenium: The United Nations and the Future World Order.* (Columbia, SC, USA: University of South Carolina Press, 1993).

Rosenau, James N. *The United Nations in a Turbulent World.* (Boulder, CO, USA: Lynne Rienner Publishers, 1992).

Ross, Alf. *Constitution of the United Nations; Analysis of Structure and Function.* (New York: Rinehart, 1950).

Rüdiger, Jutte and Annemarie Grosse-Jutte (eds). *The Future of International Organization.* (New York: St. Martin's Press, 1981).

Russell, Ruth B. *The United Nations and United States Security Policy.* (Washington, D.C., USA: Brookings Institution, 1968).

Russell, Ruth B. *The United Nations: Patterns of Constitutional Development, Development of Peacekeeping Rules.* Two papers. (Washington, D.C.: Brookings Institution, 1965).

Russett, Bruce, Barry O'Neill, and James Sutterlin. 'Breaking the Security Council Logjam'. *Global Governance.* Vol. 2/No. 1 (Jan-Apr 1996).

Russett, Bruce (ed.). *The Once and Future Security Council* (New York: St. Martin's Press, 1997).

Russett, Bruce. *Grasping the Democratic Peace: Principles for a Post-Cold War World.* (Princeton, NJ, USA: Princeton University Press, 1993).

Sahnoun, Mohamed. *How the United Nations Can be Reformed: The Recommendations of Four Former Ambassadors to the U.N.* (Washington, D.C., USA: Heritage Foundation, 1986).

Saigal, K., R. Rajagopalan and L.S. Ganesh (eds). *Science and Technology Cooperation in the Indian Ocean Region and Restructuring the United Nations: Proceedings of pacem in Maribus XXII, December 1994.* (Madras, India: International Ocean Institute Operational Centre (India), Indian Institute of Technology, Madras, 1995).

Saksena, K.P. *Reforming the United Nations: The Challenge of Relevance.* (New Delhi, Newbury Park: Sage Publications Incorporated, 1993).

Salter, Arthur Salter Baron. *The United Nations: Reform, Replace, or Supplement?* (London: David Davies Memorial Institute of International Studies, 1957).

Saxena, Jagdish Narain, Gurdip Singh and A. K. Koul (eds). *United Nations for a Better World.* (New Delhi: Lancers Books, 1986).

Schiffer, Walter. *The Legal Community of Mankind; A Critical Analysis for the Modern Concept of World Organization.* (New York: Columbia University Press, 1954).

Schoenberg, Harris O. (ed.). *Reforming the Security Council: Proceedings of a B'nai B'rith United Nations Symposium.* April 28, 1994. (New York: The International Council of B'nai B'rith, 1994).

Schoenberg, Harris O. *War No More!: A Concrete Action Plan to Revitalize the United Nations Security Council.* (New York: Center of Public Policy, 1995).

Schwartzberg, Joseph E. 'A New Perspective on Peacekeeping: Lessons from Bosnia and Elsewhere'. *Global Governance.* Vol. 3/No. 1 (Jan-Apr 1997).

Schwebel, Stephen Myron. *The Secretary-General of the United Nations: His Political Powers and Practice.* (Cambridge, MA, USA: Harvard University Press, 1952).

Scott, George. *The Rise and Fall of the League of Nations.* (London: Hutchinson & Co. Ltd., 1973).

Seara-Vazquez, Modesto. 'The UN Security Council at Fifty: Midlife Crisis or Terminal Illness?'. *Global Governance.* Vol. 1/No. 3 (Sep-Dec 1995).

Sebo, Katherine Ann Hagen. *Bureaucratization at The International Level: A Case Study of The United Nations Secretariat.* (Ann Arbor, MI, USA: University Microfilms, 1974).

Secretariat of the League. *The Aims, Methods and Activity of the League of Nations,* Geneva, 1938.

Seidl-Hohenveldern, Ignaz. 'Specialized Agencies' in Rüdiger Wolfrum (ed.), *United Nations:Law, Policies and Practice, Vol.2* (Dordrecht-Boston-London: M. Nijhoff, 1955).

Sen, Sudhir. *United Nations in Economic Development: A Need for a New Strategy.* (Dobbs Ferry, New York: Oceana Publications, 1969).

Sharp, Walter Rice. *The United Nations Economic and Social Council.* (New York: Columbia University Press, 1969).

Sherman, Frank Lester. *Partway to Peace: The United Nations and the Road to Nowhere?* (Ann Arbor, MI, USA: University Microfilms, 1987).

Sherry, George L. *The United Nations Reborn: Conflict Control in the Post-Cold War World.* (New York: Council on Foreign Relations, 1990).

Simma, Bruno (ed.). *Charter of the United Nations: A Commentary.* (Oxford, New York: Oxford University Press, 1995).

Simons, G. L. *UN Malaise: Power, Problems, and Realpolitik.* (Basingstoke, England: MacMillan Press, 1995; New York, USA: St. Martin's Press, 1995).

Simons, Geoff. *The United Nations: A Chronology of Conflict.* (New York: St. Martin's Press, 1994).

Singer, Hans. *International Development: Growth and Change.* (New York: McGraw Hill, 1964).

Singer, H. W. 'The Distribution of Gains Between Investing and Borrowing Countries'. *American Economic Review* 15. (Papers and Proceedings)(May 1950), p. 473.

Singer, H. W. 'The Distribution of Gains from Trade and Investment – Revisited'. *Journal of Development Studies* 11 (July 1975), p. 376.

Singer, Max and Aaron Wildavsky. *The Real World Order: Zones of Peace/ Zones of Turmoil.* (Chatham: Chatham House Publishers, 1993).

Singer, J. David. *United Nations Fiscal Process: Development and Practice.* (New York: New York University, 1955).

Siotis, Jean. *The Institutions of the League of Nations. The League of Nations in Retrospect,*
    (Boston-New York: Walter de Gruyter, 1983).

Siu, Philip Yeung-fai. *Realities of Prescriptive Politics: The Restructuring of the Economic*
    and Social Sectors of the United Nations System. (Ann Arbor, MI, USA: University
    Microfilms, 1984).

Smith, Edwin M. and Michael G. Schechter. *The United Nations in a New World Order: Two*
    Papers. (Monograph Series/the Keck Center for International and Strategic Studies, No. 6,
    1994).

Snider, Don M. and Stuart J.D. Schwartzstein (eds). *The United Nations at Fifty:*
    Sovereignty, Peacekeeping, and Human Rights. (Washington, D.C., USA: Center for
    Strategic and International Studies, 1995).

Society for International Development. *The United Nations and the Bretton Woods*
    Institutions: New Challenges for the 21st Century. (Bretton Woods, NH, USA, 1993).

Sohn, Louis B. 'Important Improvements in the Functioning of the Principal Organs of the
    United Nations That Can Be Made Without Charter Revision'. *American Journal of*
    International Law. 91 (4) Oct. (1997). p. 652.

South Centre. *Enhancing the Economic Role of the United Nations.*
    (Geneva, Switzerland: The South Centre, 1992).

South Centre. *The United Nations at a Critical Crossroads: Time for the*
    South to Act. (Geneva, Switzerland : The South Centre, 1992).

South Centre. *For a Strong and Democratic United Nations: A South Perspective on UN Reform.*
    (Geneva, Switzerland : The South Centre, 1996).

South Commission. *The Challenge to the South: The Report of the South Commission.*
    (Oxford: Oxford University Press,1990).

Spiry, Emmanuel. 'La Reforme des Institutions Onusiennes: Perspectives et Prospectives.
    (1985-1995).' *Studia Diplomatica.* Vol.XLVIII, (1995), No.3, p.63.

Stanley Foundation. *Restructuring of the U.N. Economic and Social System. The Stanley*
    Foundation Seventh United Nations Precedures Conference. May 21-24, 1976. (Stanley
    Foundation, 1976).

Stanley Foundation. *The United Nations: 1. Conflict management 2. Effective administration:*
    The Stanley Foundation Fourteenth United Nations Procedures Conference. May 13-15,
    1983. (Muscatine, IA, USA: Stanley Foundation, 1983).

Stanley Foundation. *UN Budgetary and Financial Impasse. Report of the 17th United Nations*
    Issues Conference Sponsored by the Stanley Foundation. February 21-23, 1986.
    (Muscatine, IA, USA: Stanley Foundation, 1986).

Stanley Foundation. *The United Nations: Mission and Management. Report of the 21st UN of*
    the Next Decade Conference Sponsored by the Stanley Foundation. June 28-July 3, 1986.
    (Quebec, Canada: Stanley Foundation, 1986).

Stanley Foundation. *Administrative and Budgetary Reform of the United Nations. Report of*
    the 18th United Nations Issues Conference Sponsored by the Stanley Foundation, February
    20-22, 1987. (Muscatine, IA, USA: Stanley Foundation, 1987).

Stanley Foundation. *The United Nations:Structure and Leadership For a New Era. Report of*
    the 22nd United Nations Issues Conference Sponsored by the Stanley Foundation. February
    22-24, 1991. (Muscatine, IA, USA: Stanley Foundation, 1991).

Stanley Foundation. *Consultation on the Role and Composition of the Security Council:*
    Report of the Co-Chairs Olara A. Otunnu and Richard H. Stanley. (New York: Stanley
    Foundation, 1992).

Stanley Foundation. *State of the United Nations: Decline or Regeneration in the Next Fifty Years.*
    *Report of the 29th UN of the Next Decade Conference Sponsored by the Stanley
    Foundation, June 19-24, 1994.* (Muscatine, IA, USA: Stanley Foundation, 1994).

Starke, Linda. *Signs of Hope: Working Towards Our Common Future.* (Oxford; New York:
    Oxford University Press, 1990).

Stassen, Harold E. *The Stassen Draft Charter for a New United Nations.* (Philadelphia,
    PA, USA: Glenview Foundation, 1985).

Stassen, Harold E. *United Nations: A Working Paper for Restructuring.* (Minneapolis, USA: Lerner
    Pub., 1994).

Steele, David. *The Reform of the United Nations.* (London, Wolfeboro, NH, USA: Croom Helm,
    c1987).

Stevenson, Ian Garth. *Constitutional Change in the United Nations.* (Ann Arbor, MI, USA:
    University Microfilms, 1971).

Stockholm Initiative on Global Security and Governance. *The Common Responsibility in the
    1990's.* (Stockholm, 22 April 1991).

Stoessinger, John George. *Financing the United Nations System.* (Washington, D.C., USA:
    Brookings Institution, 1964).

Stoessinger, John George. *The United Nations and the Superpowers: China, Russia and
    America.* (4th edn, New York: Random House, 1977).

Stoessinger, John George. *The Might of Nations: World Politics in Our Time.* (8th edn, New
    York: Random House, 1986).

Strong, Maurice. *The United Nations at Fifty: Issues and Opportunities.* (Ottawa: UN
    Association in Canada, 1997).

Sunkel, Osvaldo (ed.). *Development From Within, Toward a Neostructuralist Approach
    for Latin America.* (Boulder & London: Lynne Reinner Publishers, 1993).

Sutterlin, James S. *The United Nations and the Maintenance of Internaitonal Security: A
    Challenge to be Met.* (Westport, CT, USA: Praeger, 1995).

Sutterlin, James S. *The Imperative of Idealism: 1997 John W. Holmes Memorial Lecture in
    ACUNS Reports and Papers.* 1997 No. 3 (Providence: Academic Council on the United
    Nations System, 1997).

Szalai, Alexander. *The Situation of Women in the United Nations.* (New York: United Nations
    Institute for Training and Research, 1973).

Taylor, Paul and A. J. R. Groom (eds). *International Institutions at Work.* (London: Pinter
    Publishers Ltd., 1988).

Taylor, Paul and A. J. R. Groom. *Global Issues in the United Nations' Framework.* (New
    York: St. Martin's Press, 1989).

Taylor, Paul, Sam Daws, and Ute Asamczick (eds). *Documents on Reform of the United Nations.*
    (Dartmouth Pub. Co., 1996).

Thakur, Ramesh. 'The United Nations in a Chaning World'. *Security Dialogue*, Vol. 24, No. 1
    (1993), pp. 7-20.

Thakur, Ramesh (ed.). *The United Nations at Fifty: Retrospect and Prospect.* (Dunedin, New
    Zealand:University of Otago Press, Canberra: Peace Research Centre, Australian National
    University, 1996).

Thornburgh, Dick. *Reform and Restructuring at the United Nations: A Progress Report.* (Hanover,
    NH, USA: Nelson A. Rockefeller Center for the Social Sciences at Dartmouth College,
    1993).

The Commission on Global Governance. *Our Global Neighbourhood.* (Oxford: Oxford University
    Press, 1995).

Tinbergen, Jan. *Revitalizing the United Nations System*. (Santa Barbara, CA, USA: Nuclear Age Peace Foundation, 1987).

Tinbergen, Jan. *Supranational Decision-Making : A More Effective United Nations*. (Santa Barbara, CA, USA: Nuclear Age Peace Foundation, 1991).

Tiwari, S.C. *Genesis of the United Nations*. (Varanasi: Naivedya Niketan, 1968).

Tompkins, E. Berkeley (ed.). *The United Nations in Perspective*. (Stanford, CA: Hoover Institution Press, 1972).

Tomuschat, Christian (ed.). *United Nations at Age Fifty: A Legal Perspective*. (The Hague, Netherlands: Kluwer Law International, 1995).

Tyagi, A. R. *International Administration; an Indian Perspective*. (Delhi: Metropolitan Book Co., 1969).

U.K. Parliament, House of Commons, Foreign Affairs Committee. *The Expanding Role of the United Nations and its Implications for United Kingdom Policy*,Vol. 1. (London: HMSO, 1993).

United Nations Association of the United States of America. *A Successor Vision: the United Nations of Tomorrow: Final Panel Report, September 1987*. (New York: United Nations Management & Decision-Making project, UNA-USA, 1987).

United Nations, Charter. *A New United Nations Structure for Global Economic Cooperation*. (E/AC.62/9, 1975).

United Nations, Charter. *Comprehensive Review of the Whole Question of Peace-Keeping Operations in All Their Aspects*. (A/48/173, May 1993). (Special Committee on Peace-Keeping Operations).

United Nations, Charter. *Implementation of the Recommendations Contained in «An Agenda for Peace*. (A/47/965 5/25944, June 1993).

United Nations, Charter. *Towards Greater Order, Coherence and Coordination in the United Nations*. (E/5491, 30 April 1994).

United Nations, Charter. *Agenda for Development*. (A/48/935, 6 May 1994).

United Nations, Charter. *How Peoples Work Together; The United Nations and the Specialized Agencies*. (2nd edn, New York, 1951).

United Nations Documents. *A New United Nations Structure for Global Economic Co-operation: Report of the Group of Experts on the Structure of the United Nations System*. (E/AC.62/9).(U.N. Publication. Sales No.: E.75.II.A.7).

United Nations Efficiency Board. *UN 21: Better Service, Better Value, Better Management: Progress Report of the Efficiency Board to the Secretary General*. (New York: United Nations, 1996).

U.S. Commission on Improving the Effectiveness of the United Nations. *Defining Purpose: The U.N. and the Health of Nations: Final Report of the United States Commission on Improving the Effectiveness of the United Nations*. (Washington, D.C., USA: U.S.G.P.O, 1993).

U.S. Congress. House. Committee on Foreign Affairs. *Structure of the United Nations and Relations of the United States to the United Nations: Hearings Before the Committee on Foreign Affairs, House of Representatives, Eightieth Congress,Second Session, May 4, 5, 6, 7, 11, 12, 13, 14, 1948*. (Washington, D.C., USA: U.S.G.P.O., 1948).

U. S. Congress. House. Committee on Foreign Affairs. *To Seek Development of the United Nations into a World Federation. Hearings Before the Committee on H.Com. Res. 64*. (Washington, D.C., USA: U.S.G.P.O., 1950).

U.S. Congress. House. Committee on Foreign Affairs. Subcommittee on International
Organizations and Movements. *The United Nations at the Crossroads: Report on the 25ᵗʰ Anniversary of the United Nation, U.S. 91 Cong., Second Session.* (Washington, D.C., USA, 1970).

U.S. Congress. House. Committee on Foreign Affairs. Subcommittee on International
Organizations and Movements. *United States Role in the United Nations System: Hearings on Recommendations of the President's Commission for the Observance of the 25ᵗʰ Anniversary of the U.N. (Lodge Commission), and the UNA-USA Policy Panel on the U.N. (Katzenbach Commission), Oct. 13-14, 1971. U.S. 92 Cong., First Session.* (Washington D.C., USA, 1971).

U.S. Congress. House. Committee on Foreign Affairs. Subcommittee on International
Organizations and Movements. *Implementation of the Lodge and Katzenbach Recommendations on the United Nations.* Prepared for the Subcommittee by the Dept. of State. (Washington. D.C., USA, 1974).

US Congress. House. Committee on Foreign Affairs. Subcommittee on International
Organizations. *U.S. Participation in the United Nations and U.N. Reform: Hearing Before the Subcommittee on International Organizations of the Committee on Foreign Affairs. House of Representatives, Ninety-Sixth Congress, First Session.* (Washington, D.C., USA: U.S.G.P.O.,1979).

US. Congress. House. Committee on Foreign Affairs. Subcommittee on International
Operations. *United Nations Finances: Hearing Before the Subcommittee on International Operations and on International Organizations of the Committee on Foreign Affairs, House of Representatives, Ninety-sixth Congress, First Session, June 27 (-Nov.8) 1979.* (Washington, D.C., USA: U.S.G.P.O., 1979).

U.S. Congress. House. Committee on Foreign Affairs Subcommittee on International
Security, International Organizations and Human Rights. *Management and Mismanagement at the United Nations: Hearing before the Subcommittee on International Security, International Organizations and Human Rights of the Committee on Foreign Affairs, House of Representatives, One Hundred Third Congress, First Session, March 5, 1993.* (Washington, D.C., USA: U.S.G.P.O, 1993).

U.S. Congress. House. Committee on Foreign Affairs. Subcommittee on International
Security, International Organizations and Human Rights. *Tensions in the United States-United Nations Relations: Hearing Before the Subcommittee on International Security, International Organizations, and Human Rights of the Committee on Foreign Affairs, House of Representatives, One Hundred Third Congress, Second Session, May 17, 1994.* (Washington, D.C., USA: U.S.G.P.O., 1994).

U.S. Congress. House. Committee on Foreign Affairs. Subcommittee on International
Security, International Organizations and Human Rights. *The United Nations at Fifty: Hearing Before the Subcommittee on International Security, International Organization, and Human Rights of the Committee on Foreign Affairs, House of Representatives, One Hundred Third Congress, Second Session, October 24, 1994.* (Washington, D.C., USA: U.S.G.P.O.,1994).

U.S. Congress. House. Committee on International Relations. *The United Nations at 50: Prospects for Reform: Hearing Before the Committee on International Relations, House of Representatives, One Hundred Fourth Congress, First Session, October 24, 1995.* (Washington, D.C., USA: U.S.G.P.O., 1996).

U.S. Congress. House. Committee on International Relations. Subcommittee on International
Operations and Human Rights. *The United Nations; Management, Finance, and Reform:*

Bibliography

Hearing Before the Subcommittee on International Operations and Human Rights of the Committee on International Relations, House of Representatives, One Hundred Fourth Congress, First Session, October 26, 1995. (Washington, D.C., USA: U.S.G.P.O., 1996).

U. S. Congress. Senate. Committee on Foreign Relations. Subcommittee on the United Nations Charter. *Budgetary and Financial Problems of the United Nations.* (Washington, D.C., USA, 1954).

U.S. Congress. Senate. Committee on Foreign Relations. Subcommittee on the United Nations Charter. *Representation and Voting in the United Nations General Assembly.* (Washington, D.C., USA, 1954).

U.S. Congress. Senate. Committee on Foreign Relations. Subcommittee on the United Nations Charter. *The Status and Role of the Secretariat of the United Nations.* (Washington, D.C., USA, 1955).

U.S. Congress. Senate. Committee on Foreign Relations. *The United States and the United Nations: Hearings Before the Committee on Foreign Relations, United States Senate, Ninety-Fourth Congress, First Session, May 7, 8, 14, 15, 21, 22, and June 4, 1975.* (Washington, D.C., USA: U.S.G.P.O., 1975).

U.S. Congress. Senate. Committee on Foreign Relations. Subcommittee on the United Nations Charter. *The United Nations and the Specialized Agencies.* (Washington, D.C.: 1955).

U.S. Congress. Senate. Committee on Foreign Relations. *Proposals for United Nations Reform: Report Pursuant to Section 503 of the Foreign Relations Authorization Act, Fiscal Year 1978 (Public Law 95-105) To the Committee on Foreign Relations, United States Senate.* (Washington, D.C., USA: U.S.G.P.O., 1978).

U.S. Congress. Senate. Committee on Foreign Relations. *Reform of the United Nations: An Analysis of the President's Proposals and Their Comparison with proposals of Other Countries.* (Washington, D.C., USA: U.S.G.P.O., 1979).

U.S. Congress. Senate. Committee on Foreign Relations. *United NationsRreform: Hearing Before the Committee on Foreign Relations, United States Senate, Ninety-Sixth Congress, First Session, October 26, 1979.* (Washington, D.C., USA: U.S.G.P.O., 1980).

U.S. Congress. Senate. Committee on Foreign Relations. *Reform of the United Nations Peacekeeping Operations: A Mandate for Change: A Staff Report to the Committee on Foreign Relations of the United States Senate.* (Washington, D.C., USA: U.S.G.P.O., 1993).

U.S. Department of State. Reforming and Restructuring the U.N. System. (Washington: Dept. of State, Bureau of Public Affairs, Office of Public Communication, 1978).

U.S. General Accounting Office. *Improving the Management and Coordination of Reviews, Inspections, and Evaluations in the U.N. System: Report.* (Washington, D.C., USA: U.S.G.P.O., 1979).

U.S. Library of Congress. Congressional Research Service. *United Nations Reform: Issues for Congress.* (Washington, D.C., USA: CRS, Library of Congress, 1988).

U.S. President. *Reform and Restructuring of the United Nations System: Report by the President to the Speaker of the House of Representatives and the Chairman of the Committee on Foreign Relations of the Senate Pursuant to Section 503 of the Foreign Relations Authorization Act, Fiscal Year 1978 (P.L. 95-105).Report of the Secretary of State to the President on Reform and Restructuring of the United Nations System.* (Washington, D.C., USA, U.S.G.P.O., 1978).

U.S. President's Commission for the Observance of the Twenty-fifth Anniversary of the United Nations. *Report of the President's Commission for the Observance of the Twenty-fifth Anniversary of the United Nations.* (Washington, D.C., USA: U.S.G.P.O., 1971).

Urquhart, Brian. *Tomorrow's United Nations.*(Uppsala, Sweden: Dag Hammarskjöld Foundation, 1990).

Urquhart, Brian. *Reorganization of the United Nations Secretariat: A Suggested Outline for Needed Reforms.*(New York: Ford Foundation, 1991).

Urquhart, Brian. *For a UN Volunteer Military Force.* The New York Review of Books, 10 June 1993, pp.3-4.

Urquhart, Brian. *The United Nations Forward or Back?* (London: Wyndham Place Trust, 1994).

Urquhart, Brian and Erskine Childers. *A World in Need of Leadership: Tomorrow's United Nations.* (Uppsala, Sweden: Dag Hammarskjöld Foundation, *Development Dialogue* 1990:1-2).

Urquhart, Brian and Erskine Childers. *Towards a More Effective United Nations.* (Uppsala, Sweden: Dag Hammarskjöld Foundation, *Development Dialogue* 1991:1-2).

Urquhart, Brian and Erskine Childers. *A World in Need of Leadership: Tomorrow's United Nations; A Fresh Appraisal.* Uppsala, (Uppsala, Sweden: Dag Hammarskjöld Foundation, 1996).

Walters, Francis P. *A History of the League of Nations.* (Westport: Greenwood Press, 1952).

Waters, Maurice. *The United Nations: International Organization and Administration.* (New York: MacMillan, 1967).

Weiss, Thomas George. David P. Forsythe and Roger A. Coate. *The United Nations and Changing World Politics.* (Boulder, CO, USA: Westview Press, 1997).

Weiss, Thomas George. *NGOs, the UN. and Global Governance (Emerging Global Issues)* (Boulder, CO, USA: Lynne Riennner Publishers, 1996).

Weiss, Thomas George. David P. Forsythe and Roger A. Coate. *The United Nations and Changing World Politics.* (Boulder, CO, USA: Westview Press, 1994).

Weiss, Thomas George. *International Bureaucracy: An Analysis of the Operation of Functional and Global International Secretariats.* Lexington, (MA, USA: Lexington Books, 1975).

Weiss, Thomas George and Gordenker Leon (eds), *NGOs, the U.N; and Global Governance. (Emerging Global Issues).* (Boulder, CO, USA: Lynne Rienner Publishers, 1996).

Weiss, Thomas George. 'Round Up the Usual Suspects: The Selection Process for the UN Secretary General is in Need of Radical Overhaul'. *Peace and Security.* 6 (Autumn 1991), p. 6-7.

Whittaker, David J. *United Nations in Action.* (Armonk, New York: M.E. Sharpe, 1995).

Whittaker, David J. *United Nations in the Contemporary World.* (London; New York: Routledge, 1997).

Wilcox, Francis Orlando. *Proposals for Changes in the United Nations.* (Washington, D.C., USA: Brookings Institution, 1955).

Williams, Douglas. *The Specialized Agencies and the United Nations: The System in Crisis.* (New York: St. Martin's Press, 1987).

Wilson, Carolyn L. 'Changing the Charter: The United Nations Prepares for the Twenty-First Century'. *American Journal of International Law,* – 90(1) Jan. 1996: pp. 115-126.

World Commission on Environment and Development. Our Common Future.(New York: Oxford University Press, 1987).

World Federalists of Canada. *An Agenda forRreform of the United Nations.* (Ottawa: WFC, 1995).

Woroniecki, Jan. *Restructuring the United Nations: A Response to New Tasks, or a Substitute For Action?* (Opladen, Germany: Leske & Budrich, 1995).

Bibliography

Woroniecki, Jan. 'UN Reform: Chances, Directions, Prospects'. *Polish Quarterly of International Affairs.* – 4(1) Winter 1995:45-64.

Yepes, J. M. and Pereira da Silva. *Commentaire Thèorique et Pratique du Pacte de la Sociètè des Nations et des Statuts de l'Union Panamericaine.* (Paris: Pèdone, 1939).
Yoder, Amos. *The Evolution of the United Nations System.* (2nd edn, Washington, D.C., USA Taylor & Francis, 1993).

Zacklin, Ralph. *The Amendment of the Constitutive Instrument of the United Nations and Specialized Agencies,* (Leyden: Sijthoff, 1968).
Zolo, Danilo Cosmopolis. *Prospects for World Government.* (Cambridge: Polity Press, 1997).

INDEX

227

D

E

F

ABOUT THE AUTHORS

Kamil Idris has been Director General of the World Intellectual Property Organization (WIPO) and Secretary-General of the International Union for the Protection of Plant Varieties (UPOV), since 1997. Dr. Idris joined WIPO in 1982, becoming Deputy Director General of the Organization in 1994.

Prior to joining WIPO, Dr. Idris practised law and was a professor of international law at the University of Khartoum. Dr. Idris was an Ambassador in the Sudanese Foreign Service. He also served in the Permanent Mission of Sudan to the United Nations in Geneva and assumed the position of spokesman and coordinator of the Group of Developing Countries (Group of 77) on several important international issues.

Dr. Idris holds a PhD in International Law from the Graduate Institute of International Studies, University of Geneva (Switzerland). He has an MA in International Law and International Affairs from the University of Ohio (United States of America) and an LLB and a BA from, respectively, the University of Khartoum (Sudan) and the University of Cairo (Egypt).

Dr. Idris was a member of the United Nations International Law Commission (ILC), from 1992 to 1996. He has published extensively in various fields.

Michael Bartolo is the Ambassador and Permanent Representative of Malta to the United Nations, the Specialized Agencies and the World Trade Organization (WTO) in Geneva. Before taking up that position, Dr. Bartolo worked at the United Nations headquarters in New York, principally in the area of economic and social affairs. During his 26 years with the United Nations, he also served on the Appointment and Promotion Board and as Chairman of the Central Examination Board of the United Nations as well as Special Advisor to the President of the 45th General Assembly of the United Nations.

Dr Bartolo has a PhD in International Economics from the New School for Social Research (United States of America) as well as an MA in Economics from the University of New Hampshire (United States of America) and a BA from the University of Malta.

Dr. Bartolo's previous publications include *A Second Generation United Nations*.

NIJHOFF LAW SPECIALS

NIJHOFF LAW SPECIALS

23. E.-U. Petersmann: *The GATTWTO Dispute Settlement System*. International Law, International Organizations and Dispute Settlement. 1996   ISBN 90-411-0933-1

24. G. de Nooy (ed.): *Cooperative Security, the OSCE, and its Code of Conduct*. 1996
    ISBN 90-411-0316-3

25. M. Bertrand: *The United Nations*. Past, Present and Future. 1997
    ISBN 90-411-0337-6

26. D. Dijkzeul: *The Management of Multilateral Organizations*. 1997
    ISBN 90-411-0356-2

27. G. de Nooy (ed.): *The Role of European Ground and Air Forces after the Cold War*. 1997   ISBN 90-411-0397-X

28. M. Hilaire: *International Law and the United States Military Intervention in the Western Hemisphere*. 1997   ISBN 90-411-0399-6

29. D. Warner (ed.): *Human Rights and Humanitarian Law*. The Guest for Universality. 1997   ISBN 90-411-0407-0

30. J.C. Hathaway (ed.): *Reconceiving International Refugee Law*. 1997
    ISBN 90-411-0418-6

31. G. de Nooy (ed.): *The Clausewitzian Dictum and the Future of Western Military Strategy*. 1997   ISBN 90-411-0455-0

32. Canadian Council on International Law and The Markland Group (ed.): *Treaty Compliance: Some Concerns and Remedies*. 1997   ISBN 90-411-0732-0

33. B. de Rossanet: *War and Peace in the Former Yugoslavia*. 1998
    ISBN 90-411-0499-2

34. C.M. Mazzoni (ed.): *A Legal Framework for Bioethics*. 1998   ISBN 90-411-0523-9

35. M. Marín-Bosch: *Votes in the UN General Assembly*. 1998   ISBN 90-411-0564-6

36. L. Caflisch: *The Peaceful Settlement of Disputes between States: Universal and European Perspectives. Règlement pacifique des différends entre États: Perspectives universelle et européenne*. 1998   ISBN 90-411-0461-5

37. R. Wazir and N. van Oudenhoven (eds.): *Child Sexual Abuse: What can Governments do?* A Comparative Investigation into Policy Instruments Used in Belgium, Britain, Germany, the Netherlands and Norway. 1998   ISBN 90-411-1034-8

38. E.M. Barron and I. Nielsen (eds.): *Agriculture and Sustainable Land Use in Europe*. 1998   ISBN 90-411-9691-9

39. K. van Walraven (ed.): *Early Warning and Conflict Prevention*. 1998
    ISBN 90-411-1064-X

40. S. Shubber: *The International Code of Marketing of Breast-milk Substitutes*. An International Measure to Protect and Promote Breast-feeding. 1999
    ISBN 90-411-1100-X

41. G. Prins and H. Tromp (eds.): *The Future of War*. 2000   ISBN 90-411-1196-4

42. Choung II Chee: *Korean Perspectives on Ocean Law Issues for the 21st Century*. 2000   ISBN 90-411-1301-0

NIJHOFF LAW SPECIALS

43. K. Idris and M. Bartolo: *A Better United Nations for the New Millennium*. The United
     Nations System – How it is now and how it should be in the future. 2000
                                                        ISBN 90-411-1344-4

MARTINUS NIJHOFF PUBLISHERS – THE HAGUE / BOSTON / LONDON

*'We the peoples of the United Nations determined...
to reaffirm faith in fundamental human rights, in the
dignity and worth of the human person, in the equal
rights of men and women and of nations large and
small'* (Preamble - Charter of the United Nations)

'The United Nations shall place no
restrictions on the eligibility of men
and women to participate in any capacity
and under conditions of equality in its
principal and subsidiary organs.' (Article 8)

'The creation of conditions of stability and
well-being which are necessary for peaceful
and friendly relations among nations based
on respect for the principle of equal rights and
self-determination of peoples' (Article 55)